STUDIES IN THE COMMEDIA DELL'ARTE

STUDIES IN THE
COMMEDIA DELL'ARTE

Edited by

DAVID J. GEORGE

and

CHRISTOPHER J. GOSSIP

UNIVERSITY OF WALES PRESS • CARDIFF • 1993

British Library Cataloguing in Publication Data

A catalogue record for this book is available from the British Library.

ISBN 0-7083-1201-2

Typeset in Wales by Megaron, Cardiff
Printed in Cornwall by Hartnolls Ltd., Bodmin

Contents

The editors and contributors

DAVID GEORGE is Lecturer in Spanish at the University College of Swansea. His main area of interest is late nineteenth and early twentieth-century Spanish and Catalan drama. He has published several articles on the subject of the *commedia dell'arte* in Hispanic literature of the period, and his book *From Pierrot to Harlequin: Valle-Inclán, Lorca and the commedia dell'arte in Hispanic Literature* will appear shortly.

CHRISTOPHER J. GOSSIP holds the Chair of French at the University of New England, Armidale, New South Wales, where he is Head of the School of Modern Languages. His publications include *An Introduction to French Classical Tragedy*, and critical editions of Corneille's *Stilicon* and Cyrano de Bergerac's *La Mort d'Agrippine*.

ANDREW GREWAR is Lecturer in English at the University of Fort Hare, South Africa. He has a special interest in the influence of the *commedia dell'arte* on Shakespeare. He has written several scenarios of plays for improvisation.

TOM CHEESMAN is Lecturer in German at the University College of Swansea and specializes in teaching *Sturm und Drang* and Romantic literature, cinema history and the cultural history of 'Nature'. His study of the German street song tradition, *Shocking Ballads*, is currently in press.

JOHN TRETHEWEY is Lecturer in French at the University College of Wales, Aberystwyth. His research speciality is seventeenth-century French drama.

BRUCE GRIFFITHS is Lecturer in French at the University College of North Wales, Bangor. He has a special interest in linguistics as well as the French stage of the late seventeenth and early eighteenth centuries.

GEORGE EVANS is Senior Lecturer in French at the University College of Swansea. He has written on eighteenth-century French drama generally and on works by Lesage in particular. He is at present preparing an edition of French 'Fair' plays in collaboration with his colleague Derek Connon (see overleaf).

DEREK CONNON is Lecturer in French at the University College of Swansea. His publications include a monograph on the works of Diderot and an edition of Saurin's *Béverlei*.

GLYN PURSGLOVE is Senior Lecturer in English at the University College of Swansea. His publications include studies of the poetry of Francis Warner, and editions of works by Henry Reynolds and Richard Niccols. His *I poeti ferraresi nel Rinascimento inglese* was published in 1992.

W. GARETH JONES is Reader in Russian at the University College of North Wales, Bangor. His main research interest is the Enlightenment in eighteenth-century Russia and he is author of *Nikolay Novikov: Enlightner of Russia*. He has translated a number of Russian plays into Welsh.

SUSAN HARROW is Lecturer in French at the University College of Swansea. Her research interests focus on the relationship between Modernist poetry and the plastic arts.

GABRIEL JACOBS is Senior Lecturer in French at the University College of Swansea. He has published widely on twentieth-century French literature and culture.

CHRISTOPHER CAIRNS is Reader in Italian drama at the University College of Wales, Aberystwyth. He is a specialist in the Renaissance theatre, with interests in the *commedia dell'arte* and Dario Fo. He is general editor of Studies in Italian Theatre for the Edwin Mellen Press.

Illustrations

Acknowledgements

The illustrations in this volume have appeared by kind permission of the following:

pp. 54 and 55: Germanisches National Museum, Nürnberg.

p. 57: the Syndics of Cambridge University Library.

pp. 256 and 260: Mimmorossi Photo, Perugia, Italy.

Introduction

DAVID GEORGE

Continuing fascination with the roots of Western popular culture has given rise in recent years to much academic interest in the *commedia dell'arte*, both in its original Italian Renaissance forms and in its later developments. The present volume covers a diverse range of manifestations of this multi-faceted genre from the late sixteenth century to the present day, broadly focusing on the links between the *commedia* and popular tradition generally. However, rather than going over well-trodden ground, such as the *commedia*'s origins or its use as source material by nineteenth-century French poets, the studies in this collection – all but one from the University of Wales – explore less obvious but equally fruitful avenues like Latin American *modernista* poetry, early twentieth-century Russian drama, and music of the period immediately preceding and following the First World War. Fresh insights are also offered into major European literary figures who have adopted or have been influenced by the tradition: Shakespeare, Molière, Lesage, Marivaux, Apollinaire and Dario Fo.

Once the original *commedia dell'arte* had moved out of Italy, it was rapidly absorbed into the national cultures of other European countries, particularly France. Several Italian companies, such as the famous Gelosi, visited France in the late years of the sixteenth century. However, the first troupe really to establish itself in Paris was the one that appeared there in 1653, where it remained until it was expelled because of a performance of a play entitled *La Fausse Prude*, which contained satirical references to Mme de Maintenon. The repertoire of these Italian players, who were known as the Ancienne Troupe de la Comédie Italienne, is contained in the *Recueil de Gherardi*, published in the last decade of the seventeenth century. The author of the work, Evaristo Gherardi, was one of the most famous of the Harlequin actors. Interestingly, in the fifth edition of the *Recueil*, published in 1721, Gherardi still considers the actor to be of vital importance. Written texts had not yet replaced improvisation, and Gherardi emphasized that the actor's skill consisted not of memory but of imagination. Gherardi said, in his introduction to the 1721 edition, that the language of the plays performed by his troupe was partly French and partly Italian.

The Italians returned to Paris in 1716, led by Luigi Riccoboni, and known, logically enough, as the Nouvelle Troupe Italienne. Riccoboni found that interest in the *commedia* had faded with the absence of the Italian players, and also he faced the danger that his troupe would be compared unfavourably with the actors of the *théâtres de la foire* (see below). Riccoboni lacked an author of stature and also found the language barrier disconcerting, although he began taking steps to make a more direct appeal to his French audiences remarkably quickly. French subject matter was introduced into a play as early as two months after the troupe's arrival in France, the French-speaking actor Dominique, son of the famous Arlequin of the previous century (see below), was engaged in 1717, and scenes in French appear to have begun to figure from about the beginning of 1718. A major breakthrough came when the painter Jacques Autreau produced for Riccoboni's company a *commedia* play, *Le Naufrage au Port-à-l'Anglais*. Its performance on 20 February 1718 began the process of refinement of the *commedia*, which was one of the important French contributions to the development of the genre. Although notes in the printed text of this play, which is almost all in French, make it clear that a significant amount of the performance was in Italian, the unusually high proportion of French seems to have combined with a particularly clever exploitation of the actors' talents to produce a success much-needed to boost the troupe's flagging morale, to say nothing of their financial resources.

A further significance of Autreau's play was that the text was written down, and not improvised as it had been previously, thus increasing the role of the individual author and lessening the influence of the actor. Goldoni, one of the most significant writers of *commedia* theatre, took a similar path in Italy. Although he recognized that improvisation had a certain value, Goldoni is an important figure in the movement away from improvised scenarios to the written text and the consequent growth in the significance of the individual author.

The Italian players continued to perform in Paris until 1762 when the Italian Comedy at the Hôtel de Bourgogne obtained that the *opéra-comique* should be incorporated with them. Those actors who could play only in Italian were pensioned off and in 1779 the State Council ordered that the company of Italian players, now sixty-three years old, should be abolished and a new company formed to perform only in French. According to Goldoni, the only Italian player retained was the seventy-year-old Carlin, the Harlequin of the company, who died of apoplexy in 1783. During their long years in France, the Italian company played in French on French or Italian scenarios and Italian on Italian or French scenarios.

The best-known and best-loved *commedia* figure in the seventeenth and eighteenth centuries was Harlequin, whose evolving character was shaped by a number of great actors during this period. The original Bergamasque was a doltish character, a foil to his cunning Bergamo counterpart Brighella. Harlequin was the stupidly naïve buffoon who delighted audiences with his mistakes. With time he acquired cunning, and it is as a scheming rogue that he has passed down the centuries. Harlequin's character was changed radically in the seventeenth and eighteenth centuries, by the famous Harlequins: Dominique, Gherardi, Thomassin and Carlin – in particular Dominique and Thomassin. All these actors could perform in the spirit of the crude Arlecchino prototype, but each added a characteristic of his own to the role, with an emphasis on refinement, sensibility, grace and elegance.

Giuseppe-Domenico Biancolelli, the father of the French-speaking actor who was appointed to Riccoboni's troupe in 1717 (see above), was born in Bologna in 1640 where his parents were actors. In 1659 he was a member of a troupe that was invited by Cardinal Mazarin to perform in France, where he achieved his greatest successes, and where he was known as Dominique. Dominique was renowned for his wit and physical agility, and was a favourite with King Louis XIV. Dominique began the process of refining Harlequin, a trend which was further accentuated by another actor, whose Italian name is given variously as Tommaso Visenti, Tommaso Vicentini, Tommaso-Antonio Vicentini, Antonio Vicentini, but who is best known by the name he adopted in France, Thomassin. Born in Venice, he played in Italy for a long time before going to France with Riccoboni's Nouvelle Troupe in 1716. Like Dominique, Thomassin achieved his greatest successes not in Italy but in France. Apparently, Thomassin was able to convey emotions of mirth and pathos to his audiences. Beaumont writes:

> He had a brilliant career. Agile, gay and always original, he would set the house in roars of laughter by some inimitable display of buffoonery, then, passing almost imperceptibly from comedy to

tragedy, he would cause the same public to shed tears of sorrow – no light achievement when it is remembered that his face is covered by a mask. His physical dexterity was remarkable. In this respect he is said to have attained such a degree of perfection that he could turn a somersault with a full glass in his hand and alight on his feet without having spilt a single drop of the wine.[1]

Thomassin was one of Marivaux's favourite actors, and was the inspiration for all of the Arlequin roles he wrote, from his earliest important theatrical success, *Arlequin poli par l'amour* (1720) to the last play in which he included the character, *Les Fausses Confidences* (1737). Silvia, who shone in Marivaux's plays and spoke French fluently, was arguably the greatest actress of her day. She prolonged by her talent a waning interest in Marivaux's plays at the end of his career. Some of the other actors never acquired a good command of French, and the ability of the company to survive under these conditions is a testimony to their great miming technique, their ability to express by body movement, synchronization and ultimately by pregnant silences; some critics have stated that the *école du silence* had its roots in such a style of acting.

We shall return shortly to the peculiarly French polishing of *commedia*, but in Germany and England it was the popular spirit which survived well into the eighteenth century and was of most interest there. *Commedia* types were assimilated into German popular culture during that century, when Pulcinella, for instance, assumed a specifically German identity in the form of Hanswurst. In chapter 2, Tom Cheesman sets manifestations of *commedia* types in the context of German popular art and culture. He takes into account the theories of Bakhtin on carnivalization, and emphasizes the modernity of carnival culture. Eighteenth-century engravings and chapbooks are considered, and are illustrated in this volume. In England Harlequin was for centuries a centrepiece of pantomime, and some of the greatest of all English actors, such as Rich and Garrick, were associated with the part.

The *commedia* influenced several great European dramatists of the seventeenth century, and in many ways, such as in the use of improvisation techniques and the presence of comic types. Andrew Grewar (chapter 1) considers the influence of the *commedia* on Shakespeare with particular reference to techniques and methods, and to Shakespeare's use of stock *commedia* characters and situations, while John Trethewey (chapter 3) analyses Molière's well-known interest in the genre, and relates it to the complex question of the interaction between actors and audiences in the plays up to *L'Ecole des femmes*.

As will have already become clear, some of the most significant changes in the history of the *commedia* took place in France in the late seventeenth and early eighteenth centuries: these are analysed by Bruce Griffiths in chapter 4. He traces the repression and decline of the *commedia* in this period, and illustrates how the popular Italian provincial comic figures were replaced by recognizable types from contemporary French society. He explains how intrigue became a mere pretext for a rather static type of comedy, consisting of a series of individual sketches presided over by Arlequin. It is at this time in France that the *commedia* divided into two strands, the examination of whose characteristics is a central concern of this book: the popular and the cultivated. Griffiths also examines the traits that led to the formation of the *théâtre italien*, considers how the *commedia* is linked with the beginnings of operetta and of cabaret-style review and music hall, and speculates that the repression of the genre by the king represented the latter's attempt to remove the last surviving uncontrolled source of very public satire of his regime.

The 'refining' process of the *commedia dell'arte* was consolidated in eighteenth-century France. where the transformation of Harlequin, as has been observed, was effected. In chapter 6 Derek Connon analyses the development of Marivaux's theatre away from its *commedia* origins. He considers that this may be as much the result of Marivaux's move towards the inclusion of elements drawn from his own social milieu, as of changes in the *théâtre italien*. Connon argues that Arlequin, although polished, was still basically recognizable as the *commedia* figure, and could therefore have no place in drama which reflected the eighteenth-century trend towards realistic theatre.

At the same time as the *commedia* was being refined in eighteenth-century France, the popular tradition was alive and flourishing in the *théâtres de la foire*. These theatres originally replaced those of the Italian comedians when the latter were expelled from France at the end of the seventeenth century, but they became rivals when the Italians returned. The *théâtres de la foire* were constantly at loggerheads with the authorities and were forced, because of the numerous prohibitions placed upon them, to draw upon their inventive skills. For instance, at one stage dialogue was prohibited, so they turned to the use of dumb characters and pantomime. The musical side of the theatre developed, and as time went on the entertainment became more diversified. Acrobatics and rope dancers became part of the scene and marionette shows were included alongside harlequinade spectaculars. The *théâtres de la foire*, however, became associated with low humour and were often the subject of scorn; but their contribution to the development of the *commedia* was extremely important, and they changed some of the masks, such as Pierrot and Pulcinella.

Although in general the *théâtres de la foire* lacked authors of high quality, nevertheless, certain dramatists succeeded in raising the plays performed there to a level of literary if not moral respectability. The best-known writer for the *foires* was Lesage, whose plays use *commedia* characters to explore the relationship between high and low culture, and to make statements about questions of power structures within contemporary society. George Evans examines these issues fully in chapter 5.

Many of the important developments in the *commedia* tradition during the nineteenth century occurred in France, and involved the figure of Pierrot. This character has received extensive critical attention, and is not a subject that concerns us in the present volume. However, an understanding of Pierrot's development is a necessary context for a reading of Glyn Pursglove on Ernest Dowson (chapter 7), David George's comparative analysis of Darío and Lugones (chapter 8), Gareth Jones on Blok (chapter 9) and Susan Harrow on Apollinaire (chapter 10). What follows is a summary of the main characteristics of the Pierrot that had emerged by the end of the nineteenth century.

In the work of many a Romantic and post-Romantic Pierrot is a frustrated, but also an elegant dandy, whereas he was little more than a comic simpleton when he was first introduced into France. A key figure in the transformation of the *commedia* in general and Pierrot in particular is the eighteenth-century French painter Antoine Watteau, in whose *Gilles* the *commedia* dolt acquires an air of melancholy loneliness. Watteau, like Marivaux, refined the *commedia dell'arte*, and hinted at the presence of frustration beneath the apparently gay and frivolous masks worn by *commedia* characters and other participants in his *fêtes galantes* paintings. Watteau's transformation of the *commedia dell'arte* greatly influenced nineteenth-century French poetry. The Goncourt brothers are generally credited with stimulating interest in Watteau among poets such as Hugo, Gautier and Verlaine. Verlaine's debt to the Watteau *commedia* in his *Fêtes galantes* has been the focus of a good deal of analysis. *Fêtes galantes* captures the playful yet melancholy elegance of the Watteau world, and highlights the sadness and occasionally the bitterness behind the fantastic disguises. The importance of Watteau, then, or at least the vision of Watteau conveyed by the Goncourt brothers and Verlaine, is central to the development of the *commedia dell'arte* in eighteenth- and nineteenth-century France away from the farce and earthy humour associated with its Italian source. However, as far as Pierrot is concerned, perhaps the key figure in his development in nineteenth-century France was the famous mime, Jean-Gaspard Deburau. Robert Storey in *Pierrot: A Critical History of a Mask* emphasizes less the 'popular' inspiration of Deburau than his role in the transformation of the figure:

> A mime whom Gautier later praised as 'the most perfect actor who ever lived' and whose talents became legendary for several generations of performers, Deburau created a stage Pierrot that eclipsed all previous interpreters of the *zanni* and hung, like a white shade, over most of his pantomimic successors. This actor has often and justly been acknowledged as the godparent of the multifarious, moonstruck Pierrots who gradually found their way into Romantic, Decadent and Symbolist literature; but Deburau's real role in the transmission of the type from the popular to the literary world – and its transformation from *naïf* to neurasthenic pariah – has been only imperfectly understood, when it has been understood at all.[2]

To such an extent had the moonstruck Pierrot penetrated not only French poetry but also Parisian popular culture by the middle of the nineteenth century that Lehmann was able to note: 'leaving aside posterity, we remark simply that around 1850 Paris appeared to an onlooker like Gavarni to be alive with Pierrots'.[3] By the late nineteenth century, Pierrot, despite (perhaps even because of) the fact that he maintains something of his innocence, clearly symbolizes tragedy rather than comedy. Yet in Laforgue's poetry, in particular, Pierrot is able to maintain a certain ironic detachment from his own tragic, or potentially tragic, situation. As Lehmann puts it: '[Laforgue's] Pierrot, the fascinated but entirely lucid victim, attempts both to participate and to stand outside; to remain alive, 'a dupe', and to stand outside, 'a dilettante".[4] Indeed, Laforgue's Pierrot contains the essential duality of the nineteenth-century Pierrot figure. As King has it, he 'is both the frivolous dilettante and the Christ-like prophet-victim, but a prophet who proves to offer no positive message, he is the elegant, superior black-costumed Hamlet-like dandy, Lord Pierrot, yet he chooses to play the role of the white-faced, white-costumed simpleton'.[5] Another characteristic of the Decadent Pierrot is his sexual impotence, which converts him into almost a cult figure for some artists and writers. To quote Huerre: 'c'est justement à cause de son inhibition sexuelle que Pierrot s'est imposé d'office comme héros de la période décadente, comme héros de l'impuissance. En effet, à cette époque, les esprits sont marqués par le pessimisme qu'a engendré la défaite de 1870 et par l'inquiétude métaphysique qui accompagne les débuts du scientisme . . . L'amour devient chez Huysmans et Oscar Wilde un culte raffiné de cette impuissance'.[6] Both the whiteness of Pierrot's costume and his liaison with the moon were symbols of sterility. Perversity is a part of this cult, and Lehmann even goes a step further and highlights a philosophical side to the Pierrot/dandy figure of late nineteenth-century France: 'Pierrot − dandy, dilettante, artist − proceeds to develop his Schopenhauer pessimism, unobtrusively, into a veritable aesthetic . . . as Schopenhauer has taught − the worship of Art is a liberation from the Will, a voluntary sterility'.[7] Sterility and frustration have thus taken on a consciously aesthetic, even philosophical dimension in the *fin de siècle* portrayal of Pierrot.

Pierrot was often a reflection or projection of the persona of the poet or the painter in the Romantic and post-Romantic periods, and to some extent the vision of the frustrated, even tragic Pierrot was a way for creative artists to wear their hearts on their sleeves. Nevertheless, Laforgue, at least, is able to set some ironic distance between himself and his Pierrot persona. This is one characteristic of his Pierrot poems which has led critics to point to his modernity.

The albeit faltering and incomplete transformation of Pierrot from doltish *commedia* servant to cynical dandy exemplifies the growing gulf between the 'popular' strand of *commedia* revival and the version of *commedia*, and particularly of Pierrot, which emerges in *fin de siècle* French poetry. King puts in a nutshell the general trend in nineteenth-century French poetry away from realism:

> . . . the gulf separating the realm of art from the realm of lived experience and objective reality was an ever increasing one, and the clown, as a blatantly proclaimed actor and champion of artifice, set himself in total contrast, physically and spiritually, with his audience and society in general. A rebel against realism, or rather his audience's conception of realism, he perceived more profoundly than his audience the comedy of life, that 'all the world's a stage'; and, symbolically, by rejecting surface realism, by means of his make-up,

costume and comic mask, he was demonstrating a deeper consciousness of the illusory nature of life and death.[8]

Parnassianism, Symbolism and Decadentism represented in part a reaction against the 'populism' and vulgar excesses of Romanticism, and their versions of Pierrot admirably illustrate the point. In chapter 7, Glyn Pursglove seeks to show that the late-Victorian Ernest Dowson, in his short play, *The Pierrot of the Minute*, restates with particular force, some of the recurrent concerns of his lyrical poetry, such as mutabality and the unattainability of human love. Pursglove argues that the play offers, in its particular story of Pierrot, a 'decadent' variation on the Fall, Man (Pierrot) expelled from his briefly inhabited Garden of Joy and Knowledge.

In chapter 8 David George compares the *commedia* poetry of two Latin American *modernista* writers, Rubén Darío and Leopoldo Lugones, and concentrates on their sharply contrasting presentation of the Pierrot figure, Darío accentuating pathos, and Lugones ridicule. These differences carry over into practically all other aspects associated with their portrayal of the *commedia*, such as innocence, spirituality, love, the town/country question and, above all, the function of language. For Darío language is musical, sensuous and sometime gently humorous. Lugones sees it as sharp, even wounding, striking and unexpected.

We have discussed the Symbolist/Decadentist appropriation of the Pierrot figure, but it should be remembered that Pierrot also belongs to the other *commedia* strand mentioned earlier, namely that of popular tradition. He was thought of by some as a man of the people, and for a socially conscious painter such as Rouault he symbolized exploitation and the travails of the lower classes. A more general identification of the *commedia* with popular tradition appears in Modernist and avant-garde culture, which saw the real and vital forms of art in *commedia*, carnival, circus and pantomime . The Modernists, Expressionists and Surrealists reacted simultaneously against what they felt were the stifling limitations of Naturalism, the smug commercialism of middle-class theatre and Western culture in general, and the élitism and refinement of Symbolism and Decadentism.

Popular art as a reaction against Symbolism is found in *The Puppet Booth* by the Russian dramatist Aleksandr Blok. In chapter 9 Gareth Jones sees the play as an attempt to subvert tradition, and to negate the Symbolist movement's treatment of the *commedia*. Spectacle and mime are central elements in the play, and are firmly linked with Meyerhold's ideas on the subject.

In chapter 10 Susan Harrow examines Apollinaire's use of the Harlequin figure in the context of the way in which Modernism looked back to tradition in order to displace it. She traces the development of the figure from a Symbolist to a Cubist representation, linking the theme of *commedia* to those of alienation and anguish, and stresses the importance of popular art to the Modernists, citing Apollinaire's rehabilitation of pantomime as an example. Harlequin here embodies the spirit of creativity as opposed to Pierrot's sentimentality as the poem becomes a creation, an end in itself and not a means to an end of lyrical expression. The poet now is a constructor, a craftsman who fashions and creates an object in a much more intellectual, detached way than the typical nineteenth-century poet.

In the music of the period 1910 to the mid-1920s, too, the *commedia dell'arte*, while to an extent encapsulating nostalgia for the past, was a means by which certain composers could register distaste with the values of those who had immediately preceded them. In chapter 11 Gabriel Jacobs analyses the appropriation of the *commedia* by these composers in the broader context of their use of popular models. While recognizing the importance of this popular source, he claims that the composers in question were great and influential figures not so much because of, but rather despite their use of popular material.

In the latter half of the twentieth century, the *commedia dell'arte* has once more demonstrated not only its longevity but also its relevance to contemporary social and artistic issues. In chapter 12 Christopher Cairns identifies two trends in the vogue for the *commedia* in contemporary theatre. These are, first, the reconstruction of *commedia* costumes and working methods, and, secondly, the adaptation or selection of styles from past *commedia* traditions for modern uses. Thus, particularly since the 1960s, a deep-rooted European theatrical tradition comes face to face with contemporary social and political causes. Cairns places Dario Fo's *Harlequin* firmly in the second of these traditions and identifies a clear connection between the committed left-wing Fo and a slightly anarchic universal type reminiscent of the earliest Harlequins in their stage personalities whose most obvious incarnation is Chaplin.

With Dario Fo's hilarious harlequinades the *commedia dell'arte* has in a way come full circle. Fo brings sharply into focus the continuing fascination with a comic tradition that has endured for some four centuries. The circle is also completed in another way, which involves the figure of Harlequin. During the nineteenth century, as we have seen, Harlequin, who hitherto had been the most popular of the *commedia* servants, was supplanted by Pierrot. The latter accorded better than Harlequin with the sensibilites of the age. As the values of Symbolism and Decadentism were rejected and satirised by the Modernists, Harlequin came back into favour. His amorality, roguishness and emotional detachment were better suited to the twentieth-century sensibility, and he was perceived by writers who saw in popular art forms a rejuvenating force as an important link with the original comic spirit of the *commedia dell'arte*. Fo retains this link, as popular theatre takes on specifically political dimensions in the second half of the twentieth century.

Chameleon-like, the *commedia* tradition has adapted to the needs and moods of each succeeding epoch, receiving new sustenance in the process. With a tradition of such complexity, explanations of its unusual vigour in terms of reactions against refined intellectualism or of stock characters paradoxically allowing artists creative freedom are of necessity at best incomplete. In the final account, we can only wonder at such a powerful phenomenon, and the studies presented in this volume are therefore not intended as definitive answers to what some see as an insoluble problem, but they offer the reader an unusual opportunity to explore some of the less charted regions of the *commedia* landscape, their unity being that taken together they demonstrate the unparalleled breadth of the tradition.

NOTES

1 Cyril W. Beaumont, *The History of Harlequin* (New York, Benjamin Blom, 1967 [reprint]), 57.
2 Robert Storey, *Pierrot: A Critical History of a Mask* (Princeton UP, 1978), 94.
3 A. G. Lehmann, 'Pierrot and *fin de siècle*', in *Romantic Mythologies*, edited by I.Fletcher (London, Routledge & Kegan Paul, 1967), 209–23 (215).
4 *Ibid.*, 217.
5 Russell P. King, 'The Poet as Clown: Variations on a Theme in Nineteenth-Century French Poetry', *Orbis Litterarum*, 33 (1978), 238–52 (250).
6 Pauline Baggio Huerre, 'Etude du personnage de Pierrot' (Stanford Univ PhD, 1976), 100.
7 Lehmann, 218–19.
8 King, 244.

1 Shakespeare and the actors of the *commedia dell'arte*[1]

ANDREW GREWAR

How is it that the manuscript of Shakespeare's plays – over thirty plays – has never been found? . . . So curious a document should have been preserved . . . Who took care that not a single page of manuscript should be handed down for us to see?

Was it destroyed by Shakespeare? . . . I believe that it was, and for a very natural reason . . . and because he was a very human being, and more of a literary man than an actor . . .

In my opinion the Dramas were created by Shakespeare in close collaboration with the Manager of the Theatre and with the actors; . . . and I believe that a glimpse of the manuscript of the plays would reveal a mass of corrections, additions, and cuts made in several handwritings. I believe that the improvisators – and the comedians of that day were great improvisators – contributed a great deal to the Comedies, and not a little to several of the Tragedies.

That the poetry and beauty of some of the unique figures in the Plays were born of Shakespeare's imagination I do not doubt, but I do most decidedly doubt whether the other part, the huge material side of the dramas came from the poet. We should be less astounded at Shakespeare's accomplishment were his Dramas less complete, if they lacked their grossness, their popular appeal, their naturalness, which, added to the sublimity of their poetic imagery, makes them seem too complete for one man to have created alone.

The naturalness of the Dramas was, I believe, wafted to England from Italy. Italy had awakened just previous to the birth of Shakespeare to a new sense of Drama. It was red hot, spontaneous, natural . . . It was not a literary effort – quite the reverse. It was good talk, wonderful patter . . .

I claim that Shakespeare's works are the fruit of a poet's collaboration with this newly formed dramatic art.

Edward Gordon Craig[2]

I

Between 1910 and 1914, Gordon Craig published over a dozen articles on the improvised Italian comedy in his theatrical journal, *The Mask*. But in spite of this, and in spite of the provocation offered by his essay on Shakespeare's plays, few of the thousands of people who have since written about Shakespeare have made even a passing reference to the *commedia dell'arte*. Craig's attempts to interest his countrymen in the links between the drama of early Renaissance Italy and that of Elizabethan England seem to have gone largely unheeded.

Of course Craig was not the first to write about the *commedia dell'arte*, nor even the first to suggest that it influenced Shakespeare, and several other, more scholarly writers have considered the topic since him.[3] Writers on the *commedia dell'arte* have indeed often claimed rather glibly that Shakespeare was influenced by the improvised drama.[4] But by and large, Shakespeare scholars have relegated the *commedia dell'arte* to the occasional gloss on an unfamiliar word such as 'pantaloon'.

Outstanding exceptions to this neglect of the Italian comedy are to be found in three monumental works of scholarship: *Italian Popular Comedy*, by Kathleen Lea, and *Masks, Mimes and Miracles* and *The World of Harlequin*, both by Allardyce Nicoll.[5] Lea discusses the connections of the *commedia dell'arte* with Elizabethan theatre, whereas Nicoll looks at the Italian popular comedy more generally. Both Lea and Nicoll find evidence of the influence of the *commedia dell'arte* on Shakespeare, although Lea is more cautious in her conclusions than Nicoll. But neither of them refers to Craig's belief that the actors may have contributed substantially to Shakespeare's plays by improvising their lines during performance.[6]

There are several scholars who have investigated the popular dramatic tradition and the links between English and Italian Renaissance drama, but who have had little to say about the *commedia dell'arte*.[7] On the other hand, there are some who have noted that certain features of Shakespeare's plays resemble aspects of the *commedia dell'arte*, and who have suggested his use of it as a source for some of his plots.[8] A few writers besides Kathleen Lea and Gordon Craig have discussed the practice of extempore acting on Shakespeare's stage and its relation to the *commedia dell'arte*.[9] But as far as I am aware, no one has ever challenged or even mentioned Craig's remarkable claim that the original actors improvised parts of

Shakespeare's plays after the manner of the *commedia dell'arte*. The subject seems to have been almost entirely ignored.

This lack of critical response to the ideas expressed by Craig seems symptomatic of a wider neglect by scholars, not only of the *commedia dell'arte*, but of theatre conventions and theatre history in general, due in part, no doubt, to their treatment of plays, particularly Shakespeare's plays, as literary texts. Where the text is held to be sacrosanct, Craig will no doubt be viewed as a dangerous heretic. His ideas may have seemed particularly iconoclastic at the time he was writing. This century, however, has seen a shift away from a strictly literary interpretation of drama. 'After a quarter-century during which scholars have been preoccupied with Shakespeare's text and Shakespeare's poetry sometimes to the exclusion, or denigration, of character and plot, the pendulum is swinging back to the more purely dramatic side of his art', wrote Bullough, more than thirty years ago.[10] There has been a renewed interest in the actor's part in interpreting a play, in theatrical and dramatic conventions, particularly those of popular theatre, and in oral as opposed to literary traditions, as may be seen in the writing of Eric Bentley, Muriel Bradbrook, John Russell Brown, Northrop Frye or Frances Yates, among others.

We need to look at Shakespeare's plays, then, in the broader context of early Renaissance theatre practice. If Craig is right, we may find in the plays traces of the Italian players' craft. Are there indications of extempore playing by the Lord Chamberlain's Men, the original actors? What scenes or roles might have been improvised by the players, and to what extent? We shall have to look at what has been discovered about the methods of the actors, both of the early *commedia dell'arte* and of the Elizabethan stage, if we are to assess Craig's contention. But to begin with, what contact, if any, may there have been between Shakespeare and the *commedia dell'arte*?

II

There is no direct evidence that Shakespeare came into contact with Italian comedians, but there are records of Italian players in England as early as 1546, and of at least a further six visits by them before 1578.[11] In January of that year, one 'Drousiano, an Italian commediante', and his troupe performed in London, having been granted a licence to do so by the city's Privy Council. Winifred Smith has pointed out that this must have been Drusiano Martinelli, who, like his more famous brother,

Tristano Martinelli, was one of the first actors to play the part of Arlecchino. Both were associated with the Confidenti, but were also to become members of the renowned Gelosi troupe. They had recently played together in Antwerp, and probably in Paris too.[12]

According to Lea, 'by 1591 the visits of Italian comedians [to England] were evidently common enough for spies to choose the habit of tumblers as a safe disguise'.[13] Besides the likelihood that Shakespeare actually saw the performances of such players in London or Paris, there is the virtual inevitability of contact between English and Italian actors, in England or abroad, over a period of several decades. It is also clear from contemporary records that the Elizabethan public was perfectly familiar with the Italian comedy. References to the main characters of the *commedia dell'arte* are found in many English plays of the period, indicating that audiences were sufficiently acquainted with the Italian types to make them 'a safe subject for allusion'.[14] Thomas Nashe made an early reference to the Masks of the *commedia dell'arte* in his vigorous defence of the English actors against Puritan censure:

> Our Players are not as the players beyond Sea – a sort of squirting baudie Comedians that haue whores and common Curtizens to playe womens partes, and forbeare no immodest speech or vnchast action that may procure laughter – ; but our Sceane is more statelye furnisht than euer it was in the time of *Roscius*, our representations honourable and full of gallant resolution, not consisting, like theirs, of a Pantaloun, a Whore, and a Zanie, but of Emperours, Kings, and Princes; whose true Tragedies . . . they do vaunt.[15]

As Lea points out, the chief *commedia dell'arte* masks, Zanni, Pantalone and Arlecchino were known 'in their Anglicized forms of Zany, Pantaloon and Harlaken'.[16] Now, according to the *Oxford English Dictionary*, the earliest documented use of the word 'pantaloon' in English occurs in a stage direction from the 'stage plot' or outline of a play called *The Dead Man's Fortune*. This is one of several such plots believed to have been found among the papers of Edward Alleyn at Dulwich College. 'Written in two columns on paper mounted on pasteboard', with 'a hole cut near the top to enable [its] being hung on a peg in the playhouse' as a guide to the actors during performance, it is thought to have been 'in the possession of Alleyn's company, the Lord Admiral's Men', and to have been drawn up for use by an amalgamated company of the Lord Admiral's Men and Lord Strange's Men some time between 1590 and 1592.[17]

In this stage plot, which consists almost entirely of a list of entrances and necessary props, Pantaloon (spelt Panteloun) is attended by his man, an equivalent of Zanni but with the more English, yet suitably clownish, name of Peascod (Pesscodde). In true *commedia dell'arte* manner the old man is cuckolded by his young wife, Asspida. Her lover is one Validore. Mention is also made of Validore's man, Sam, and a maid, Rose. These characters appear only in 'what seems to be the farcical subplot of a tragi-comedy'.[18] The subplot seems to have had all the elements of farce found in the repertoire of the *commedia dell'arte*: 'Enter panteloun whiles he speakes validore passeth ore the stage disguisde then Enter pessecode to them asspida to them the maide wth pesscodds apparell;' or 'Enter aspida & validore disguisd like rose wth a nother flasket of clothes to them the panteloun'.[19] Sketchy as it is, this plot of the jealous old man, Pantalone, cuckolded by the deceits of his wife and servants, bears a distinct resemblance to some of the earliest known *scenari*, those published in 1611 by Flaminio Scala and associated with the famous Gelosi troupe.[20]

But, for us, one of the most significant details of *The Plot of the Dead Man's Fortune* is that it contains the direction 'Enter Burbage', referring to none other than Richard Burbage. It is interesting to find him at the age of about twenty acting in a play with distinct features of the *commedia dell'arte*. His acting career had started at the age of thirteen, and he was already a notable actor by 1590. From what we know, he was to play the lead in virtually all of Shakespeare's plays. It is not clear what part he played in the *Dead Man's Fortune*, though Greg has suggested it was the fairly major role of the magician Urganda.[21]

The name Burbage is also found in another of these stage plots, *The Platt of the Secound Parte of the Seuen Deadlie Sinns* (?1592).[22] In fact, this plot contains the names of most of the combined Admiral's–Strange's company: Thomas Pope, George Bryan, Richard Cowley, John Duke, Augustine Phillips, John Sincler, and William Slye, among others. (Pope and Bryan are first heard of in 1586 – 'at Elsinore, of all places', as Gurr remarks – where, together with the clown Will Kemp, they were entertaining Danish royalty.[23]) These were the players who with Shakespeare and Burbage were to form the Lord Chamberlain's Men in 1594. They were listed in the First Folio as having acted in all of Shakespeare's plays and praised by Heywood in his *Apology for Actors* as among the chief actors of the age. Greg considers 'reasonable enough' the speculation that the young Shakespeare may have played Henry VI in the performances in which the plot of *The Seven Deadly Sins* was used.[24]

John Payne Collier, in his *Annals of the English Stage* (1831), was apparently the first to note the possibility that these plots show a direct link between the *commedia dell'arte* and Elizabethan drama. Surprisingly, this was not because of the name 'Pantaloon' in *The Dead Man's Fortune*, but because he thought the plot outlines themselves were equivalent to the Italian *scenari*, and that the plays must have been presented impromptu.[25] Later scholars have disputed this, however. Lea, for example, says that these stage plots were merely prompter's aids such as were used in scripted plays, and that the *commedia dell'arte scenari* were more explicit, describing 'every turn of the plot as it is to be presented in action'. Greg, too, finds no evidence that the plots were actually used in improvised performances.[26]

But there is no reason to suppose that plot outlines like these were *not* used back-stage in extemporary performances, even if these stage plots were not in fact the equivalents of *scenari*, as Collier thought. In fact, an improvised play would be more likely to require just such an aid. The *scenari* contained in a collection such as Locatelli's may have been elaborations of such plot outlines made for use during performance. Greg even admits at one point that it would be difficult 'to refute the suggestion' that at least the sub-plot of *The Dead Man's Fortune* might have been 'rendered by the actors impromptu'.[27]

So in spite of the caution expressed by Lea and Greg, it seems that as early as 1590 most of the actors who were to work with Shakespeare – and perhaps Shakespeare himself – were not only acquainted with the stock characters of the *commedia dell'arte*, but may actually have been using its comic conventions and the technique of improvisation in the plays they were performing.

III

It is not entirely surprising, then, to find Shakespeare himself providing the *OED*'s next historical reference to 'pantaloon' in *The Taming of the Shrew* (?1590–91). The name is twice used to refer to Gremio, first in a stage direction: *Enter Baptista with his two daughters, Katerina & Bianca, Gremio a Pantelowne, Hortentio suter to Bianca* (I.i.45/322),[28] and again later, during Bianca's 'music' and 'grammar' lessons. Disguised as the pedant Cambio, and under the pretence of 'construing' Ovid's Latin, Lucentio attempts to explain the situation to Bianca:

> *Hic ibat*, as I told you before, *Simois*, I am Lucentio, *hic est*, sonne vnto Vincentio of Pisa, *Sigeia tellus*, disguised thus to get your loue, *hic*

steterat, and that Lucentio that comes a wooing, *Priami*, is my man Tranio, *regia*, bearing my port, *celsa senis*, that we may beguile the old Pantalowne. (III.i.31–6/1246–51)

Besides this direct reference to Pantalone, the scene shows various devices common in the scenarios of the *commedia dell'arte*: the inversion of the roles of master and servant, the servant wooing in the place of the master, the lover disguised as a pedant in order to gain access to the *innamorata*, and very possibly also the *lazzo* of the Latin 'translation'. And as in the plot of *The Dead Man's Fortune*, the word 'pantaloon' is used as if to indicate a class of foolish old men: '*the* Pantaloon'.

As we see, the Pantaloon is not the *Shrew*'s only link with the Italian comedy. But before we consider such parallels more closely, let us consider other references by Shakespeare to the *commedia dell'arte* masks. *Love's Labour's Lost* (?1594–5) contains one of the earliest examples in English of the use of the word 'zany', from *zanni*, the general name for the clownish servant. Clearly Shakespeare takes the word to mean 'servant', 'follower' or 'imitator' as well as 'clown'. Thus Berowne calls Boyet,

> Some carry tale, some please-man, some sleight sanie:
> Some mumble newes, some trencher Knight, some Dick,
> That smyles his cheeke in yeeres, and knowes the trick
> To make my Lady laugh, when shees disposd.
> (V.ii.463–66/2213–17)

And in *Twelfth Night* (?1601), Malvolio with a nasty twist reverses the master–servant relationship when he uses it to refer to those (such as Olivia!) who laugh at the jokes of his enemy, the fool Feste:

> I protest I take these Wisemen, that crow so at these set kinde of fooles, no better than the fooles Zanies. (I.v.83–4/365–7)

Shakespeare's only other direct reference to the masks shows most clearly his acquaintance with them. It is found, of course, in *As You Like It* (?1599–1600), in Jaques' well-known depiction of the Seven Ages of Man:

> All the world's a stage,
> And all the men and women, meerely Players;
> They haue their *Exits* and their Entrances,
> And one man in his time playes many parts,
> His Acts being seuen ages. At first the Infant,

Mewling, and puking in the Nurses armes;
Then, the whining Schoole-boy with his Satchell
And shining morning face, creeping like snaile
Vnwillingly to schoole. And then the Louer,
Sighing like Furnace, with a woful ballad
Made to his Mistresse eye-brow. Then, a Soldier,
Full of strange oaths, and bearded like the Pard,
Ielous in honor, sodaine and quicke in quarrell,
Seeking the bubble Reputation
Euen in the Cannons mouth: And then, the Iustice
In faire round belly, with good Capon lin'd,
With eyes seuere, and beard of formall cut,
Full of wise sawes, and moderne instances,
And so he playes his part. The sixt age shifts
Into the leane and slipper'd Pantaloone,
With spectacles on nose and pouch on side,
His youthfull hose well sau'd, a world too wide,
For his shrunke shanke, and his bigge manly voice,
Turning againe toward childish trebble, pipes,
And whistles in his sound. Last Scene of all,
That ends this strange euentfull historie,
Is second childishnesse and meere obliuion,
Sans teeth, sans eyes, sans taste, sans euery thing.

(II.vii.139–66/1062–89)

Here we have a vivid and accurate portrait of four of the *commedia dell'arte* masks as they strutted on the Renaissance stage: 'No one who has studied the prints representing the early Venetian type', says Nicoll,

> can turn to the 'Seven Ages of Man' and deny that Shakespeare had seen a real Pantalone. His leanness, his spectacles, his pouch – all are there to testify to the exactitude of the dramatist's knowledge. Perhaps it may even be true that, in this famous speech, Shakespeare's imagination had been fired by witnessing the Italian *amoroso* (lover), Capitano (soldier), Dottore (justice), and Pantalone whom he has thus introduced at their appropriate cues.[29]

IV

Now that we have looked at some of the ways that the *commedia dell'arte* may have been encountered by Shakespeare and the direct references he made to it, let us consider some of the parallels that exist between his plays and those of the Italian players.

As I see it, there are two main areas to be considered. First, there are the techniques or methods of the *commedia dell'arte*, namely the art of improvised acting and the clowning or *lazzi* of the zanies. Second, there are its materials, by which I mean the stock characters and the stock situations in which they seem fated to find themselves. Northrop Frye has pointed out the similarities of the plot conventions in Shakespeare's comedies and romances to those in the *commedia dell'arte*, and their relation to popular folklore and to myth. Along with the plots came the characters of the Italian comic repertoire, both of which he adopted and adapted to his own ends, as Oscar Campbell has argued.[30] Even a brief comparison of the characters of his early comedies with the *commedia dell'arte* masks shows that Shakespeare made extensive use of the traditional types, the 'character myth' of comedy, as Eric Bentley terms it.[31] This is a vast area deserving extended treatment and I shall not be able to discuss Shakespeare's use of these comic conventions within the scope of this essay. I shall therefore confine myself here to a discussion of the techniques of improvisation and the possible traces of the actors' art to be found in his plays.

As the name itself indicates, the main feature of the *commedia dell'arte* was the supremacy of the professional actors. I have already mentioned some of the possible links between the English actors and the Italian comedians. Obviously there were differences in the circumstances and methods of the Italian and English players, but what is important is the fact that both groups were professionals. It is surely not mere chance that the flowering of drama in Renaissance Italy and England coincided with the professionalism of companies such as the Gelosi or the Lord Chamberlain's Men. Like that of the *commedia dell'arte*, Shakespeare's theatre was very much a theatre of the actors.

Their importance is shown, for instance, in the fact that Shakespeare seems to have written with the members of his company in mind for the various parts. 'Working in close association with a regular company of players,' says Martin Holmes, 'he would become instinctively familiar not only with their individual characters and capabilities, but with the sound, pace and effect of their different voices upon the stage.'[32] This may be why we sometimes find that, as in the reference to Burbage in *The Dead Man's Fortune*, an actor's name is used in a stage direction instead of the character's. Kemp and Cowley, for example, were assigned the speeches of Dogberry and Verges in the 1600 Quarto edition of *Much Ado About Nothing*.[33] And the 1599 Quarto of *Romeo and Juliet* has the direction *Enter Will Kemp* at the end of Act Four, instead of *Enter Peter*. Playing the comic servant or zany, he engages in repartee with the musicians, gives them all quibbling nicknames, and plays a typically clownish, riddling game of one-upmanship before he leaves, 'taking off the edge of lamentation for Juliet's supposed death'.[34] 'In each case,' notes John Russell Brown, 'the actor seems to have dominated Shakespeare's creating mind.'[35] On the basis of these references to the actors, T. W. Baldwin long ago argued that they played certain 'lines' or specialized roles, such as the clown, the braggart, or the 'fat fool'. He seems oblivious, though, of the similarity of such a practice to the methods of the *commedia dell'arte* actors.[36]

The importance of the actors in Shakespeare's theatre is also shown by the frequency with which they appear *in propriae personae*, as themselves. The motto of the Globe Theatre, *Totus mundus agit histrionem*, is echoed in Jaques' 'All the world's a stage, and all the men and women merely players', as well as in Macbeth's vision of despair:

> Life's but a walking Shadow, a poore Player,
> That struts and frets his houre vpon the Stage,
> And then is heard no more.   (V.v.24–6/2004–6)

In both *Hamlet* and *The Taming of the Shrew*, troupes of strolling players perform a play within the play, drawing our attention indirectly to the convention of the theatre itself. They are clearly professionals who are held in some esteem, both by Hamlet and the Lord who appears in the Induction of *The Shrew*. On the other hand, the distinctly amateur dramatic efforts of Bottom and his 'rude mechanicals' in *A Midsummer Night's Dream* are gently satirized, as are those of Armado and company in the Pageant of the Nine Worthies in *Love's Labour's Lost*.

Christopher Sly and the other characters in *The Shrew*'s Induction are undoubtedly English, in contrast to the very Italianate play that is performed for them. Does this reflect anything more than the fact that Italian players were fashionable in England at the time? Polonius reminds us that (like the actors of the *commedia dell'arte*) the players visiting Hamlet in Elsinore have a wide repertoire of both scripted and improvised plays, for, as Nicoll notes, the 'lawe of writ' and the 'liberty' 'may well be an allusion to the literary and improvised styles':[37]

> The best actors in the world, either for Tragedie, Comedy, History, Pastorall, Pastoricall Comicall, Historicall Pastorall, Tragicall-Historical: Tragicall-Comicall-Historicall-Pastorall: scene indeuidible, or Poem

vnlimited. *Sceneca* cannot be too heauy, nor *Plautus* too light, for the
lawe of writ, and the liberty these are the only men.

(Ham.II.ii.392–7/1327–33)

This brings us to the feature of the *commedia dell'arte* that is central
to this discussion: improvisation. If the actors played such an important
part in Shakespeare's theatre, what evidence is there that they actually
contributed materially to the text of the plays, as Craig asserted?

According to Lea, the 'extemporall witte' so much praised by the
Elizabethans, of entertainers such as Richard Tarlton and Will Kemp,
'refers to their talent for composing rhymes upon given themes'. This,
she says, was the primary meaning of the word 'extempore': 'To a
theme the Italians were expected to fit a plot, the Englishmen a rhyme.'[38]

In *Love's Labour's Lost* the braggart, Don Adriano de Armado, and
the pedant, Holofernes, are both satirized for their pretensions as
extemporizing poets: 'Assist me, some extemporal god of rhyme', cries
Armado dramatically, 'for I am sure I shall turn sonnet. Devise, wit;
write pen; for I am for whole volumes in folio' (I.ii.167–70/475–7). The
absurd conceits of the 'sonnet' he appends to his love-letter to
Jaquenetta testify more to the outrageous extravagance of his self-
importance than to the generosity of his muse:

> Thus dost thou heare the nemean Lion roare,
> Gainst thee thou Lambe, that standest as his pray:
> Submissiue fall his princely feete before,
> And he from forrage will incline to play.
> But if thou striue (poore soule) what art thou then?
> Foode for his rage, repasture for his den.   (IV.i.81–6/1019–24)

And the pedant, Holofernes, delivering an equally absurd 'extemporal
epitaph' on the death of the deer killed by the Princess, explains his
talent with false modesty:

> This is a gyft that I haue simple: simple, a foolish extrauagant spirit,
> full of formes, figures, shapes, obiects, Ideas, aprehentions, motions,
> reuolutions. These are begot in the ventricle of Memorie, nourisht in
> the wombe of *pia mater*, and deliuered vpon the mellowing of
> occasion: But the gyft is good in those in whom it is acute, and I am
> thankfull for it.   (IV.ii.62–9/1144–50)

The term 'extempore' was also applied to acting, but this, says Lea,
was only a secondary meaning. We find it used in this sense in
Midsummer Night's Dream, but such acting does not seem to be viewed
very seriously:

SNUG   Haue you the Lyons part written? Pray you, if it bee, giue it
mee: for I am slowe of studie.
QUINCE   You may do it extempore, for it is nothing but roaring.

(I.ii.58–61/313–16)

On the other hand, there is Falstaff's suggestion: 'What shall wee bee
merrie, shall wee haue a play extempore?' and the telling rehearsal of
'real-life' roles that follows (H IV Pt 1, II.iv.270–71/1210–11). Moreover, in the comedy or 'kind of history' enacted before Christopher Sly,
there is the boast of Petruchio, a less ridiculous braggart than Armado.
'Where did you study all this goodly speech?' asks Kate scathingly after
a sally of extravagant and astonishing compliments. 'It is *extempore*,
from my mother wit', is his swift reply. 'A witty mother, witlesse else
her sonne', is hers, no less swiftly 'improvised' (Shr.II.i.262–4/1065–7).
Do these references to extempore playing indicate more than simply
that Shakespeare was aware of the practice?

It is tempting to think so, but then we have Hamlet's advice to the
players, which seems to end our speculations about Shakespeare's
opinion of improvisation on the stage:

> . . . and let those that play your clownes speake no more then is set
> downe for them, for there be of them that wil themselues laugh, to set
> on some quantitie of barraine spectators to laugh to, though in the
> meane time, some necessary question of the play be then to be
> considered, that's villanous, and shewes a most pittifull ambition in
> the foole that vses it.   (III.ii.36–44/1765–72)

This is the stern voice of the playwright, 'jealous in honour' of the
written word, it seems. The speech may be an attack on the clowning of
Will Kemp, who had left the Lord Chamberlain's Men in 1599,
apparently on bad terms with Shakespeare, and having danced his
famous morris-dance from London to Norwich in 1600, was in
Germany or Italy when *Hamlet* was first performed (?1600–1). In the
pirated first Quarto there is a longer version of this speech, which,
ironically enough, may have been an impromptu comment by Burbage,
who of course played Hamlet.[39] Here, as Lea says, 'the reprimand of the
clown is remarkably personal':

> And then you have some agen, that keepes one sute
> Of jests, as a man is known by one sute
> Of Apparell, & Gentlemen quotes his ieasts downe
> In their tables, before they come to the play, as thus:
> Cannot you stay till I eate my porrige? &, you owe me

> A quarter's wages: & my coate wants a cullison:
> And, your beere is sowre: &, blabbering with his lips
> And thus keeping in his cinkapase of ieasts,
> When, God knows, the warme Clowne cannot make a iest
> Unlesse by chance, as the blind man catcheth a hare.

Harrison notes that Shakespeare may have been particularly annoyed because Kemp joined the rival company, Worcester's Men at the Rose Theatre, 'almost next door to the Globe', after his return from abroad late in 1601. He did apparently rejoin the company, but it is not known when, nor whether he ever took Hamlet's advice. 'Probably,' suggests Lea, he 'continued with his 'pitiful ambition' to the end of his days.'[40] David Wiles, in his thorough study of Shakespeare's clowns, has suggested that Worcester's Men offered Kemp a greater opportunity than did the Lord Chamberlain's of displaying his unique talents as a performer.[41]

Kemp's place was taken by Robert Armin, a very different kind of comedian. Kemp's act was that of the rough country bumpkin – played in roles such as Launce, Launcelot Gobbo, Costard or Grumio. By contrast, Armin played the court jester or fool, and provided Shakespeare with a dry, ironic voice for the roles of Feste, Lavache, Touchstone and Lear's Fool.

It has frequently been suggested that there was an unusual degree of collaboration between Shakespeare and Armin, who had been a playwright himself before joining the Lord Chamberlain's Men.[42] And despite the fact that he was one of the new breed of what Malvolio contemptuously called 'these set kind of fools', as opposed to the traditional extemporizing clown, he may well have contributed jokes and stage business and his professional knowledge of fooling to the parts he played. Guy Butler has suggested that some of the obscure quips made by Touchstone in *As You Like It* were skirmishes in the 'running battle between the witty fool and the clownish fool': 'I remember,' says Touchstone,

> when I was in loue, I broke my sword vpon a stone, and bid him take that for comming a night to *Iane Smile*, . . . and I remember the wooing of a peascod instead of her; from whom I tooke two cods, and, giuing them her againe, said with weeping teares, weare these for my sake.   (II.iv.46–8/790–97)

Butler identifies Stone as the tavern fool John Stone, and Peascod as none other than the clown of the Admiral's–Strange's Men, who played the zany to Pantaloon in *The Dead Man's Fortune*![43]

It is tempting to speculate as to whether Kemp had taken the part of Peascod, but there is no mention of him in any of the stage plots. Although *The Seven Deadly Sins* has the following scene as part of the representation of Sloth –

> Enter sardanapa . wth the Ladies to them A
> Messenger . Th Goodale to him will foole
> Runing   A Larum

– an earlier scene appears to indicate that the part of 'will foole' was played by John Duke, another early member of the Lord Chamberlain's Men.[44] However, we find that Kemp was in fact working with the Admiral's–Strange's Men around 1592–3, just at the time that they are thought to have been using the stage plots. The title page of *A Knacke to Knowe a Knave*, registered in January 1594, gives the play,

> Newlie set foorth, as it hath sundrie times bene played by Ed. Allen and his companie. With Kemps applauded Merrimentes of the men of Goteham, in receiving the King into Goteham.

But the roles of the 'mad men of Goteham' must have been largely improvised, for apart from a few Dogberry-like malapropisms on the part of the miller, little remains of Kemp's 'applauded merrimentes'.[45]

If the author (Nashe?) of *An Almond for a Parrat* is to be believed, Kemp's fame seems to have spread among *commedia dell'arte* actors before 1590:

> . . . comming from Venice the last Summer, and taking Bergamo in my waye homeward to England, it was my happe, soiourning there some four or fiue dayes, to light in felowship with that famous Francatrip' Harlicken, who . . . enquired of me whether I knew any such Parabolano here in London as Signior Chiarlatano Kempino.[46]

'It is pleasing to imagine', says Nicoll, that this 'Harlicken' was Tristano Martinelli, whose brother Drusiano had been to London, but the tale is most likely Nashe's fiction.[47] Whether or not it is true, there are definite records of Kemp visiting Italy in 1601. This may be the basis for a scene in John Day's play, *The Travailes of Three English Brothers* (1607), where a character named Kemp is shown taking part in some 'extemporall merriment' with an Italian Harlaken, for the entertainment of their host:

> HARLAKEN   Marry Sir, first we will have an old Pantaloune.
> KEMP   Some iealous Coxcombe.

HARLAKEN   Right, & that part will I play.

KEMP   The iealous Cox-combe.

HARLAKEN   I ha plaid that part ever since . . .

KEMP   Your wife plaid the Curtizan.

HARLAKEN   True, & a great while afore, then I must have a peasant to my man, & he must keepe my wife.

KEMP   Your man, & a peasant, keepe your wife, I have knowne a Gentleman keepe a peasants wife: but 'tis not usual for a peasant to keepe his maisters wife.

HARLAKEN   Oh tis common in our countrey.

KEMP   And ile maintain the custome of the country.
   offers to kisse his wife

HARLAKEN   What do you meane sir?

KEMP   Why to rehearse my part on your wives lips: we are fellowes, & amongst friends & fellowes you knowe all things are common.

HARLAKEN   But she shall bee no common thing, if I can keepe her severall: then sir we must have an *Amorado* that must make me Cornuto.

KEMP   Oh for loves sake let me play that part.

HARLAKEN   No yee must play my mans part, & keepe my wife.

KEMP   Right, & who so fit to make a man a Cuckold as hee that keepes his wife.

HARLAKEN   You shall not play that part.

KEMP   What say you to my boy?

HARLAKEN   I, he may play it and you will.

KEMP   But he cannot make you iealous enough?

HARLAKEN   Tush I warrant you, I can be iealous for nothing.

KEMP   You should not be a true *Italian* else.

HARLAKEN   Then we must have a Magnifico that must take up the matter betwixt me & my wife.

KEMP   Any thing of yours, but Ile take up nothing of your wives.

HARLAKEN   I wish not you should, but come, now am I your Maister.

KEMP   Right, & I your servant.

HARLAKEN   Lead the way then.[48]

Kemp is obviously able to 'play the Fool's zany' with a vengeance! If there is any truth in this, Kemp was a master of the sort of extempore wit needed for the play envisaged here. He seems utterly at home in the role of the servant who undermines his master's authority at every turn.

V

But the fact that Kemp is depicted as able to act in 'a true extempore comedy' in Italy, says Lea, 'does not prove that these methods were practised in England.' 'No amount of licence to rhyme and gag brings the impromptu element in English drama into line with the Italian practice of improvisation.' What would have been lacking, above all, she says, is 'the discipline of co-operation which was the secret of the improvising comedians.'[49]

Despite Lea's argument, it may yet be instructive to enquire whether this was in fact so. If we look again at Hamlet's description of the clown's 'gagging' we find that it comes closer to Riccoboni's definition of Arlecchino's *lazzi* than to improvised acting as such: 'We give the name of *lazzi* to the actions of Harlequin or other masked characters when they interrupt a scene by their expressions of terror or by their fooleries. These have nothing to do with the subject on hand, and to it return must always be made.'[50]

Hamlet's complaint may simply be against an indulgence in *lazzi* and playing to the 'groundlings'. 'Let those that play your clowns speak no more than is set down for them', he says. It is just possible, at least in parts of some of Shakespeare's plays, that what was 'set down' was the plot rather than a complete script. The Italian comedians were aware of the dangers of interrupting the plot for the sake of a few cheap laughs, as we see from Perrucci:

> The actors, having heard [from the *corago* or director] what they have to do in the matter of entering as well as in the treatment and termination of the scenes, will be able with their companions to rehearse the scenes and devise among themselves some new lazzi or something after their own fancy. One must take care, however, not to depart so much from the argument as not to be able to return to it, and be prudent in this respect so that the audience may not, owing to long and persistent lazzi, lose the thread of the story or have difficulty in understanding it again.[51]

Supposing that Shakespeare did in fact allow the actors a degree of freedom to improvise, what indications of this might we expect to find in the plays? Are there comic devices peculiar to the improvised performances of the *commedia dell'arte* that he or his actors may have known and used?

Nicoll describes the use by the Italian improvisators of rhyming couplets for exits (*uscite*), and endings of speeches (*chiusette*). This is a common enough poetic practice in Elizabethan drama, and its extensive use by Shakespeare is hardly extraordinary. Were the English playwrights indebted to Italian models in this, perhaps, whether literary or *dell'arte*? The possible currents of influence are obscure.

In the *commedia* the lovers in particular made much use of conceits (*concetti*), upon which they might base a soliloquy or fashion a dialogue.[52] According to Lea, *concetti* are 'brief speeches containing some witty paradox or comparison. . . . It falls to the lady to catch the idea of the conceit, and return it in graceful dialogue'. A sustained conceit is found in the following 'dialogue of unrequited love':

HE   Behold a lover who offers you his heart.

SHE   I do not accept the fumes of an incense that does not please me.

HE   I am a moth-like lover fluttering round your lovely light, and caring nothing for death.

SHE   A foolish insect if it courts its destruction, and a stupid heart to seek death in my face.

HE   Rather, a noble fly if it prefers a shining tomb above an obscure life, and my heart, rejoicing in your beautiful fire, cares not that it is burnt to ashes.[53]

Another common device in the *commedia dell'arte* was that of repeating what the previous actor had said, in different words. Lea gives an example of a dialogue of 'mutual disdain' between two lovers:

SHE   The bonds . . .

HE   The chains . . .

SHE   . . . that bind . . .

HE   . . . that fetter . . .

SHE   . . . this soul . . .

HE   . . . my heart . . .

SHE   . . . crack!

HE   . . . burst!

. . .

SHE   I say I detest you . . .

HE   I say I abhor you . . .

SHE   . . . and that I cannot endure the sight of you any more.

HE   . . . and that I cannot bear to be with you any more.

SHE   Do you not know, these bonds . . .

HE   Do you not know, these shackles . . .

SHE   . . . which you said were of gold . . .

HE   . . . which you said were of diamond . . .

SHE   . . . are proved false.

HE   . . . were only of glass.[54]

'Ridiculous as this is,' comments Nicoll, 'one could imagine its having an electrical effect . . . when uttered by two performers gifted in this kind.'[55]

The exchanges between Benedick and Beatrice in *Much Ado About Nothing* are marked by the way they echo one another's quips. They are far more witty, but much of the time they are engaged in a similarly constructed, if more elaborate, dialogue of reciprocal scorn, where each echoes the other's sentiments, and picks up and plays with a word or image used by the other:

> BEATRICE   I wonder that you will still be talking, signior Benedicke, no body markes you.
> BENEDICKE   What, my deere lady Disdaine! are you yet liuing?
> BEATRICE   Is it possible Disdaine should die while she hath such meete foode to feede it, as signior Benedick? Curtesie it selfe must conuert to Disdaine, if you come in her presence.
> BENEDICKE   Then is curtesie a turn-coate, but it is certaine I am loued of all Ladies, onlie you excepted: and I would I could finde in my heart that I had not a hard heart, for truely, I loue none.
> BEATRICE   A deere happinesse to women, they would else haue beene troubled with a pernitious suter, I thanke God and my cold blood, I am of your humour for that, I had rather heare my dog barke at a crow, than a man sweare he loues me.
> BENEDICKE   God keepe your Ladiship stil in that mind, so some Gentleman or other shall scape a predestinate scratcht face.
> BEATRICE   Scratching could not make it worse, and twere such a face as yours were.
> BENEDICKE   Well, you are a rare parrat teacher.
> BEATRICE   A bird of my tongue, is better than a beast of yours.
> BENEDICKE   I would my horse had the speed of your tongue, and so good a continuer, but keep your way, a Gods name, I haue done.
> BEATRICE   You always end with a iade's tricke, I knowe you of olde.   (I.i.99–124/110–39)

The dialogue sounds remarkably similar to that of Berowne and Rosaline at *their* first encounter in *Love's Labour's Lost*:

> BEROWNE   (*to Rosaline*)
> Did not I dance with you in *Brabant* once?
> ROSALINE
> Did not I dance with you in *Brabant* once?
> BEROWNE
> I know you did.
> ROSALINE   How needles was it then
> To aske the question?

BEROWNE   You must not be so quicke.
ROSALINE
Tis long of you that spur me with such questions.
BEROWNE
Your wit's too hot, it speedes too fast, twill tire.
ROSALINE
Not till it leaue the rider in the mire.
BEROWNE
What time a day?
ROSALINE
The houre that fooles should aske.
BEROWNE
Now faire befall your maske.
ROSALINE
Fair fall the face it couers.
BEROWNE
And send you manie louers.
ROSALINE
Amen, so you be none.
BEROWNE
Nay then will I be gon.   (II.i.113–26/591–604)

The fact that the last part of this exchange is rhymed does not mean that
it could not have been produced impromptu. As we have seen, the
English entertainers were renowned for their extempore rhymes, and
Kemp was as famous for his extempore rhyming jigs as Tarlton before
him.

We find very much the same type of exchange in the verbal skirmishes
between Petruchio and that other Katherine, even more 'curst' than
Beatrice:

PETRUCHIO
Hearing thy mildnesse prais'd in euery Towne,
Thy vertues spoke of, and thy beautie sounded,
Yet not so deepely as to thee belongs,
My selfe am moou'd to woo thee for my wife.
KATHERINE
Mou'd, in good time, let him that mou'd you hether
Remoue you hence: I knew you at the first
You were a moueable.
PETRUCHIO   Why, what's a moueable?
KATHERINE
A ioyn'd-stoole.

PETRUCHIO   Thou hast hit it: come sit on me.
KATHERINE
Asses are made to beare, and so are you.
PETRUCHIO
Women are made to beare, and so are you.
KATHERINE
No such Iade as you, if me you meane.
PETRUCHIO
Alas good *Kate*, I will not burthen thee,
For knowing thee to be but yong and light.
KATHERINE
Too light for such a swaine as you to catch;
And yet as heauie as my waight should be.
PETRUCHIO
Shold be, should: buzze.
KATHERINE   Well tane, and like a buzzard.
PETRUCHIO
O, slow-wing'd Turtle, shall a buzard take thee?
KATHERINE
I for a Turtle, as he takes a buzard.
PETRUCHIO
Come, come you Waspe, y'faith you are too angrie.
KATHERINE
If I be waspish, best beware my sting.
PETRUCHIO
My remedy is then to plucke it out.
KATHERINE
I, if the foole could finde it where it lies.
PETRUCHIO
Who knows not where a Waspe does weare his sting?
In his taile.
KATHERINE   In his tongue?
PETRUCHIO   Whose tongue.
KATHERINE
Yours if you talke of tales; and so farewell.
PETRUCHIO
What with my tongue in your taile. Nay, come again,
Good *Kate*, I am a Gentleman.
KATHERINE   That Ile trie.
                    She strikes him
                    (Shr.II.i.191–214/999–1025)

Peter Bryant points out the similarity of much of the language of *The Shrew* to the bawdy jigs that were so popular at the time, many of them sharp and witty exchanges in the war of the sexes.[56] One wonders whether the Lord Chamberlain's Men did not have one or more boy actors, such as Richard Cowley or Alexander Cooke, perhaps, who specialized in this type of spicy repartee for certain female parts.

Besides echoing the other's conceits, or rhyming, an improvising actor could also display his wit by punning on the other's words. Many of the exchanges between the couples mentioned, and many other bits of comic dialogue, are based on quibbling wordplay, and this might be another indication of improvisation. Dr Johnson deplored Shakespeare's fondness for puns: 'A quibble, poor and barren as it is, gave him such delight that he was content to purchase it by the sacrifice of reason, propriety, and truth.' One reason for his objections may have been the bawdiness of many of the puns. While he commends Shakespeare for the 'ease and simplicity' of his dialogue, he remarks that,

> In his comic scenes he is seldom very successful when he engages his characters in reciprocations of smartness and contests of sarcasm; their jests are commonly gross, and their pleasantry licentious; neither his gentlemen nor his ladies have much delicacy nor are sufficiently distinguished from his clowns by any appearance of refined manners.[57]

Perhaps it was not Shakespeare, but the improvising actors who were responsible for the quibbling and much of the bawdiness.

Besides the puns and the echoing of poetic conceits already mentioned, where the actors provoked the audience's amusement or admiration with sustained play on words or images, the *comici* had recourse to other types of verbal or physical *lazzi* as a way of sustaining a scene. Richard Andrews has observed that traces of the *commedia dell'arte* in scripted drama may be indicated by the presence of a type of 'elastic' gag used by the improvising actors. This was a joke which could be drawn out at will by the performers, according to the audience's response, often simply by the device of suspending the punchline.

A series of such jokes, Andrews suggests, could have provided a 'modular', easily memorized structure for an improvised scene. He has found such gags in various Italian plays written after the mid-sixteenth century, particularly in the *commedie ridicolose* of Briccio and Verucci. These fully scripted plays apparently date from around the turn of the seventeenth century, and seem to have been attempts by amateurs 'to reproduce something like the *commedia dell'arte* experience in private performances among friends . . . ' They contain elements which reappear in Molière's plays, leading Andrews to propose that they show Molière's use of what may originally have been *commedia dell'arte* techniques for improvised performance.

Andrews gives several interesting examples of the type of 'elastic' gags he believes gives evidence of *commedia dell'arte* influence in scripted drama. The first is the delaying of even the most banal event, such as the opening of a door. Here Andrews cites the scene between the two Dromios in the *Comedy of Errors* (III.i) as an example of this form of *lazzi*, although he believes the dialogue shows the playwright's hand as well as the voice of two clowns 'settling down to milk a situation absolutely dry, however long it takes'.[58]

A second such trick has one actor reading a document (usually the Dottore or pedant, with atrocious mangling of Latin) accompanied by a translation into absurd or suggestive everyday Italian. Lucentio's Latin 'translation' in *The Shrew*, mentioned earlier, may bear traces of this gag. So may the bawdy English lesson given to the Princess Katherine by Alice her maid in *Henry V* (III.iv). Launce's 'cate-log' of the milkmaid's virtues and vices, read out by Speed as a 'feed' to Launce's licentious quibbles, is a similar gag (III.i.276–359).

These last also resemble another *lazzi* which could easily be prolonged. This is simply that of working through a list, typically, says Andrews a 'list of suitors'. He cites as an example the scene in *The Merchant of Venice* (I.ii) where Portia declines each of the suitors listed by Nerissa, with mocking dismissal, until finally Bassanio is named. It is interesting that an earlier version of the same scene is to be found in *The Two Gentlemen of Verona*, played between Julia and her maid, Lucetta, where Julia names her would-be lovers and Lucetta gives her opinion 'which is worthiest love' (I.ii.1–21). There is another echo of this list of suitors in *The Shrew*:

> KATHERINE
> > Of all thy sutors heere I charge thee tel
> > Whom thou lou'st best: see thou dissemble not.
> BIANCA
> > Beleeue me sister, of all the men aliue
> > I neuer yet beheld that speciall face
> > Which I could fancie more then any other.
> KATHERINE
> > Minion thou lyest: Is't not *Hortensio*?

BIANCA
  If you affect him sister, heere I sweare
  Ile pleade for you my selfe, but you shal haue him.
KATHERINE
  O then, belike, you fancie riches more:
  You wil haue *Gremio* to keepe you faire.
BIANCA
  Is it for him you do enuie me so?
  Nay then you jeste, and now I wel perceiue
  You haue but iested with me all this while:
  I prithee sister Kate, vntie my hands.
KATHERINE   (*strikes her*)
  If that be iest, then all the rest was so.   (II.i.8–20/816–28).

Besides these sorts of devices, a further aid to improvisation used by
the *commedia dell'arte* actors was to arrange themselves in symmetrical
patterns if there were many actors on stage, and to pattern their
dialogue accordingly. Many of the *scenari* demonstrate such symmetry
in the grouping and entrances of characters.[59] Tim Fitzpatrick has
analysed Scala's *scenari* to show how they are contrived to group the
actors in pairs.[60] One couple might echo or parody the utterances of
another pair, or display contrasting responses to a situation. Fitzpatrick
notes that this binary patterning often forms a chain: 'A loves B, but B
loves C, who in turn is in love with D, who loves A'. A neater summary
of the main plots of *Twelfth Night* or *A Midsummer Night's Dream*
would be hard to find!
   Lea also mentions the common device of deliberate repetition of a
joke, a phrase or an action for comic effect: 'When something happens
three times in succession we laugh whether it is a joke or not. Why? The
professional comedians did not linger over the problem but made use of
the fact.'[61]
   Many of these devices appear in the courtship scenes in *Love's
Labour's Lost*: when the King and his three lords first meet the Princess
and her three ladies (II.i), and in the Masque of the Muscovites (V.ii),
where they all meet again, disguised and masked. In the latter scene, for
example, the couples step forward, each in turn. They exchange a few
conceits in rhyming couplets, the men are mockingly repulsed, the
ladies at last agree to 'hold more chat' 'in private', and they retire to
make way for the next couple. Berowne and Katharine are the accepted
wits of the company, as Benedick and Beatrice are in *Much Ado*. Their
exchanges with their masked partners are particularly mocking as they

echo the other couples. The final couplets delivered by each pair should be noted. The scene begins with Rosaline refusing to dance with the King, who mistakes her for the Princess, and continues:

KING
Prise you your selves: What buyes your company?
ROSALINE
Your absence onely.
KING   That can neuer be.
ROSALINE
Then cannot we be bought; and so adue,
Twice to your Visore and halfe once to you.
KING
If you denie to daunce, lets holde more chat.
ROSALINE
In priuat then.
KING   I am best pleasd with that.
The King and Rosaline talke apart
BEROWNE   (*to the Princesse, taking her for Rosaline*)
White handed Mistres, one sweet word with thee.
PRINCESSE
Honie, and Milke, and Suger: there is three.
BEROWNE
Nay then two treyes, an if you grow so nice,
Methegline, Wort, and Malmsey; well runne dice:
There's halfe a dosen sweetes.
PRINCESSE   Seuenth sweete adue,
Since you can cogg, Ile play no more with you.
BEROWNE
One word in secret.
PRINCESSE   Let it not be sweete.
BEROWNE
Thou greeust my gall.
PRINCESSE   Gall, bitter,
BEROWNE   Therefore meete.
Berowne and the Princesse talke apart
DUMAIN   (*to Maria, taking her for Katherine*)
Will you vouchsafe with me to change a word?
MARIA
Name it.
DUMAIN   Faire Ladie.
MARIA   Say you so? Faire Lord
Take that for your faire Lady.

DUMAIN   Please it you,
As much in priuat, & Ile bid adieu.
Dumaine and Maria talke apart
KATHARINE
What, was your vizard made without a tongue?
LONGAUILL *(taking Katherine for Maria)*
I know the reason (Lady) why you aske.
KATHARINE
O for your reason, quickly sir, I long?
LONGAUILL
You haue a double tongue within your Maske,
And would afforde my speachles vizard halfe.
KATHARINE
Veale quoth the Dutch-man, is not veale a Calfe?
LONGAUILL
A Calfe faire Ladie.
KATHARINE   No, a faire Lorde Calfe.
LONGAUILL
Let's part the word?
KATHARINE   No, Ile not be your halfe:
Take all and weane it, it may proue an Oxe.
LONGAUILL
Loke how you butt your selfe in these sharpe mocks.
Will you giue hornes, chast Lady? Do not so.
KATHARINE
Then die a Calfe, before your hornes do grow.
LONGAUILL
One word in priuate with you ere I die.
KATHARINE
Bleat softly then, the Butcher heares you crie.
Longaville and Katherine talke apart
                                         (V.ii.224–55/1974–2005)

We notice the quibbles, the way in which a particular conceit is caught up and tossed back and forth, and in the final exchange, the *double entente* of some of the puns.

A very similar scene is found in *Much Ado About Nothing*, in the masked dance of Act II, scene one. In exactly the same way, the final words spoken by each couple in the dance seem to be a cue for the next couple to make a turn:

DON PEDRO *(to Hero)* Lady will you walke a bout with your friend?
HERO So, you walke softly, and looke sweetly, and say nothing, I am yours for the walke, and especially when I walk away.

DON PEDRO   With me in your company.

HERO   I may say so when I please.

DON PEDRO   And when please you to say so?

HERO   When I like the fauour, for God defend the lute should be like the case.

DON PEDRO   My visor is Philemons roofe, within the house is Ioue.

HERO   Why then your visor should be thatcht.

DON PEDRO   Speak low, if you speak loue.

They moue aside

BALTHASAR   (*to Margaret*) Well, I would you did like me.

MARGARET   So would not I for your owne sake, for I haue many ill qualities.

BALTHASAR   Which is one?

MARGARET   I say my praiers alowd.

BALTHASAR   I loue you the better, the hearers may cry Amen.

MARGARET   God match me with a good dauncer.

BALTHASAR   Amen.

MARGARET   And God keepe him out of my sight when the daunce is done: answer Clarke.

BALTHASAR   No more words, the Clarke is answered.

They moue aside

VRSULA   (*to Anthonio*) I know you well enough, you are signior Anthonio.

ANTHONIO   At a word, I am not.

VRSULA   I knowe you by the wagling of your head.

ANTHONIO   To tell you true, I counterfeit him.

VRSULA   You coulde neuer doe him so ill well, vnlesse you were the very man: heeres his drie hand vp and downe, you are he, you are he.

ANTHONIO   At a word, I am not.

VRSULA   Come, come, do you thinke I do not know you by your excellent wit? can vertue hide it selfe? go to, mumme, you are he, graces will appeere, and theres an end.

They moue aside

BEATRICE   (*to Benedicke*) Will you not tell me who tolde you so?

BENEDICKE   No, you shall pardon me.

BEATRICE   Nor will you not tell me who you are?

BENEDICKE   Not now.

BEATRICE   That I was disdainefull, and that I had my good wit out of the hundred mery tales: wel, this was signior Benedick that said so.

BENEDICKE   Whats he?

BEATRICE   I am sure you know him well enough.

BENEDICKE   Not I, beleeue me.

BEATRICE   Did he neuer make you laugh?

BENEDICKE   I pray you what is he?

BEATRICE   Why he is the princes ieaster, a very dul fool, only his gift is in deuising impossible slaunders; none but Libertines delight in him, and the commendation is not in his wit, but in his villanie for he both pleases men and angers them, and then they laugh at him and beate him: I am sure he is in the Fleete, I would he had boorded me.

BENEDICKE   When I know the gentleman, I'll tell him what you say.

BEATRICE   Do, do, heele but break a comparison or two on me, which peraduëture, (not markt, or not laught at) strikes him into melancholy; and then theres a partrige wing saued, for the foole will eate no supper that night.   (II.i.82–131/494–547)

Foakes comments that *Much Ado*'s 'happiest' quibbles seem to 'arise naturally out of the narrative context'.[62] This is demonstrated by the way in which Ursula's teasing remark to Antonio, 'Can virtue hide itself? . . . Graces will appear', and Beatrice's 'His gift is in devising impossible slanders', hint at the play's central theme: Don John's slandering of Hero, and the fact that her virtues, although thereby obscured, cannot remain hidden forever.

Improvisation would not necessarily preclude the type of organic unity we might expect to find only in a written play. Bethell comments on the relevance to the theme of the play of what is 'perhaps an *ad hoc* invention of the actor [Robert Armin] who played the Fool' in *King Lear*, that is, the 'prophecy' addressed directly to the audience at the end of Act Three, scene two. As Bethell points out, direct address is a common convention of popular drama, and he cites the monologue of Launce with his dog Crab in *The Two Gentlemen of Verona* as another example of it:[63]

LAUNCE   Nay, 'twill bee this howre ere I haue done weeping: all the kinde of the *Launces*, haue this very fault: I haue receiu'd my proportion, like the prodigious Sonne, and am going with Sir *Protheus* to the Imperialls court: I think *Crab* my dog, be the sowrest natured dogge that liues: my Mother weeping: my Father wayling: my Sister crying: our Maid howling: our Catte wringing her hands, and all our house in a great perplexitie, yet did not this cruell-hearted Curre shedde one teare: he is a stone, a very pibble stone, and has no more pitty in him then a dogge: a Iew would haue wept to haue seene our parting: why my Grandam, hauing no eyes, look you, wept her selfe blind at my parting . . .

Bryant remarks that this latter scene 'has the appearance of an interpolated comic interlude', although it is thematically related to the rest of the play, presenting comic inversions of situations in the main plot. It seems almost certain that the part was played by Will Kemp, and Bryant suggests that Shakespeare may have been influenced by the 'characteristics of his clowning act'.[64] One characteristic of the English version of the comic servant seems constant: the name Launce, like Peascod, has bawdy connotations, which we may be sure Kemp would have played up to in presenting the character. Other such characteristics include the favourite verbal tricks of the stand-up comedian: bawdy puns, malapropisms, bathos, logical absurdities, and of course the wonderfully elastic gag of showing the audience 'the manner of' his parting:

> LAUNCE   This shooe is my father: no, this left shooe is my father; no, no, this left shooe is my mother: nay, that cannot bee so neyther: yes; it is so, it is so: it hath the worser sole: this shooe with the hole in it, is my mother: and this my father: a veng'ance on't, there 'tis: Now sir, this staffe is my sister: for, looke you, she is as white as a lilly, and as small as a wand: this hat is *Nan* our maid: I am the dogge: no, the dogge is himselfe, and I am the dogge: oh, the dogge is me, and I am my selfe: I; so, so: now come I to my Father; Father, your blessing: now should not the shooe speak a word for weeping: now should I kisse my Father; well, hee weepes on: Now come I to my Mother: Oh that she could speake now, like a mou'd woman: well, I kisse her: why there 'tis; heere's my mothers breath vp and downe: Now come I to my sister; marke the moane she makes: now the dogge all this while sheds not a teare: nor speaks a word: but see how I lay the dust with my teares.   (II.iii.1–30/566–98)

Kemp's clowning act is very reminiscent of Arlecchino's, also known for his *lazzi* of crying. And Launce is very like Launcelot Gobbo in *The Merchant of Venice*, or the servant, Peter, in *Romeo and Juliet*. A favourite trick of the *zanni* was to parody the passions of the lovers, just as Launce does with his 'cate-log', or as Touchstone does when he tells of how he wooed Jane Smile. It is possible that Shakespeare's clowns also improvised their performances, and that their best quips (or even their worst!) were recorded and incorporated into the plays.

But then again, the contribution of the comedians may have been minimal. The fact that 'Shakespeare's language is that of "spoken words which have strayed on to the page"', and that 'his plays bring us close to the oral tradition' so that 'we may even be in doubt whether an entire play is a garbled version of Shakespeare or the work of someone else', may be due to his 'fantastically acute' 'ear for a phrase' and his immersion in his theatrical craft as an actor-playwright, as Bradbrook and Frye have argued.[65]

We must not forget either – as Craig conveniently does when he speaks of a 'mass of corrections, additions, and cuts made in several handwritings', in Shakespeare's manuscript – the testimony of Heminge and Condell, his first editors:

> His mind and hand went together: And what he thought, he vttered with that easinesse, that wee haue scarse receiued from him a blot in his papers.[66]

This is borne out by the sections of the manuscript of *Sir Thomas More* that could have been written by Shakespeare. Fido observes:

> There are no lengthy corrections . . . In a passage of 140 lines, Shakespeare made only eighteen alterations, and in every case he simply struck out one word or part of an uncompleted word, and raced on with his instant substitution . . . Shakespeare's creative mind . . . seems to be that of an impassioned participant actor or enrapt spectator.[67]

Here we have a picture of the poet himself as an expert 'improvisator'. But the fact that he willingly collaborated with other writers could indicate that he may also have happily accepted the extempore contributions of his fellow actors.

What conclusions may we reasonably draw on the matter? Even if we deny the claim that they made substantial contributions to his plays, the actors clearly played a great part in Shakespeare's conception of his characters, and he would almost certainly have created parts suited to the company's talents, with actors playing particular 'lines'. But it may go further than that. The early plays, particularly the comedies, may contain dialogue and pieces of clowning which were invented by the actors on the spur of the moment during rehearsals or performances, and some of the roles played by Will Kemp provide examples of this. Robert Armin may well have played the 'set fool' as opposed to Kemp's extempore clowning, but, as has been suggested, he may not have been above making impromptu comments himself.[68] The same may be true of Richard Burbage. It has even been argued that Shakespeare himself improvised his part as an actor in one of Jonson's plays.[69] This means he may have done the same in his own plays, too.

Besides the clowns' 'gagging', it is possible that improvisation was deliberately called for in some of the comic roles. The rhyming couplets, bawdy puns, quibbles and conceits in the exchanges between the lovers in many of the early comedies may be the traces of such practices. On the other hand, they may merely show Shakespeare's use as a dramatist of the type of comic devices originally found in the improvisation of the Italian players.

Shakespeare's clear acquaintance with the *commedia dell'arte* raises the possibility that he saw performances of the Italian comedians during their visits to England, or that he had extended contact with someone familiar with the *commedia dell'arte* repertoire and conventions. The name William Kemp immediately springs to mind, but Thomas Pope may also have been such a source. It does seem likely that Shakespeare learnt much of his stage-craft from the actors he worked with throughout his career, and that they in turn had picked this up from the *commedia dell'arte* troupes. The stage plot of *The Dead Man's Fortune* is particularly suggestive in this respect.

Perhaps Kemp, Bryan or Pope had brought back certain of the methods and materials of the *commedia dell'arte* from their Continental travels, and when they joined up with the Admiral's– Strange's Men these resulted in the *Plot of the Dead Man's Fortune* and the other stage plots. Perhaps Shakespeare's poetic gift was first discovered when he was called on to improvise a part in a play such as the revival of Tarlton's *Seven Deadly Sins*. For of course, he is first heard of in Robert Greene's attack on the players as an actor-turned-playwright: 'There is an vpstart Crow, beautified with our feathers, that with his *Tygers heart wrapt in a Players hide*, supposes he is as well able to bumbast out a blank verse as the best of you; and being an absolute *Iohannes fac totum*, is in his owne conceit the onely Shake-scene in a countrie.'[70]

Whatever our conjectures and conclusions on points such as these, Craig's suggestions are clearly not as outrageous as they might appear at first, and the link between Shakespeare and the *commedia dell'arte* is an area of theatre history that deserves further attention. Furthermore, the comparison gives us a broader view of Shakespeare's craft, and this is valuable in itself. As Bullough says, 'Without a knowledge of the material available to him neither his debts nor the transcendent scope of his creative energy can be assessed.'[71]

NOTES

1 This article was originally published as 'The Clowning Zanies: Shakespeare and the Actors of the Commedia dell'Arte', in the journal of the Shakespeare Society of Southern Africa, *Shakespeare in Southern Africa*, 3 (1989), 9–32, edited by Professor Guy Butler and Dr Lawrence Wright of Rhodes University. It has since been revised, and new material has been added.

2 Edward Gordon Craig, 'Shakespeare's Plays', *The Mask*, 6 (1913–14), 163–5.

3 Early writers who deal with the topic include: Karl Mantzius, *A History of Theatrical Art in Ancient and Modern Times, 3: Drama in the Age of Shakespeare*, trans. Louise von Cossel (New York, Peter Smith, 1904), 1–5; Winifred Smith, 'Italian and Elizabethan Comedy', *Modern Philology*, 5 (April 1908), 555–67; 'A Comic Version of *Romeo and Juliet*', *Modern Philology*, 7 (October 1909), 217–20; and *The Commedia dell'Arte: A Study in Italian Popular Comedy* (New York, Columbia University Press, 1912); and Max J. Wolff, 'Shakespeare und die Commedia dell'arte', *Jahrbuch der deutschen Shakespeare-Gesellschaft*, 46 (1910), 1–20.

4 For example, Pierre Louis Duchartre, *The Italian Comedy: The Improvisation, Scenarios, Lives, Attributes, Portraits and Masks of the Illustrious Characters of the Commedia dell'Arte*, trans. Randolf T. Weaver (New York, John Day, 1928, reprinted with a supplement, New York, Dover, 1966), 23, 80, 127; Thelma Niklaus, *Harlequin Phoenix, or the Rise and Fall of a Bergamask Rogue* (London, Bodley Head, 1956), 127–8; or Giacomo Oreglia, *The Commedia dell'Arte* (London, Methuen, 1968), 147.

5 Kathleen M. Lea, *Italian Popular Comedy: A Study of the Commedia dell'arte, with Special Reference to the English Stage*, 2 vols. (Oxford, Clarendon Press, 1931). Allardyce Nicoll, *Masks, Mimes and Miracles: Studies in the Popular Theatre* (London, Harrap, 1949) and *The World of Harlequin: A Critical Study of the Commedia dell'Arte* (Cambridge University Press, 1963).

6 The essay quoted from is the last of a series of articles by Craig on the relationship between Shakespeare and the actors. Although Lea discusses extemporal acting in Elizabethan England, none of these articles is listed in her otherwise complete bibliography of Craig's publications on the *commedia dell'arte*.

7 These include S. L. Bethell, *Shakespeare and the Popular Dramatic Tradition* (London, Staples, 1944); Muriel Bradbrook, *The Rise of the Common Player* (Cambridge, Mass., Harvard University Press, 1962); Leo Salingar, *Shakespeare and the Traditions of Comedy* (Cambridge University Press, 1974); and Robert Weimann, *Shakespeare and the Popular Tradition in the Theater* (Baltimore, Johns Hopkins University Press, 1978).

8 Important early studies of this link are those by Henry David Gray, 'The Sources of *The Tempest*', *Modern Language Notes*, 35 (June 1920), 321–30; and Oscar J. Campbell, '*Love's Labour's Lost*, Restudied', and '*The Two Gentlemen of Verona* and Italian Comedy', *University of Michigan Publications*, 1 (1925), 3–45, 49–63; and 'The Italianate Background of *The Merry Wives of Windsor*', *University of Michigan Publications*, 8 (1932), 81–117. These were followed by

Frances A. Yates, *A Study of 'Love's Labour's Lost'* (Cambridge University Press, 1936), 173–82; John Robert Moore, 'Pantaloon as Shylock', *Boston Public Library Quarterly*, 1 (1949), 33–42; F.D. Hoeniger, 'Two Notes on *Cymbeline*', *Shakespeare Quarterly*, 8 (1957), 132–3; Helen Andrews Kaufman, '*Trappolin Supposed a Prince* and *Measure for Measure*', *Modern Language Quarterly*, 18 (1957), 113–24; Robert C. Melzi, 'From Lelia to Viola', *Renaissance Drama*, 9 (1966), 67–81; Barbara H.C. de Mendonça, '*Othello*: A Tragedy Built on a Comic Structure', *Shakespeare Survey*, 21 (1968), 31–38; and most recently, Ninian Mellamphy, 'Pantaloons and Zanies: Shakespeare's 'Apprenticeship' to Italian Professional Comedy Troupes', in Maurice Charney (ed.), *Shakespearean Comedy* (New York, New York Literary Forum, 1980), 141–51.

9   Sir E. K. Chambers, *The Elizabethan Stage*, 4 vols. (Oxford, Clarendon Press, 1923), 2: 553–4; Louis B. Wright, 'Will Kemp and the *Commedia dell' Arte*', *Modern Language Notes*, 41 (1926), 516–20; Lea, *Italian Popular Comedy*, 381–8; George C. Taylor, 'Did Shakespeare, Actor, Improvise in *Every Man in His Humour?*', in James G. McManaway, Giles E. Dawson and Edwin E. Willoughby (eds.), *Joseph Quincy Adams Memorial Studies* (Washington, Folger Shakespeare Library, 1948), 21–32; Evert Sprinchorn, Introduction, in Oreglia, *Commedia dell'Arte*, xiii–xv; Eugene Steele, 'Verbal Lazzi in Shakespeare's Plays', *Italica*, 53 (1976), 214–22.

10 Geoffrey Bullough (ed.), *Narrative and Dramatic Sources of Shakespeare*, 8 vols. (London, Routledge & Kegan Paul, 1957 – 75), 1: xi.

11 Louise George Clubb. 'Italian Comedy and *The Comedy of Errors*', *Comparative Literature*, 19 (1968), 241. Cf. Chambers, *Elizabethan Stage*, 2: 261–65.

12 Smith, 'Italian and Elizabethan Comedy', 556–7; Chambers, *Elizabethan Stage*, 2: 263; Nicoll, *Masks, Mimes and Miracles*, 308–9. See also William Schrickx, '*Commedia dell'Arte* Players in Antwerp in 1576: Drusiano and Tristano Martinelli', *Theatre Research International*, 2 (1976), 79–87.

13 *Italian Popular Comedy*, 352, 357.

14 Ibid., 374.

15 Thomas Nashe, *Pierce Penilesse his Supplication to the Diuell* (1592), in *The Works of Thomas Nashe*, 4 vols. ed. Ronald B. McKerrow (Oxford, Blackwell, 1958), 1: 215; cf. Chambers, *Elizabethan Stage*, 4: 239.

16 Lea, *Italian Popular Comedy*, 374.

17 W.W. Greg (ed.), *Henslowe Papers, being documents supplementary to Henslowe's Diary* (London, Bullen, 1907), 128–9, 133; *Dramatic Documents: Commentaries*, 89–90. Cf. Andrew Gurr, *The Shakespearean Stage*, 2nd ed. (Cambridge University Press, 1980), 36–8.

18 Lea, *Italian Popular Comedy*, 388.

19 Greg, *Henslowe Papers*, Appendix II, 3, 134–5.

20 Henry F. Salerno (trans.), *Scenarios of the 'Commedia dell'Arte': Flaminio Scala's 'Il Teatro delle favole rappresentative'* (New York University Press, University of London Press, 1967), 47–54, 396–7.

21 Greg, *Dramatic Documents from the Elizabethan Playhouses: Commentaries* (Oxford, Clarendon Press, 1931), 100, 103; cf. Gurr, *Shakespearean Stage*, 34–41, 89–90.

22 Greg, *Henslowe Papers*, 129–32, 149, 151–2; cf. *Dramatic Documents: Commentaries*, 70–93 passim. The stage plots of *The Dead Man's Fortune* and *2 Seven Deadly Sins* are believed to be the earliest of the extant plots, with *The Dead Man's Fortune* probably the earliest of all.

23 Gurr, *Shakespearean Stage*, 34. See Chambers, *Elizabethan Stage*, 2: 273.

24 Greg, *Henslowe Papers*, 149. There are two other tantalizing links between Shakespeare and these stage plots. First, there is the fact that one of the central characters in the plot of *The Dead Man's Fortune* is named Laertes. And the handwriting in which the plot of *2 Seven Deadly Sins* is written has been identified with Hand C in the book of *Sir Thomas More*, Shakespeare's being thought to be Hand D: see Greg, *Dramatic Documents: Commentaries*, 4; Peter Alexander (ed.), *William Shakespeare: The Complete Works*, (London & Glasgow, Collins, 1951), Appendix, 1345–51; Martin Fido, *Shakespeare* (London, Hamlyn, 1978), 71–5.

25 John Payne Collier, *The History of English Dramatic Poetry to the Time of Shakespeare: And Annals of the Stage to the Restoration* (London, John Murray, 1831), 393–405.

26 Lea, *Italian Popular Comedy*, 129–30; Greg, *Henslowe Papers*, 127.

27 Greg, *Dramatic Documents: Commentaries*, 98, n.

28 All references to Shakespeare's plays are to the Oxford Shakespeare: *William Shakespeare: The Complete Works, Original-Spelling Edition*, eds. Stanley Wells, Gary Taylor, John Jowett, and William Montgomery (Oxford, Clarendon Press, 1986). References are to the act, scene and line numbers as given in the Alexander edition of Shakespeare, followed by the line numbers given in the Oxford Shakespeare. I give the approximate dates for the plays as conjectured by Stanley Wells and Gary Taylor, *William Shakespeare: A Textual Companion* (Oxford, Clarendon Press, 1987), 109–34.

29 Nicoll, *Masks, Mimes and Miracles*, 346–7. Cf. Lea, *Italian Popular Comedy*, 377, n.

30 Campbell, '*The Two Gentlemen of Verona* and Italian Comedy', 63; and 'The Italianate Background of *The Merry Wives of Windsor*', 101ff.

31 Frye, *Natural Perspective*, 12–14, 21–3, 30, 44–8, 57–61; *The Secular Scripture: A Study of the Structure of Romance* (Cambridge, Mass., Harvard University Press, 1978), 28–9, 111; Bentley, *Life of the Drama*, 52–3.

32 Martin Holmes, *Shakespeare and his Players* (London, Murray, 1972), 25.

33 David L. Stevenson, Textual Note, *Much Ado About Nothing*, Signet Classic Shakespeare (New York, New American Library, 1964), 132. See Gareth Lloyd Evans, 'Shakespeare's Fools: The Shadow and the Substance of Drama', in Malcolm Bradbury and David Palmer (eds.), *Shakespearian Comedy*, Stratford-upon-Avon Studies 14 (London, Arnold, 1972), 146.

34 Note to *Romeo and Juliet*, 4.5.100, by T. J. B. Spencer (ed.), New Penguin Shakespeare (Harmondsworth, Penguin, 1967), 266.

35 John Russell Brown, 'Laughter in the Last Plays', in John Russell Brown and Bernard Harris (eds.), *Later Shakespeare*, Stratford-upon-Avon Studies 8, (London, Arnold, 1966), 106.

36 T.W. Baldwin, *The Organization and Personnel of the Shakespearean Company*

(Princeton, Princeton University Press, 1927), ch. 9, 229ff.

37 Nicoll, *Masks, Mimes and Miracles*, 347. Nicoll follows Collier, *History of English Dramatic Poetry*, 399, and Smith, 'Italian and Elizabethan Comedy', 560, in this interpretation of the phrase.

38 *Italian Popular Comedy*, 384. Cf. Gurr, *Shakespearean Stage*, 85–7.

39 Harold Jenkins, Note, *Hamlet*, Arden Shakespeare (London, Methuen, 1982), 289. This extract is not included in the Wells–Taylor edition. I quote from Lea, *Italian Popular Comedy*, 386. Cyrus Hoy, Textual Commentaries, *Hamlet*, A Norton Critical Edition (New York, Norton, 1963), 100, notes that the folio text of *Hamlet* shows evidence of interpolations made by the actors, such as repetition of catch-phrases, 'gagging', etc.

40 G. B. Harrison, Note, *The Tragedy of Hamlet, Prince of Denmark*, Penguin Shakespeare (Harmondsworth, Penguin, 1937), 170. Lea, *Italian Popular Comedy*, 386.

41 David Wiles, *Shakespeare's Clown: Actor and Text in the Elizabethan Playhouse* (Cambridge University Press, 1987), 82.

42 Cf. Robert Hillis Goldsmith, *Wise Fools in Shakespeare* (Liverpool, Liverpool University Press, 1958), 41; S.L. Bethell, 'Shakespeare's Actors', *Review of English Studies* 1, n.s., 3 (July, 1950), 197; Evans, 'Shakespeare's Fools', 146.

43 Guy Butler, 'Shakespeare and Two Jesters', *Hebrew University Studies in Literature and the Arts*, 11.2 (1983) 164, 180.

44 Greg, *Henslow Papers*, Appendix 2, 131.

45 W. Carew Hazlitt (ed.), *A Select Collection of Old English Plays*, originally published by Robert Dodsley (1744), 15 vols. (London, Reeves & Turner, 1874), 6: 565–8. See John Payne Collier's 'General Introduction' (1851) to vol. 6: 23; Chambers, *Elizabethan Stage*, 4: 24; Wright, 'Kemp and *Commedia dell'Arte*', 519.

46 McKerrow (ed.) *Works of Thomas Nashe*, 3: 342. Cf. Lea, *Italian Popular Comedy*, 350; Wright, 'Kemp and *Commedia dell'Arte*', 517–8.

47 Nicoll, *Masks, Mimes and Miracles*, 279.

48 Quoted in Lea, *Italian Popular Comedy*, 381–82. Cf. Nicoll, *Masks, Mimes and Miracles*, 279–80; Chambers, *Elizabethan Stage*, 2: 326.

49 Lea, *Italian Popular Comedy*, 382, 386–7.

50 Luigi Riccoboni, *Histoire du théâtre italien* (Paris, 1728), 65; quoted in Nicoll, *Masks, Mimes and Miracles*, 219–20.

51 Perrucci, *Arte rappresentativa*, trans. and ed. by Craig, 'The Commedia dell' arte or Professional Comedy: Directions as to the Preparation of a Performance from a Scenario', *The Mask* 4 (1911–12) 112.

52 Cf. Nicoll, *Masks, Mimes and Miracles*, 218–19; *World of Harlequin*, 35–9.

53 Lea, *Italian Popular Comedy*, 105–6.

54 Ibid., 108–9.

55 Nicoll, *Masks, Mimes and Miracles*, 236.

56 Eric Peter Bryant, 'Shakespeare's Early Comedies: Studies in *The Comedy of Errors*, *The Taming of the Shrew*, and *The Two Gentlemen of Verona*', (Rhodes University Ph.D. thesis 1970), 89–90, 221–5.

57 Samuel Johnson, *Dr Johnson on Shakespeare*, ed. William K. Wimsatt (Harmondsworth, Penguin, 1969) 60, 66–7, 68.

58 Richard Andrews, 'Scripted theatre and the *commedia dell'arte*', (unpublished paper, 1990), 10–11.

59 Muriel Bradbrook has argued that this formal patterning of the action was widely used on the Elizabethan stage, in *Themes and Conventions of Elizabethan Tragedy* (Cambridge University Press, 1935) 25–8.

60 Tim Fitzpatrick, 'Commedia dell'Arte and Performance: The Scenarios of Flaminio Scala', *Renaissance Drama Newsletter, Supplement no. 5*, (Warwick University, 1985).

61 *Italian Popular Comedy*, 194–5.

62 R. A. Foakes, Introduction, *Much Ado About Nothing*, New Penguin Shakespeare (Harmondsworth, Penguin, 1968), 9.

63 Bethell, *Popular Dramatic Tradition*, 84–6. On the convention of direct address, see Peter Davison, *Popular Appeal in English Drama to 1850* (London, Macmillan, 1982). See also Harold S. Brooks, 'Two Clowns in a Comedy (to say nothing of the Dog): Speed, Launce (and Crab) in *The Two Gentlemen of Verona*', *Essays and Studies*, n.s. 16 (1963), 91–100. Was the sure-fire *lazzi* of the dog on stage perhaps also something Kemp learnt from the Italian comedians? It is interesting that the puppet, Punch, an English descendant of the *commedia dell'arte* mask Pulcinella, is traditionally accompanied by a small performing dog, Toby.

64 See Bryant, 'Shakespeare's Early Comedies', 174–82, 226–9.

65 Bradbrook, *Shakespeare: The Poet in his World* (London, Methuen, 1978) 51–2; Frye, *Natural Perspective*, 22–3.

66 John Heminge and Henry Condell, 'To the Great Variety of Readers', in Alexander, *Shakespeare's Works*, xxvii.

67 Fido, *Shakespeare*, 75.

68 See Bethell, *Popular Dramatic Tradition*, 85; 'Shakespeare's Actors', 193–7. Cf. Goldsmith, *Wise Fools*, 41; Brown, 'Last Plays', 105–10.

69 Taylor, 'Did Shakespeare, Actor, Improvise?', in McManaway, Dawson and Willoughby, *Joseph Quincy Adams Memorial Studies*, 21–32.

70 Robert Greene, *Greene's Groats-worth of Wit bought with a Million of Repentance* (1592), quoted in Chambers, *Elizabethan Stage*, 241–2.

71 Bullough, *Narrative and Dramatic Sources*, 1: xii.

2 Performing omnivores in Germany *circa* 1700

TOM CHEESMAN

> ... the inner logic of consumer culture depends upon the cultivation of
> an insatiable appetite ... [1]

The short-lived popular vogue discussed in this chapter lies on the
margins of the tradition with which this book is concerned. I will locate
the 'performing omnivore' or 'gluttony artist' vogue within a cultural
historical process understood in terms of Bakhtin's theory of carnival
and the grotesque body, especially as that theory has been extended, to
incorporate a range of more recent studies in anthropology, social
history, psychoanalysis and textual theory, by Peter Stallybrass and
Allon White in *The Politics and Poetics of Transgression* (1986).[2] My
approach shares common ground with recent work on *commedia
dell'arte* and related aspects of popular theatre in Germany. There the
focus of research has moved on from efforts in the 1960s to trace the
influence of Italian (and Franco-Italian) theatrical traditions on German
literary comedy (Hinck 1965),[3] to efforts towards understanding the
significance of genuinely popular and, in particular, predominantly
non-literary theatrical practices in historical context.

> The question of the influence of *commedia dell'arte* on German-
> language theatre has come to the fore again recently amid growing
> interest in forms of the *Volkstück* (popular drama), in popular theatre
> as a 'theatre of laughter', an 'alternative theatre' belonging to a
> 'culture of carnivalesque laughter'.[4]

Thus the opening words of Otto Schindler's succinct foreword to a new
edition of fourteen manuscript scenarios from eighteenth-century
Vienna. Vienna was the site of the earliest firmly established
Volkstheater in German-speaking Europe, and of the most prominent,
cosmopolitan tradition of improvisational, stereotypical comedy.[5]

The back cover of Schindler's book quotes Lessing's foreword to his edition of *Entwürfe ungedruckter Lustspiele des italiänischen Theaters* ('Drafts of unpublished comedies of the Italian theatre') (1758): 'uncontestably, among all civilized peoples, we Germans have most need of means of assistance in this kind of poetry.' Despite his then fairly unusual advocacy of this type of unruly theatre (and it is an advocacy of a politely poetical variety of it), Lessing like other writers of his time was in fact instrumental in the 'literarization, moralization and institutionalization of the stage' which, Schindler indicates, had successfully marginalized any improvisational traditions by the end of the eighteenth century. Already by the late seventeenth century, a division had been established between 'high' and 'low' cultures that led to the 'aestheticization' and 'domestication' of the archetypal unruly servant figure, Hanswurst, where he appeared in high culture at all (his career is well summarized in a recent Bakhtin-inspired paper by Richard Sheppard).[6] Nestroy and Raimund, the popular Viennese comedian-manager-authors who became internationally renowned in the early nineteenth century (when Goldoni and Gozzi were also celebrated among German Romantic travellers and readers), did so on the basis of their published texts; whereas the essence of popular theatre in practice lies in spontaneity and dialogue (literal and Bakhtinian) with the immediate audience – and in disrespectful challenge to limits and authorities of all kinds, including the authority which was and is vested in fixed, literary texts in high culture.

The influence of *commedia dell'arte* in German dramatic literature of the seventeenth and eighteenth centuries, as Hinck described it, revealed a long tradition behind Nestroy and Raimund's work. But he stressed that this line of German reception of *commedia dell'arte* was predominantly mediated in writing, by the courtly Parisian *Théâtre italien* and the works of Molière, Marivaux and other authors. As regards popular theatrical practice, research in the 1960s by Hansen and Asper (students of Hinck who worked in Viennese archives) showed that a complex of English and French as well as Italian influences went into the melting pot of popular drama.[7] But such arguments about 'influence' (mostly, about which versions of the Hanswurst character are more genuinely German, or Austrian, and which are imitations of Italian, French or English precursors), though at that time they challenged earlier, decidedly nationalistic and myth-laden histories of German popular theatre, have meanwhile come to seem less interesting than questions of contextual interpretation – and equally, the linear narrative model of literary history used by Hinck has come to seem suspect in many ways. However, German writers' persistent recourse to *commedia dell'arte* models (figures, motifs, dramatic devices, plots) in comedy texts is far easier to establish than the presence and significance of those performance traditions which, in theatre history, are associated (if often loosely) with the term *commedia dell'arte*.

Pictorial and other historical documents testify to the presence of Italian troupes in German-speaking countries from the middle of the sixteenth century to the eighteenth (when there was, briefly, an established Italian theatre in Vienna). A recent essay, also drawing on Bakhtin, Peter Sprengel's account of Italian-inspired comedy at the court of Bavaria in the late sixteenth century,[8] focuses on the carnivalized master–servant relationship which frescoes and songs, and a few other surviving documents, show to have been the central feature of this 'comedy of the body, of situations and of dialogue' (p.11). Most documents of *dell'arte* theatre omit details of the physical gags or routines (*lazzi*) which comprised the core of this comedy. But Sprengel quotes from a fascinating source, a Tirolean doctor's treatise of 1610, in which *commedia dell'arte* episodes are used as didactic *exempla*. As Sprengel puts it, Hippolyt Guarinoni's interest was in the 'grotesque body' in Bakhtin's sense: the supra-individual body in its cycle of self-reproduction, consumption and expurgation, represented in ways that emphasize its functional openings onto the world. In most of Guarinoni's twenty-two examples from *commedia dell'arte*, Zanni excels in eating and/or in defecating: the servant 'appears as a specialist in the maximization of pleasure through taking in food or evacuating fecal matter.' Quoting Guarinoni, Sprengel continues: 'Recalling a performance which he apparently saw in Padua, Guarinoni describes "Zane [Zanni] in the Italian comedy, who was especially given to eating and gluttony" and therefore "fervently desired that his throat might stretch from Padua all the way to Constantinople, so that the finest macaronis and noodles, which at the time he was eating, one fistful after another, on the public square, might not slip down into his stomach so quickly" and "the pleasure of tasting them might last the longer". ' (p.12). As the next best thing to his Gargantuan fantasy, Zanni half-swallows the noodles, holding on to them with his hand down his gullet for as long as possible.

Grotesque eating performances such as this feature prominently in *commedia dell'arte* traditions as they do in carnivalesque, 'low', popular performances (and narratives) generally. In the German itinerant theatre of the seventeenth and eighteenth centuries, the numerous manifestations of the comical personage were variously designated Zanni, Harlekin, Pickelhering, Hans Supp (Jean Potage), Hans Stockfisch, Hanswurst and so on. In his study, Asper sets out their common characteristics: aside from peasant background, materialist world-view, fecal language, association with ghosts and the dead, and sexual rapacity, greed for food and drink is an essential trait. It is immediately signalled by the name, in most cases. In fact in the performing omnivores under discussion here, all these features, apart from sexuality, can be discerned (and perhaps there are hints of sexuality too). But let us concentrate on eating.

Performing, rather than just afflicted,[9] human omnivores may have been common in many places and at many times; they are well-documented in nineteenth- and twentieth-century Western popular culture;[10] but there is a remarkable cluster of highly distinctive German sources dating from the first decade of the eighteenth century. A comparable phenomenon is the international 'hunger artist' vogue of around the turn of the present century – its rise and fall is documented in Kafka's short story *Ein Hungerkünstler* (1922; translated as 'A Fasting Showman'), and it survived, obscurely, in German fairgrounds until the 1950s.[11] This has certain antecedents in early modern pseudo-miracles (young girls who apparently ate nothing at all gained fame and fortune, or, if revealed as frauds, suffered terrible penalties) but it emerged as a still more lucrative masculine touring profession, exciting scientific as well as popular interest, in the 1880s.

Similarly, 'gluttony artistry' has many antecedents in traditional culture, but its emergence as a form of showmanship seems to be quite precisely dateable; and as with the hunger artists, the phenomenon was briefly the object of universal and in part scholarly interest, and then dropped into the underworld of popular entertainment, where it still pursues a scarcely-noticed existence. Its sudden conspicuousness is a problem: one feels that it is symptomatic of some cultural historical necessity – a complex web of determinations acting on mass psychology, on the mentality of central European townspeople. But what and how? I will suggest a way of answering this question by taking into consideration both the historical context, and the internal logic of the gluttony artist vogue. I will start with the latter.

This internal logic seems to govern *only* those performances and stories which date from the decade in question. It is a narrative pattern or 'deep structure' common to all the documented manifestations of the vogue. The pattern amounts to an etiological explanation of the claimed affliction with an insatiable, indiscriminating appetite. In short, this kind of human monster appears as the *lone survivor of a mass fatal catastrophe*: and after presenting the sources I will argue that this pattern may be understood as a commentary on the cultural historical process of the time: as an example of popular culture, in the form of the grotesque body, commenting on its own subjugation by a newly hegemonic culture of individual decorum.

My first source for the vogue, the latest, is best described as an engraving to play with. It dates probably from 1709. (See p. 54.) *A pretty engaged couple of market-singers* are performing and selling a *Zeitungslied*, 'news-song', holding up a large placard and standing on a low, rickety bench. This bench, in German *Bänkel*, a market-place mountebank's minimal improvised stage, gives their trade speciality its name, *Bänkelsang*.[12] Itinerant performer-traders of this type, a familiar sight at markets and fairs all over continental Europe from the sixteenth century to the twentieth, sold ballad sheets and chapbooks to crowds outdoors by not merely singing them but also telling the shocking story with the help of often very large, elaborate painted placards divided into picture frames. This was therefore a form of proto-cinema and of early popular 'news'-paper in one, complex institution. The oldest, richest and longest-lasting tradition in Europe is as a matter of fact the Italian *cantastorie*: *cantambancos* were still performing in some regions in the 1960s, narrating the Kennedy assassination, for example, in mournful ballads illustrated by placards.[13]

The title of this engraving is obviously ironic: the unprepossessing couple are dressed in rags and tatters, the man has a wooden leg (as street singers indeed often did). Their sheets read: 'Wahrhaffte Geschicht so geschehen Anno 7901' ('True story which happened in 7901') – the anagram probably encodes '1709'.[14] Their placard shows a grotesquely caricatural man brandishing a huge sword and carrying a corpse between his teeth, with the motto: 'Auf ein mahl 3,000 Mann gefressen und 10,000 Mann erschlagen' ('At one time/ meal [a pun!] ate 3,000 men and killed 10,000'). The caption at the foot reads:

Ein schönes verlobtes Paar Marck-Singer.
Wer dañ was nues will erfahren ünd erseher's
Ein recht Wuñder geschicht, so dieses Jahr geschehen,
so Ochsen 20.ʰ Kuh, 1000 Schaff, fraß einer allein
Heb nür mein Daffel auf, darünter wird Er sehn.

1a. 'A pretty engaged couple of market-singers' performing and selling a
     Zeitungslied, 1709 (see p. 53).

Ein schönes verlobtes Paar Marck-Singer.

Wer dañ was neues will erfahren ûnd ersehen
Ein recht Wûnder geschicht, so dieses Jahr geschehen,
50 Ochsen 20 Kûh, 1000 Schaff, fraß einer allein
heb nûr mein Daffel auf, darûnter wird Er sehn

1b.   'A pretty engaged couple of market-singers' (see p. 56).

Wer dann was neues will erfahren und ersehen
Ein recht Wunder geschicht, so dieses Jahr geschehen
10 Ochsen 20ig Kuh, 1000 Schaff, fraß einer allein
Heb nur mein Daffel auf, darunter wird er seyn.

Who wants to learn and see something new
A real wonder-story that happened this year
10 oxen, 20 cows, 1000 sheep one single man ate
Just lift up my picture and he'll be underneath.

The picture-within-the-picture, printed separately, can be lifted to reveal a rear-end view of an enormously fat person defecating, and the euphemistic motto: 'Ey, hat er sie gefressen ein, so mus ers husten auch allein' ('Ah, if he's eaten them up, he'll have to "cough" it all on his own').

The story is of massacre, Gargantuan gorging, cannibalism, and Gargantuan evacuation. At first sight this source might appear to contradict my assertion that the underlying narrative pattern in these representations of omnivorousness is one of mass catastrophe – survival – insatiability. Here the survivor of the mass fatality also apparently perpetrates it. However, Elias Canetti's reflections on mass psychology can be adduced in support of the notion that in this sort of context of fantasy, of mythical and psychological logic, perpetrator and survivor are two sides of one coin. As is indicated by the experience of guilt felt by the most innocent survivors of major accidents, disasters and genocides, one kills in order to be a survivor; another achieves survival (as if) through the deaths of others.[15] At most, this source provides a variant of the basic narrative.

In my second source (opposite), from Nuremberg, the postulated narrative pattern is occluded in a different way: it has to be deduced from the context. If the 1709 engraving, especially the singers' placards, is quintessentially grotesque, this relatively realistic (and classically designed) image suggests more specific connections with popular dramatic and carnival traditions. In this depiction, the performing omnivore who toured cities in 1701 has several features in common with Hanswurst/Harlekin: the phallic stick tucked into his belt, the outsize, shapeless hat, the peasant status (though his dress is bourgeois), as well as of course the gestures of outrageous eating. But he surpasses most comical stage figures in sheer omnivorousness. The caption relates that this man, in 1701,

2.   A 1701 portrayal of the 'gluttonous Bohemian' (see p. 56).

... in various places in Austria and Saxony, to the great amazement of many trustworthy people, swallowed and devoured a living cat, with skin and hair, and other things no less, such as gravel, metal, raw meat, felt, hide, glass and such like, with great appetite; a whole calf suffices only to break his fast, and he is also reputed to have eaten two small children, in Bohemia; while his brother, his twin, and another such glutton, is supposed to have eaten a Jew alive, in Prague. He was captured in a wood, and now, for money, he is both displayed to people, and also given all kinds of unnatural things to swallow by them.

The capture in the wood is depicted on the backdrop behind the Bohemian – it gives a hint of possible relatedness to the Wild Man of popular cultural tradition, a figure who shares certain demonic properties with early versions of Harlequins and Hanswursts. The broader connection with carnival traditions is apparent from the fact that the pig he is shown in the act of eating is the 'emblematic animal' of carnival, and Jews (his supposed brother's supposed victim) were one of carnival's traditional 'enemies'; while cats have many associations with popular magic, sex and violence.[16]

The Bohemian's presence in Leipzig, at the Michaelmas fair in 1701, is attested in Vogel's chronicle of the city published in 1714. His account was shortened in *Theatrum Europaeum*, the compendium of chronicles published in Frankfurt in 1717 (quoted first below); and it was reproduced in full in Zedler's *Universal-Lexicon* in the article on *Vielfresser*, Gluttons (1746).[17]

Es zog auch dieses Jahr ein sogenenneter Vielfraß herum/ der da Katzen mit Haut und Haar/ Steine/ Werck/ und dergleichen mehr unnatürlicher Weise wahrhafftig fraß und verschluckte/ und anbey versicherte/ dieses nicht aus Vorwitz oder Muthwillen/ sondern aus Noth und wegen seines unnatürlichen Appetits und Hungers zu thun/ die Schuld dessen allen auff seine Eltern werfend/ die da mit dem Schaafhüten sich genähret. Denn da sein Vater einst dem Wolff ein halbzerrissenes Schaaf abgejaget/ sey seine schwangere Mutter darzugekommen/ und hätte einen unordentlichen Lusten bekommen/ von diesem halbzerfleischten Aas zu essen/ welches aber ihr Mann durchaus nicht zugestanden/ und damit gemachet hätte/ daß dero Leibes-Frucht dieser unnatürliche Vielfraß/ mit einem so greulichen und unersättlichen Hunger und Appetit angestecket worden wäre.

This year a so-called glutton also toured, who truly ate and swallowed cats with skin and hair, stones, pieces of metal and such like in an unnatural manner, affirming that he did this not out of immodesty or mischievousness, but out of necessity and due to his unnatural appetite and hunger, throwing the blame for all this upon his parents, who had made their living as shepherds. For once, as his father had chased a wolf away from a half-dismembered sheep, his pregnant mother had arrived and had been seized by an extraordinary desire to eat this half-mangled carrion, which her husband by no means permitted her to do, with the result that the fruit of her body (this unnatural glutton) was infected with such a terrible and insatiable hunger and appetite.

Vogel himself gives a still more stupendous account of the man's feats (he ate whole dogs and sheep as well as cats, and stones as large as chestnuts, which could be heard rattling in his belly), and stresses that he exhibited himself for money, while the biography is substantially the same: the pregnant mother 'hatte sich an einem Wolffe . . . versehen' (literally: 'mis-saw herself upon a wolf', that is, came under the wolf's pernicious influence by looking at it). Vogel's account ends (this time in Zedler's fuller text):

> Dieser Stein-Fresser muste ein Paar Tage in dem neuen Zucht-Hause, welches den 30. des Herbst-Monats des gedachten Jahres zuerst bewohnet worden war, Brod essen, und bekam hernach seinen Lauf-Zettel, damit sich niemand an ihm versehen möchte.

> This stone-eater had to spend a few days in the new jail, which had received its first inmate on 30 September of the same year, eating bread, and was then expelled from the city, in order that no one might see him and come under his pernicious influence.

These academic accounts of the gluttonous Bohemian reveal less about him than about the continuing force, in scholarly circles, of such ancient popular notions as lycanthropy, the evil eye, and women's original sinfulness and frightful subhumanity (especially when pregnant). This construction of the omnivore leaves little or no trace of the popular model I am trying to recreate. However, that can be explained as a consequence of the differentiation of 'high' from 'low' culture. An echo of the idea of mass death may be detected in the wolf's attack on the sheep; but that is stretching a point. On the other hand the idea certainly is present in the broadside's caption, if one recalls what 'from Bohemia' would have meant in about 1700. Bohemia was known at this time as a region of widespread famine, plagues, armed rebellions crushed with dreadful violence, punitive taxation and the concerted persecution of Protestants by a new nobility, installed by the Habsburgs, who recruited them among the soldiers of fortune who had won them the Thirty Years War. So the gluttonous peasant's son appeared as a traumatized survivor of those conditions: total defeat, destruction of a culture.

My last source testifies to the fact that the famous 'Bohemian' was not a unique figure, but was actually profiting from a distinct vogue for performances, depictions and narratives of outrageous omnivorousness which preceded him (as well as continuing at least for several years after his brief appearance in the historical record). This source is of special interest because it involves citation of a 'low' cultural text in a 'high', pedagogical context. It is the first-act finale of a school play written by a master, Johann Leonhard Frisch, and performed on the 126th anniversary of the school's foundation by boys at the Berlin grammar school, Das Graue Kloster ('Greyfriars') in 1700.[18] This fascinating text, *Die entdeckte und verworfene Unsauberkeit der falschen Dicht- und Reimkunst (The Uncovered and Repudiated Uncleanliness of the False Art of Poetry)*, was an early battle-cry in the long bourgeois campaign against popular 'dirt'. In each scene, a boy presents an example of an 'unclean' form of poetry (sometimes a modish form of literary verse, sometimes a text from oral tradition), and this is criticized in terms of classicist aesthetics and the Enlightenment doctrine of virtuous reasonableness as the path to personal self-improvement and prosperity, and general social decorum. Here, the text is that of a street song about a monstrous glutton. Two schoolboys enter: Wedigen, playing the 'Beginner in the Art of Poetry', faces a false temptation represented by Jannigke, who re-enacts a mountebank-singer's performance (or enacts re-enacting it):

JANNIGKE   Who was here but the news-singer? He was carrying his rickety stool and his pole around from place to place, and wherever he found a few people gathered together, he got up on the stool and started shouting.

WEDIGEN   What was the news story then?

J.   First he invited everyone up, the way he does, and I heard him call out to everyone, with roughly these words: Hear ye, my lords, what happened in a genteel city in Brandenburg, there took place a wonderful story with a monk of a friary known as the Grey Monk. All this monk's brothers in the monastery died of a great sickness, one after another. Finally he was left all on his own in the monastery. Then it happened that he was plagued by a great hunger, so that he could not eat his fill, and he had to beg from door to door, and the whole city could not give him enough to eat, and there are still people today in this same city who swear to it and tell it on their civil oath. This story, he went on, is printed on this sheet (here he showed his printed song) and the poor monk is painted here, as my lords see (here he struck the picture hanging from a pole, with a stick). The song though went to the tune 'There's a lovely lady lives in this land, Her qualities are many'.

W.   Go on, sing me some of it, or tell me a few verses; since you can remember the introduction so well, the song will be even better preserved in your memory.

J.   This is how it began:
   Come hither all you dear people,
   Hear ye what I have to tell,
   About a monk who sorely
   Was plagued by hunger-pain.
   He said: Here comes Brother Hermann
   Bringing his empty gut,
   O help him fill his belly.
   Give him what your good will – –

The tune referred to is that of a very popular historical mock-epic in septets, using erotic metaphors, concerning Bernhard von Weimar's conquest of Breisach, in December 1638: a typical news-ballad tune of the time.[19] At the start of the second verse the performance is regrettably interrupted by the 'Guide to the aspiring Poet', played by a (senior?) boy called Schadebrod:

SCHADEBROD   Silence! Be quiet! This fable has been known here for a hundred years, and he was singing it as a new wonder-story.[20]

W.   How much for such a song?

J.   Threepence.

S.   Off! Off! Off you go and learn by heart the introduction and text of an edifying sermon; that would be more profitable to remember. You ought to know, though, that a student of true poetry should not design to listen to nor to read such abuses as this.

W.   But what is all this about Brother Hermann, since it's supposed to have happened here?

S.   There are some who say, after an old tradition, that he was the last monk of this friary, and went begging with rhymes door to door, almost as in the news-singer's words; but he has attached many lies to the circumstances: that his brothers in the order all died of a great sickness; that he is supposed to have had an insatiable hunger. If anything about it is true, then learn from it this: that you learn righteousness, so you may not go begging. This Friary School is devoted to the former, and the latter is where many end up, who abuse the noble art of poetry or other gifts of God; so that though not so grossly as Brother Hermann, yet in a subtler way they have to beg with rhymes.

The last word goes to Franke (again, a schoolboy), who develops, in alexandrines, the equation between sickness, begging, and abuse of poetic art which Schadebrod has established:

Who honours God's name, must hate such people,
For their godless mouth often takes it in vain.
Who loves reason and truth, must shun their worthless trash,
Which is often wholly false, often false in part.
And who honours songs and their melodies,
Through which the fire of devotion is awakened in hearts,
Must avoid such a yowling as a plague
Which infects many with nausea before they notice.
Here we revile the abuse of our rhymes,
Which runners of this kind are guilty of in high degree.
For out of this abomination emerges a contempt,
As is to be expected, for our noble art.
There runs the mob to hear these wretched songs
And often buys out of pity for the poor man,
Whose limbs all shake from the force of shouting,
And all believe him feverish with poverty.
And often standing here with this market poet
Are his wife and child, singing along to the wonders;
The crowd concludes that he's in great need,
Since he begs for his penny so fearfully.
If then a true poem once comes before the people's eyes
They believe it's from the very same Parnassus
Where battered benches serve as the high seat,
And only news-singers join the choir of Muses.
Some do say that hereby wonders are publicised,
Which otherwise the people would never hear.
Since here the ground of truth is challenged, it'd be better
To hear nothing than to hear this trash.

It is striking that the two elements in the (undoubtedly genuine) ballad which are challenged by Schadebrod/Frisch are references to mass death, and to freakish hunger. The monk is the traumatized survivor of an epidemic, as the Bohemian is the traumatized survivor of conditions in Bohemia, and the monster of 1709 is the survivor of the mass killings he himself has carried out. This common narrative pattern is what makes the omnivore vogue of the 1700s unique (as far as I have been able to establish) in the history of representations of grotesque eating. The story, then, is that an individual survivor of a catastrophe which destroys masses of people is gripped by an animal desire to consume which breaks down all conventional cultural constraints. The catastrophe in question might, on one level, be taken to be the Thirty Years War, which had ended half a century previously. Certainly there was a so-called *Freßwelle* – an 'eating wave' – in Germany after the two wars of this century: when food became available again at last, people gorged themselves. The plight of Bohemia around 1700 was also due essentially to the aftermath of the Thirty Years War. But the delay seems unaccountable, quite apart from the fact that staged presentations such as these need not be reflections of real social behaviour. I think it is more pertinent that, where the Thirty Years War is concerned, to audiences in Berlin, Vienna, Nuremberg or Leipzig, Bohemia represented the continuance of a disaster which for them was of the *past*: so I want to argue that what was actually at stake in this vogue was historical change.

There is much to be said for seeing the years around 1700 as marking a watershed in German cultural history. I have already referred to the distinction between 'high' and 'low' cultures as having become institutional in these years. A highly symbolic marker of the arrival of a new hegemony is the foundation of the Academy of Sciences in Berlin, in 1700 exactly. Its president, Leibnitz, is renowned for formulating, in his theory of monads, perhaps the most systematic philosophical application of bourgeois individualism ever conceived. In these years, a German national consciousness emerged; the infrastructure of modern nation states was established (Berlin became the capital of an expansionist kingdom, rather than of a minor Electorate, in 1701); the lineaments of a modern, bourgeois civil society based on literary communication (periodical newspapers and journals, reading clubs, etc.) appeared. The German language, crucially, attained respectability for the first time: the first university lecture in German, rather than Latin, was held in 1695 – and Frisch was one of an army of linguisticians and grammarians who advanced the vindication of German as a literary language over the next decades.[21] The Pietist movement (a renewal of Protestantism) in tandem with the Enlightenment movement united professionals, churchmen and not a few nobles and merchants in a forward-looking campaign to regulate, rationalize and purify society and culture. The period is characterized by the foundation of new institutions of learning and discipline, including many prisons and workhouses, such as the one in Leipzig of which the Bohemian was one of the first inmates. The new century, often dubbed 'the century of *Bildung*' (education, cultivation of taste and manners), opened with a sense of a radical shift in the constellation of cultural power, which was threatening to all carnivalesque, collective popular traditions. The famed, emblematic moment which completed this development came in 1737, when Hanswurst was ceremoniously 'expelled' from the stage in Leipzig by Karoline Neuber's theatre troupe, acting out the recommendation of the classicist grammarian and poetologist, Gottsched.

In this context, the gluttony vogue can be seen to amount to a representation of the modern, monadic, bourgeois individual being born out of the ashes of that festive collectivity which was traditionally celebrated in carnivalesque rites. In the narrative pattern I discern, the grotesque body of the whole society which lives in carnivalesque imagery and performances is, so to speak, compressed into a single man's body: his insatiability – which possibly breaches even carnival's norms when he eats glass and stones – amounts to a paradoxical attempt to re-enact carnival, alone ('allein', as the 1709 print stresses twice). The audiences may equally well have 'read' these performances, and the images and texts which both commemorated them and assisted secondary recreations of them, as stereotypical satires of a gluttonous monk, a gluttonous peasant, a gluttonous swordsman; or they may have seen a comment on the conspicuous consumption which was being practised by some classes in the expanding capitals of German states; they may have seen the 'naturalness', healthiness and propriety of their own relatively newly-acquired urban manners confirmed by a monstrous spectacle from 'the past', or 'far away', or 'the distant future' ('7901'); or they may, just possibly, have seen such manners carnivalized, challenged as unnatural themselves. As they laughed, they surely were dimly aware that they were paying to spectate at a peculiar perversion of traditional festive pleasures.

Space does not permit me to develop this argument in full here. Where popular entertainments are studied in view of cultural historical processes, the significance of grotesque eating certainly deserves closer attention (among body functions generally). Norbert Elias's influential account of the process of civilization since the Renaissance suggests a fairly consistent increase in self-control over social behaviour, particularly manners of consumption.[22] But another analysis can be suggested, departing from Bakhtin's recognition that the 'classical' body image – decorous, self-enclosed, smooth-surfaced, immobile and pedestalized, with an individual face – is opposed by and to an organized disruptive counter-image: that of the grotesque body. Both continue to exist, but in altering relations of power: their visibility is a matter of struggle among and within people. As the grotesque body has been repressed in bourgeois mentality, it has taken every sort of bizarre form in art and in life.[23] Among them, perhaps foremost among them is the material basis of the changes Elias describes: the expansion of food production in Europe and the expropriation and exploitation of global food resources by Europeans: their collective self-transformation, to adopt Zanni's image, into the gullet of the world.

The history of the West over the last three or four hundred years or so can indeed be said to have involved a progressive collapse of all restraint, perhaps not on table-manners, but certainly on the desire to consume. Imperialism and technology have so reduced material constraints that well-off people, certainly in large towns in rich countries, can eat more or less anything anytime, and most of them usually want to. Not only do they want to because they can; they can, because trend-setting early modern Europeans wanted to. The rationalism of Frisch's Enlightenment, while it preached decorum, also presented itself as the recipe for unceasing improvement of the efficiency of exploitation of labour, land and other resources, including language, in order to secure ever more differentiated pleasures. 'Good taste' also meant, and means, tasting ever more of more different things. It is arguable that carnival culture, for all its more than obvious limitations and largely because of them, contained (contains?) an ecological aspect (and it is at least partly for that reason that it is currently so interesting) in its insistence on cyclical time, the recycling of the same. It was (is?) therefore somewhat resistant to the Faustian project of modernity which has reduced the world to its present sorry state.

To bring these speculations to a preliminary conclusion, I quote Robert Graves's version of a pertinent Greek legend, recently re-examined by Kate Soper. Her essays collected in *Troubled Pleasures: Writings on Politics, Gender and Hedonism* (1990) explore the anxieties of New Leftists in the 1980s. She notes that 'insatiability is indissociable from modernity' and 'also the curse of our times'; but not only of our times. As a 'lesson glimpsed early in our culture' which ought to be heeded now, she cites the legend of Erysichthon ('earth-tearer') and his

66   STUDIES IN THE *COMMEDIA DELL'ARTE*

punishment for profaning a natural temple to Demeter, goddess of fertility:

> At the head of twenty companions, Erysichthon dared invade a grove which the Pelasgians had planted for her at Dotium, and began cutting down the sacred trees, to provide timber for his new banqueting hall. Demeter assumed the form of Nicippe, priestess of the grove, and mildly ordered Erysichthon to desist. It was only when he threatened her with his axe that she revealed herself in her splendour and condemned him to suffer perpetual hunger, however much he might eat.[24]

The utter insatiability of the gluttony artists who seized the German mass imagination around 1700 echoes this legend as a comedy, perhaps no less uncanny then than it is now. The traces of the vogue which I have discussed point to a simultaneous trauma and delight accompanying the dissolution of a culture founded on the ancient rhythm of hunger and feasting, and its replacement by a culture founded on the promise of unlimited growth in individual conspicuous consumption.[25]

NOTES

1 Mike Featherstone, in idem et al, eds, *The Body. Social Process and Cultural Theory* (London, Sage, 1991), 178.

2 Peter Stallybrass and Allon White, *The Politics and Poetics of Transgression* (London, Methuen, 1986).

3 Walter Hinck, *Das deutsche Lustspiel des 17. und 18. Jahrhunderts und die italienische Komödie: Commedia dell'arte und Théâtre italien* (Stuttgart, Metzler, 1965).

4 Otto G. Schindler, ed., *Stegreifburleske der Wanderbühne. Szenare der Schulz-Menningerschen Schauspielertruppe* (St. Ingbert, Werner J. Röhrig, 1990), 5. (All translations here and below are mine).

5 Beside other works referred to here, see W.E. Yates and John R.P. McKenzie, eds, *Viennese Popular Theatre. A Symposium* (University of Exeter, 1985); J.M. Valentin, ed., *Volk – Volksstück – Volkstheater im deutschen Sprachraum des 18. – 20. Jahrhunderts*, (Bern, Peter Lang, 1986); and, more broadly, Jürgen Hein, ed., *Volksstück. Vom Hanswurstspiel zum sozialen Drama der Gegenwart* (Munich, Beck, 1989).

6 Richard Sheppard, 'Upstairs–Downstairs. Some Reflections on German Literature in the Light of Bakhtin's Theory of Carnival', in idem, ed., *New Ways in Germanistik* (New York, Berg, 1990), 278–315, here esp. 298f.

7 Helmut G. Asper, *Hanswurst. Studien zum Lustigmacher auf der Berufsschauspielerbühne in Deutschland im 17. und 18.* Jahrhundert (Emsdetten, Lechte, 1980); and Günther Hansen, *Formen der Commedia dell'arte in Deutschland*, (Emsdetten, Lechte, 1984).

8 Peter Sprengel, 'Herr Pantalon und sein Knecht Zanni. Zur frühen Commedia dell'arte in Deutschland' in *Wanderbühne. Theaterkunst als fahrendes Gewerbe* (Berlin, Gesellschaft für Theatergeschichte, 1988), 5-18.

9 See e.g. Marc Feldman, '*Pica*: Current Perspectives', in *Psychosomatics*, 27 (1986), 519–23. Indiscriminate eating is reported as an element of various syndromes including starvation. A recent mass outbreak of earth-eating in central Africa (reported in May 1991 in Britain) was caused by a rumour that eating earth would cure AIDS.

10 See Hans Scheubl, *Showfreaks und Monster. Sammlung Felix Adanos*, (Cologne, Dumont, 1974), 145f.; 'Signor Saltarino' (H. W. Otto), *Fahrend Volk* (Leipzig, J. J. Weber, 1895), 148ff., and older editions of the annual *Guinness Book of Records*. An earlier example is indicated by a handbill from a popular comedy performed in Nuremberg in 1769: *Der teutsche Franzos oder der wunderliche Jahrmarkt von Rumpelsdorff* ('The German Frenchman or the Amazing Revelston Fair'). This stars, beside 'Hanswurst as a modern Robinson', and among various fairground characters, a 'Monsieur Mangetout'. Cited in Max Pirker, ed., *Teutsche Arien* (Vienna etc., 1927), vol.I, 389.

11 See Breon Mitchell, 'Kafka and the Hunger Artists', in Alan Udoff, ed., *Kafka and the Contemporary Critical Performance* (Bloomington, Indiana University Press, 1987), 236–55.

12 Wolfgang Braungart, ed., *Bänkelsang* (Stuttgart, Reclam, 1985); Leander Petzoldt, *Bänkelsang* (Stuttgart, Metzler, 1974); and Tom Cheesman, 'Bänkelsang' (unpublished D. Phil. thesis, Oxford, 1989), and *Shocking Ballads* (monograph in preparation).

13 A. Altamura, *I cantastorie e la poesia popolare italiana* (Naples, F. Fiorentino, 1965); G.B. Bronzini, 'Zwischen mündlicher und schriftlicher Überlieferung. Die Erzählkunst der Bänkelsänger und die Balladentradition in Italien', in Stefaan Top and Eddy Teilemans, eds, *Aspects of the European Broadside Ballad*, (Brussels, Centrum voor Vlaamse Volkscultuur, 1982), 107–88; Walter Hirdt, *Italienischer Bänkelsang* (Frankfurt, Klostermann, 1979).

14 Many thanks to Dr Axel Janecke of the Germanisches Nationalmuseum, Nuremberg, for this information.

15 Elias Canetti, *Crowds and Power*, tr. Carol Stewart (Harmondsworth, Penguin, 1987), 265–326 ('The Survivor').

16 Jews, cats and pigs all straddle conceptual categories and so feature prominently in traditional transgressive rites. See Stallybrass and White 1986, ch. 1 and pp. 53–64; and Robert Darnton, *The Great Cat Massacre and Other Episodes in French Cultural History* (Harmondsworth, Penguin, 1984), 91–9. For the background in anthropology, see Mary Douglas's seminal *Purity and Danger. An Analysis of Concepts of Pollution and Taboo* (London, RKP, 1966).

17 Johann Jakob Vogel, *Leipziges Geschicht-Buch oder Annales . . .* (Leipzig, Fr. Lauchischens Erben, 1714), 936.; *Theatrum Europaeum . . .*, vol. XVI (Frankfurt

a.M., Anton Heinscheit, 1717), 486; *Grosses vollständiges Universal-Lexicon* . . . , vol.XLVIII (Leipzig and Halle, J. H. Zedler, 1746), 1101.

18 The original is lost, but the play was republished in facsimile in 1890: L. H. Fischer, ed., *Johann Leonhard Frischs Schulspiel von der Unsauberkeit der falschen Dicht- und Reimkunst*, Berlin (Schriften des Vereins für die Geschichte Berlins no.26).

19 See Lutz Röhrich and R.W. Brednich, eds, *Deutsche Volkslieder*, vol. I (Düsseldorf, Schwann, 1965), no. 62.

20 No trace of the story of the singing monk could be found in histories of Berlin or of Das Graue Kloster. The school was founded on the site of a dissolved Franciscan friary, and the last friar, Peter (Otto von Golitz), was accorded a 'most honourable' burial by the (Lutheran convert) Elector of Brandenburg, his personal friend, in 1571, according to Martin Diterich, *Berlinische Kloster- und Schul-Historie* (Berlin, C. G. Nicolai, 1732), 34.

21 Frisch's works between the school play (his first publication) and his death in 1743 include, beside treatises on birds and insects, several bilingual dictionaries, editions of German grammars, and school text-books on classical and modern languages; he pioneered the study of Slav languages (*Allgemeine deutsche Biographie*, vol. VIII, 1878, 93–5). On the wider development, see Eric A. Blackall, *The Emergence of German as a Literary Language* (Cambridge University Press, 1957), ch. 1.

22 Norbert Elias, *The Civilising Process*, 2 vols (Oxford, Blackwell, 1978 and 1982). Cf. S. Mennell, 'On the Civilising of Appetite', in Mike Featherstone et al., eds, *The Body. Social Process and Cultural Theory* (London, Sage, 1991), 126–56.

23 See here Stallybrass and White 1986; and Allon White, 'Hysteria and the End of Carnival: Festivity and Bourgeois Neurosis', in Nancy Armstrong and Leonhard Tennenhouse, eds, *The Violence of Representation. Literature and the History of Violence* (London and New York, Routledge, 1989), 157–70.

24 Quoted from Robert Graves, *The Greek Myths* (Harmondsworth, Penguin, 1955), vol. I, 89, in Kate Soper, *Troubled Pleasures* (London and New York, Verso, 1990), 271 (and cf. p. 81).

25 This paper has been through a number of drafts, and there were several variant oral performances in 1990. I am very grateful for the responses of audiences at the German Department of Swansea U.C, at the Folklore and Cultural History section of the Akademie der Wissenschaften of the GDR, in Berlin, and at the Music Department of the University of Rostock. Friends and colleagues who kindly read and commented helpfully on earlier drafts include Gerd Baumann, Kate Hodgkin, Audrey McMullan, Ros Brown-Grant and the present editors, and the late Andrew Duff-Cooper. I remain responsible for all inaccuracies etc. Felix Adanos of Vienna and Heiner Vogel of Leipzig provided essential insights into German fairground traditions; and for their researches on my behalf I am indebted to Dr Erika Karasek of the Museum für Volkskunde (Pergamon-Museum), Berlin, Dr Eva Rysava of the National Museum of Prague, Dr Elisabeth Schneider of the Österreichische Nationalbibliothek, Vienna, and Dr Axel Janecke of the Germanisches Nationalmuseum, Nuremberg.

3   Stage and audience in the *commedia dell'arte* and in Molière's early plays

JOHN TRETHEWEY

The nine early Molière plays I want to discuss here are very varied, comprising the two prose scenarios, *La Jalousie du Barbouillé* and *Le Médecin volant*, which are the only remaining complete *canevas* (out of thirteen for which we have names) associated with Molière and his troupe, two one-act comedies, *Les Précieuses ridicules* and *Sganarelle ou le Cocu imaginaire* (the first in prose, the second in verse), two three-act verse comedies, *L'Ecole des maris* and *Les Fâcheux*, and three five-act verse comedies, *L'Etourdi*, *Dépit amoureux* and *L'Ecole des femmes*. The two scenarios cannot be dated. The earliest firm date we have for a Molière play is the year 1655 when, according to the *Registre* of La Grange, *L'Etourdi* was premièred in Lyon.[1] The influence of the *commedia dell'arte* on Molière does not end with *L'Ecole des femmes*, the last, the most successful and most important play with which I deal in this essay. But limitations of time and space prevent me from advancing any further into the playwright's career, even in a restricted topic like that of use by characters of audience address and audience awareness.[2] I am therefore covering roughly seven or eight years of Molière's career, of which the last five were the beginning of his success in Paris, culminating in *L'Ecole des femmes*, first performed in December 1662.[3]

The published literary or dramatic sources of these various plays have been studied exhaustively. A couple of them are from prose stories – *La Jalousie du Barbouillé* (*Decameron*, seventh day, fourth story) and *L'Ecole des femmes* (Maria de Zayas via Scarron, and Straparola). Others have Italian *commedie erudite* for sources (*Le Médecin volant*, *L'Etourdi* and *Dépit amoureux*[4]), one, *L'Ecole des maris*, owes much to a Spanish *comedia* (Hurtado de Mendoza, *El marido hace mujer*, 1643), and finally three seem to owe nothing to printed sources (*Les Précieuses ridicules*, *Sganarelle* and *Les Fâcheux*). Molière, then, to the extent that he relies on the published work of others, does not, as we shall see, differ greatly, in his choice of subject matter and source material, from the inventors of *commedia dell'arte* scenarios.

His short preface to *L'Amour médecin* (1666) is often quoted as a professional's sound advice to the lay reader: 'on sait bien que les comédies ne sont faites que pour être jouées; et je ne conseille de lire celle-ci qu'aux personnes qui ont des yeux pour découvrir dans la lecture tout le jeu du théâtre' ('everyone knows that plays are only written to be performed; and I suggest that this one should be read only by those with eyes to discover in the text all the action which takes place on stage'). Playtexts exist to be *acted*, and to be bedecked with all the finery that designers, choreographers, musicians and other theatrical professionals can bestow on them, 'des grâces dont ils ont toutes les peines du monde à se passer' ('charms which they would have all the trouble in the world to do without').[5] What is more the reader, whether layperson, would-be interpreter or scholar, must have the imagination to supply tones of voice, accompanying gestures and unspoken reactions. However where, as in *commedia dell'arte*, there is no 'text' in the accepted sense, where there is only the experienced professional actor's memory, 'stored with phrases, *concetti*, declarations of love, reproaches, deliriums, and despairs',[6] evolved and perfected over the years, then the reader/interpreter/scholar is often compelled to work backwards, as it were, from the texts and interpretations of a Molière, in the hope of reconstructing the traditions and conventions of performance evolved by the entertainers. This is certainly true where the relationship between stage and audience is concerned, for Molière's texts, though short on stage directions, give us more clues than the brief descriptions of sketches that the *commedia dell'arte* has bequeathed to us. The professional aims of the latter were perhaps rather different from those of Molière, but the techniques and experience of the Italian troupes were undoubtedly an inspiring example for one who was not initially a writer but 'un comédien qui peu à peu [allait] se mettre à écrire' ('An actor who bit by bit [was] to begin writing').[7]

Not that records are completely lacking. It is well known that the *commedia dell'arte* regards speech as only one ingredient in a theatrical entertainment, sometimes dispensable, sometimes endowed with more – or less – or another – meaning than that which the words alone suggest. Flaminio Scala, publishing fifty of his sketches in *Il Teatro delle favole rappresentative* (1611), provides summaries indicating hardly any dialogue, preferring 'to present to the world his plays in their scenario form, leaving to the beauty of the imagination (which thrives on the excellence of its own language) the creation of its speeches.'[8] At other times, plays were ' "comédies mixtes", in which certain written passages were bound together by scenes of pure improvisation'.[9] Whatever the case, it is plain that neo-classical *vraisemblance* (verisimilitude), or any other ideal of realism, was completely disregarded by troupes of the *commedia dell'arte* whose memorized and oft-repeated material included not only set speeches for all occasions but also *lazzi* (literally 'clowning', 'gags' – a very necessary ingredient to fill in gaps, especially between improvised episodes where a familiar piece of 'business' would provide a welcome relief from the strain of ad-libbing), mime, juggling, acrobatics, animal acts, dancing, and vocal and instrumental music. Theatrical illusion in the neo-classical sense was unimportant to them, even when, patronized by the rich and the high-born, they were given the use of elaborate stages and machinery like Palladio's Theatre at Vicenza used by Flaminio Scala.[10] Machines and elaborate perspective scenery were not to be scorned, of course, when available, but the basic patterns of plot, *lazzi* and stock characters – many wearing masks – remained the same, even in grand surroundings.

The varied list of performance and entertainment ingredients given above indicates that *commedia dell'arte* owed little to classical theory governing tragedy and comedy (apart perhaps from the unities of time and place, vaguely observed). In addition, the attitude of these players to their spectators was not that of classical theatre where actors play characters living in a universe of their own, ignoring the audience. Despite the use of a stage generally built high, so that the feet of the performers were at eye level to a standing spectator, audience address, and even mingling with the audience, were common. Duchartre tells us that 'as a rule, there were two ladders placed at either side from the ground to the stage, and on the rungs of these one or two players . . . would perch after having finished their turns in the performance.'[11] Certain *lazzi* required actors to mix with the audience or acknowledge their presence. Sometimes this mixing called for agility. In the 'Lazzo of Running along the Balcony Rail' (obviously devised for a theatre), Arlecchino 'leaps from the stage to the first spectator box and runs around the outer railings of three sets of balconies'. Or an absurd attempt at imitating reality is made which soon breaks down, as in the 'Lazzo of the Chase' where, 'with a drawn sword the Captain chases Coviello. They remain on the stage in a stationary position as they mime running, each slightly out of reach of the other. As they run, each begins to acknowledge the audience's response.' And a frank, mocking destruction of theatrical illusion is undertaken in the 'Lazzo of the Interruption' in which, 'in the middle of the performance, actors walk into the audience while other actors are speaking on the stage. The off-stage actors begin to shout ridiculous and irrelevant phrases.'[12] There are many such routines involving actors talking to spectators, mingling or sitting with them, recognizing them as old friends, taking a dislike to individuals and insulting them. They are familiar routines to anyone who has frequented modern companies who keep up the traditions, including that of 'working an audience', or British pantomime or music hall where many of the traditions of *commedia dell'arte* live on.

Yet despite these displays of agility and skill and these mockeries of dramatic convention, one element of drama is never abandoned, and that is the thread of narrative. However often it is interrupted, and however thoroughly it is mocked or subverted, the story-line – again, as in British pantomime – always survives. The spectators are never fobbed off with a series of 'turns'. Furthermore, the stories chosen for these scenarios can be remarkably complex ones, sometimes of very respectable provenance, to judge by the examples provided by Flaminio Scala's collection. As these companies wandered further and further afield, from the mid-sixteenth century onwards, enhancing their reputation, particularly in France, their basic material and their techniques did not appear to change – not, at all events, until after the period with which we are concerned.[13] Classical 'new comedy' and *commedie erudite* are plundered or adapted, as are, above all, Renaissance romances with all their complexities of plot, sub-plot, disguise, misunderstanding, kidnappings, shipwrecks, substitutions and mistaken identities. Of course, these stories cannot be staged in their entirety, after the manner of Shakespeare's comedies, nor are they taken as seriously as were their romance sources. We are witnesses, usually, to the final hours before a complicated dénouement, full of remarkable coincidences and revelations, our understanding of which is ensured by a series of narrations, in the form perhaps of a prologue, expository dialogues or soliloquies. The amount of dramatic *action* devoted to developing the plot is usually minimal. Consequently, the characters who would appear as serious and central in the original romances are now upstaged by the comic stock characters, and can in any case no longer be taken very seriously, since their heroic or courtly attitudes and aspirations, their transports and posturings, are openly derided or parodied. We are enjoying a form of theatre, therefore, which cheerfully undermines the conventions of romance while clinging to the very necessary narrative framework that they provide.

Molière's personal experience of the *commedia dell'arte*, and his debt to it, have been much studied and commented upon,[14] and yet no one has been able to define exactly where the line runs which divides this Italian influence from that of native French farce, with its simpler, more homespun plots recalling fabliaux rather than romances. Undoubtedly, sketches and plays like *La Jalousie du Barbouillé*, *Sganarelle*, *L'Etourdi*, *Le Mariage forcé*, *Le Médecin malgré lui* and *George Dandin* owe not a little to native French tradition which preferred to exploit a rustic or a petty bourgeois setting and the comic potential of the husband–wife relationship – 'la farce conjugale', as Raymond Lebègue calls it.[15] The two traditions have in any case much in common, and by the early seventeenth century, the merging of Italian practices with French was so far advanced that only by naming actors, companies and nationalities can one make any sure distinction. The famous French *farceurs* of the first half of the century, Tabarin, Gaultier-Garguille, Bruscambille, Turlupin, Guillot-Gorju and Jodelet, whether street entertainers or attached to one or other of the established theatres of the time, all owed much to the Italians as far as dress, make-up and routines were concerned, but in general (though not always) preferred to be *enfarinés* rather than to wear masks, and, naturally, used only French instead of a mixture of languages.[16]

As for Molière, when one attempts to separate the influences of the two traditions in his theatre, one is quickly confused. The sketch, *La Jalousie du Barbouillé*, would seem to be typically French in that it has a simple plot and is concerned with the quarrels of a husband and wife. Yet that simple plot has been borrowed, as I have already noted, from a Renaissance Italian *novella* – admittedly more akin to a fabliau than to romance.[17] As for the mask tradition,[18] the extent of Molière's debt to it has recently been brought into question. It has been accepted, from Molière's own day, that the French actor learned much of his comic technique by sharing theatres – first the Petit-Bourbon and then the Palais-Royal – with a troupe of Italians including Tiberio Fiorilli who played Scaramouche. But it has been pointed out that these theatres were of quite modest size, which may have suggested, first to the Italian and subsequently to the Frenchman, that facial expression could be effectively used there for refining and enlarging the range of emotions that could be conveyed to the audience. Thus it could be argued that a famous actor in a tradition noted for its use of masks taught another famous actor how to do without them. It may have been the influence of Fiorilli which caused Molière to evolve from the masked Mascarille to the bare-faced Sganarelle.[19]

Caution is necessary, however, as far as the period which I am covering is concerned. Molière and his troupe returned to Paris, after a thirteen-year sojourn in the provinces, in October 1658, and began officially to share the Petit-Bourbon with the Italians from the beginning of November. From that date the apprenticeship (such as it was) of Molière to Fiorilli begins: 'Scaramouche enseignant, Elomire estudiant', as the caption to the frontispiece of the hostile *Elomire hypocondre* (1670)[20] puts it. Molière, a thorough professional, would be able to absorb quickly anything of a technical theatrical nature. He would need to. By 11 July 1659, Fiorilli and the Italians had left for Italy on 'sabbatical leave', and did not return until January 1662.[21] Molière's character Sganarelle appeared in Paris for the first time shortly before that 'sabbatical' period began – in *Le Médecin volant* which was played at the Petit-Bourbon on 18 April 1659. That sketch, it is generally agreed, was inspired by one of many possible Italian sources. We have, however, no means of knowing when or under what circumstances Molière's version was first devised, and scholars surmise that it may well date from his period in the provinces.[22] The question of the extent and nature of Molière's debt to Fiorilli, and whether the Italian's influence played any part in the creation of the character Sganarelle, must therefore remain open.

The further, equally germane question of who or what provided Molière with inspiration in the matter of character–audience relations is just as hard to answer. It goes almost without saying that such a relationship must, in large measure, have been the product of personal experience, of an individual coming to appreciate his own strengths and weaknesses as well as 'learning a trade' from others. The relationship must also have varied from production to production, even from performance to performance. As a young actor, and then as a touring actor-manager, Molière was perforce made familiar with drama of every sort, from farce to classical tragedy,[23] acquiring knowledge of a wide range of techniques and conventions, and performing in many venues, from *tripots* to noble households. Only with the success of *L'Ecole des femmes* did works of his own begin to predominate in the repertoire instead of those of Corneille and other contemporaries.

It is evident, from what is known of Molière's repertoire in the provinces and during his first four years in Paris, that the troupe preferred more complex, more calculated, more controlled forms of theatre than those associated with the Italians. Even in the two scenarios there is evidence, not yet of loftier preoccupations, but certainly of a desire to define beforehand the shape of an entertainment, to establish more or less clearly what is to be said and when. The words are nearly all provided in these little comedies: there is certainly room for ad-libbing or prearranged unwritten dialogue, but (provided there is plenty of non-verbal inventiveness) little needs to be added in the form of spoken exchanges. In *Le Médecin volant*, for instance, speeches occasionally suggest quite precise actions and movements and need to be spoken as written, as when, in scene iv, Sganarelle disguised as a physician, announced by Sabine, makes a belated entry, so that Gorgibus must ask her: 'Où est-il donc?' ('Where is he then?') and Sabine must reply in three stages: 'le voilà qui me suit; tenez, le voilà.' ('There he is, following me; look, there he is.') As far as improvisation is concerned, in *La Jalousie du Barbouillé* apparently only the chaotic ending of scene vi is left entirely to the actors' ingenuity, and in *Le Médecin volant*, only Gros-René's *galimatias* in scene iii *obviously* remains untranscribed, for the actor René Berthelot (alias Du Parc) to fill out with material from stock (Gros-René being his role in this and other sketches and plays).[24]

Fraternization with the audience, or acknowledgement of its presence, varies in quantity or in potential in Molière's plays according to the amount of comedy or farce in the text. One can well imagine that in a *commedia dell'arte* sketch the audience is constantly solicited for applause or reactions, when some acrobatic feat has been accomplished, or when a character confides his schemes to the spectators, or seeks their sympathy, or approbation. Sometimes it is just as overt in a Molière sketch, as when in *La Jalousie du Barbouillé* the hero points to the audience as witnesses of his innocence: 'Demandez plutôt à ces Messieurs qui sont là-bas dans le parterre.' ('Ask rather those gentlemen there in the pit.') At other times, it is, as it were, optional, as in a soliloquy, where – so long as the text does not decree that absent characters, personified objects or abstractions be addressed – classical conventions may be observed, or not, according to the decision of actor or director.[25]

In addition to such obvious exchanges between stage and audience, there are also in Molière (as there must also have been in *commedia dell'arte*) instances of passive audience collusion furnished by dramatic irony. Where a character shares (or thinks he shares) with the spectators, knowledge which is hidden from other characters, then he may, for dramatic or comic effect, invest his speeches with double meaning for their benefit. Under such circumstances, an audience is given a sense of superiority by knowing itself to be addressed, even when the character 'in the know' is ostensibly speaking to another. Instances of this sort of irony would not be easy to pinpoint in *commedia dell'arte*, but can be found without difficulty (as I hope to show) in the dialogues of Molière.

Now, as I have said, Molière must have learned his trade, not only by experience and trial-and-error, but also from the Italians and from traditional French farce. Undoubtedly the relationship between stage and audience in the native sketches was one in which collusion with the spectators, addresses to them, various forms of exploitation of them or of individuals for comic purposes, were a common part of the tradition, perhaps more so than in the *commedia dell'arte*. At the same time features such as the wearing of masks, their association with stereotypes used many times over in many sketches, improvization, the mingling of dramatic action with byplay of various sorts and with displays of theatrical skills, all that belongs to the world of Italian comedy which, as we have seen, was also not averse to fostering and exploiting a relationship with the audience.

Classicism, however, the other great formative influence on Molière, abhors farce, and in the interest of preserving the 'dramatic illusion' not only banishes open, direct audience address, but even looks critically upon any stage practice or convention which might endanger the spectator's 'willing suspension of disbelief'. To quote the intelligent, if dogmatic Abbé d'Aubignac's *Pratique du Théâtre* of 1657: 'La partie de l'Hôtel de Bourgogne élevée et environnée de toile peinte, où se joue la Tragédie, est le lieu représentant et l'image d'un autre, et celui qui y est représenté par cet espace, soit la salle du Palais d'Horace, ou de celui d'Auguste, est dans la Tragédie le lieu véritable, ou du moins qu'il faut regarder comme véritable.' ('The part of the Hôtel de Bourgogne which is raised and surrounded with painted canvas, where the Tragedy is played, is the place which represents and is the image of another place, and that which is represented there by this space, whether it be a room in the palace of the Horace family, or that of Augustus, is, in the Tragedy, the real place, or at least one must regard it as such.') But d'Aubignac is not here making a rule exclusively for tragedy. Let me quote him again: 'Il [*the character*] fait tout comme s'il n'y avait point de spectateurs, c'est-à-dire tous les personnages doivent agir et parler comme s'ils étaient véritablement roi, et non pas comme étant Bellerose, ou Mondory, comme s'ils étaient dans le palais d'Horace à Rome, et non pas dans l'Hôtel de Bourgogne à Paris; et comme si personne ne les voyait et ne les entendait que ceux qui sont sur le théâtre agissants et comme dans le lieu représenté.'[26] ('The character does everything as if there were no audience: that is to say that all the characters must act and speak as if they were truly kings, and not Bellerose or Mondory; as if they were in the Horaces' palace in Rome, and not in the Hôtel de Bourgogne in Paris; and as if no one could see or hear them except those who are on the stage, and as if in the place which is being represented.') In other words, 'the dramatic action, in all its aspects, must be represented as an image of reality',[27] and the job of dramatist and actors is to do their best to persuade the audience to accept that. Such an influence obviously runs counter to that of the farce traditions. At the same time, it would be possible for a dramatist to keep the two worlds separate, by distinguishing fairly rigorously between genres, keeping one law for tragedy and for polite comedy, and another for farce and 'low' comedy. Not so Molière: it was Boileau's complaint, for instance, that he could not keep farce out of his plays, so that the only one the satirical poet admired unreservedly was *Le Misanthrope*.[28] As far as the theatrical illusion is concerned, therefore, one can expect Molière to do undogmatically whatever he thought was appropriate to a particular subject and occasion, and even to a particular moment or character in a play.

As a generalization, one can say that certain Molière characters are 'privileged' by being aware of audience and by being therefore able to address it. The central comic character is frequently thus privileged. Le Barbouillé in *La Jalousie du Barbouillé* is such a one, opening the play with a monologue, largely – not wholly – addressed to us, in which he sets out his complaints against his unfaithful wife, and in general when something upsets him he expresses his frustration to us, as when he is enraged by the pedantic, loquacious Docteur (scenes ii, vi). But he by no means has the audience to himself in this most *invraisemblable* of scenarios. All the characters may speak to us and be aware of us: Angélique the wife of Le Barbouillé, for instance, alone on stage in scenes viii and x; and Le Docteur, whose feverish speeches in the above-mentioned scenes are more than just pedantry and garrulity: they are an act, performed in direct competition with Le Barbouillé, an act for which he openly solicits audience appreciation and applause.

Les Précieuses ridicules is perhaps a special case in that the characters taking part are all named after the actors of Molière's troupe who originally appeared in it under their stage or even their personal names, as was frequently the case in farce. Thus the actors La Grange and Du Croisy were the 'amants rebutés', the familiar names Magdelon, Cathos and Marotte thinly disguised the forenames of the actresses Madeleine Béjart, Catherine de Brie and Marie Ragueneau, while Gorgibus, Mascarille and Jodelet were already well-known stage personalities about whom I have more to say below. Obviously, under these circumstances, firmly delineated characters were not what Molière had in mind. The absurd pretensions, the mock-*précieux* language and the extravagant dress of the young ladies and the fake nobles add up to a tableau which must have the air of being enjoyed as much by the actors as by the audience, and which cannot be regarded as a true reflection of any sort of reality. Caricature is plainly the weapon in use here: every absurdity must be clearly recognizable. The accumulated features are more important than character portrayal. La Grange in scene i suggests that his valet Mascarille is a self-deceiving fool but nevertheless provides him, in ways which are left unexplained, with the clothing and the opportunity to display his 'bel esprit'. They are therefore working together (with Jodelet as a knowing third party) in a conspiracy of which the play's dénouement must be a part. Mascarille's folly is also belied by his and Jodelet's sly, ironic references in scene xi to their real stations in life, to 'des lieux où il faisait fort chaud' (kitchens) and 'gens de service' (servants). These inconsistencies do not matter, however. What is important is the virtuoso display of comic extravagance by all the actors, and the allusions to identifiable people, manners, language and literature, all of which elements are too outrageous, too exaggerated, too obviously without bitterness, to cause offence to the supposed victims of the attack – the habituées of the Hôtel de Rambouillet and Madeleine de Scudéry and her friends and admirers. Molière's play may suggest satire, it may foreshadow comedy of manners, but it is essentially a good-natured piece of entertainment within the traditions of farce.

Another point worth making about this play and the others by Molière of this period is the, by now, obvious one that they have characters in common. The seventeenth-century audience therefore, if it knew Molière's troupe and the theatre, recognized these familiar types, and was aware of a continuity, not only in the characters, but also in the actors who habitually played them, making them more 'real' in their way than the plays or playlets in which they were acting. Le Barbouillé, for instance, is the aforementioned Gros-René. La Grange, in his *Registre*, actually calls the sketch *La Jalousie du Gros-René*. He is a fat man, noted for drunkenness and gluttony. He turns up as a valet in *Le Médecin volant*, in *Dépit amoureux* and again in *Sganarelle ou le Cocu imaginaire*. He is also obviously the central character of the lost scenario, *Gros-René Escolier*, recorded by La Grange as having been played on various occasions between 1659 and 1664. Gros-René is capable of self-advertising and making jokes and puns about his features, as in the opening scene of *Dépit amoureux*: 'Je . . . suis homme fort rond de toutes les manières' (lines 13–14).

Gorgibus is another familiar name in the cast list of *La Jalousie du Barbouillé*. This foolish-old-man role was that of François Bedeau, known as L'Espy, brother of the more famous Jodelet (Julien Bedeau).[29] Both brothers, already old (their appearance on the professional stage is first recorded at Angers in 1603), joined Molière in 1659. The role of Gorgibus may well have existed before that year (there is a lost scenario entitled *Gorgibus dans le sac* recorded by La Grange in his *Registre* as having been played six times between January 1661 and July 1664), but L'Espy made it his own until his retirement in 1663, playing that part, not only in *La Jalousie*, but also in *Le Médecin volant*, *Les Précieuses ridicules* and finally in *Sganarelle*. Throughout these plays, Gorgibus is frequently left alone with the audience, and expresses to them his curiosity, his anger or frustration, his over-bearing self-confidence, or reveals his plans before going on to fail to realize them. His brother Jodelet had been playing similar games with audiences for years as a foolish, cowardly valet, and parts – indeed plays – had been specially written for him by a variety of dramatists including Scarron, d'Ouville and both Pierre and Thomas Corneille. It is noticeable that when Molière's troupe acquired him, at Easter 1659, a number of these plays were immediately revived, including Corneille's *Le Menteur*, Thomas Corneille's *Le Geôlier de soi-même*, and Scarron's *Jodelet ou le maître-valet*. The one part that Molière wrote for him, that of the Vicomte de Jodelet in *Les Précieuses ridicules*, is not a taxing one, comprising relatively few lines and an indication towards the end, where dancing is called for, that this vicomte is not very agile (end of scene xii). It obviously takes account of Jodelet's age. But the part also has that element of self-advertising which I have already mentioned, reminding the audience that here is a character who transcends any given dramatic role, who therefore is closer to them, in a way, than is the action of which he is condescending to be part. His famous appearance, with a face made pallid by the application of make-up (he is an *enfariné*), has to be accounted for to the two ignorant young *précieuses* – the only persons on or off stage who do not recognize him – by the pretence that 'il ne fait que sortir d'une maladie qui lui a rendu le visage pâle comme vous le voyez' (sc. xi, p. 280), ('he has just got over an illness which made his face pale, as you see'). And his lack of agility is also accounted for by this same 'maladie', an ironic explanation which gives the explainer Mascarille and the audience the chance to collude in further deception of the foolish young ladies.

The two remaining repeated roles I have to deal with are those that Molière created for himself: Mascarille and Sganarelle. Mascarille in fact wore a mask, enabling Molière to stay young, and to play this lively, disabused, resourceful, Scapino-like valet until as late as 1670, when the last revivals of *L'Etourdi* during Molière's lifetime are recorded by La Grange (Scapin himself went on until July 1671). He turns up in only three published texts: *L'Etourdi, Dépit amoureux* and *Les Précieuses ridicules*. His part as the Marquis de Mascarille in *Les Précieuses* is his most famous, but he is just as much to the fore, initiating all the action, in the full-length, five-act *L'Etourdi* as sharp valet to a dull young master, the *étourdi* of the title. Like Gorgibus and others, he is given the privilege of addressing us, of taking us into his confidence, of tipping us the wink as he deceives or mocks someone. His exchanges with the foolish old man Anselme in Act I, scene v, can be taken as an example, not only of his confidences to the audience (Anselme too, in fact, has this very privilege in this very scene), but also of yet another situation in which the audience is in the know and in collusion with one character while a second is, ironically, ignorant of what is *really* going on and of what is *really* being said. Anselme tells us that he has just received a purse containing two thousand francs, and he rashly displays it. Mascarille resolves to steal it from him, and tells us how he proposes to go about it.

> O Dieu! la belle proie
> A tirer en volant! chut: il faut que je voie
> Si je pourrais un peu de près le caresser,
> Je sais bien les discours dont il le faut bercer.
> *(And then, to Anselme:)*
> Je viens de voir, Anselme, . . . votre Nérine.   (215–19)

Oh God! What a prey to take in flight! Hush! I must see if I can get close to him and flatter him. I well know what sort of speeches to lull him with . . . Anselme, I've just seen your girl-friend Nérine.

We then watch Mascarille as he flatters and distracts the old man and waits for his chance to remove the purse, watch him deliberately almost give the game away as he does so, and then drop his booty in a corner ready to be picked up later. At the same time, the flattery which Mascarille metes out to the old man is to some extent double-edged, dangerously close to mockery; in fact he likes to live a dangerous life in order to show off his dexterity to us. He pretends to Anselme that the lady Nérine loves him, and underlines the folly of this *senex* with plays on words which *could* give the game away if Anselme were only a little brighter; mocking him, therefore, and at the same time flattering us, the audience. That is how the valet proceeds throughout the play. Again, in II, ii, having put about the lie that Pandolfe is dead, Mascarille speaks to Anselme about it with an irony which is all for the audience and not at all for the distracted old man:

ANSELME   Etre mort de la sorte!
MASCARILLE   Il a certes grand tort:
       Je lui sais mauvais gré d'une telle incartade.
ANSELME   N'avoir pas seulement le temps d'être malade!
MASCARILLE   Non, jamais homme n'eut si hâte de mourir.   (500–3)

ANSELME   To die like that! MASCARILLE It is certainly very wrong of him. I'm annoyed with him for playing such a prank. ANSELME Not even having time to be ill! MASCARILLE No, never did a man make such haste to die.

His stupid master, the *étourdi* Lélie, on whose behalf these tricks are played, manages every time to undo all the good work that is being done for him, exasperating Mascarille more and more, so that he must find an outlet for his frustration. We thus become his *confidents*, the only persons privileged to see the true extent of his rage and scorn, or savour the full flavour of his mockery. In III. iv, for instance, when Lélie is failing to hide from Léandre the fact that Mascarille is his servant, the latter's exclamations, in the course of a disastrous three-way conversation, are all addressed exclusively to us:

Fut-il jamais au monde un esprit moins sensé? . . .
             Encore! il va tout découvrir . . .
Ah! le double bourreau, qui me va tout gâter,
Et qui ne comprend rien, quelque signe qu'on donne!   (1053–63)

Was there ever in the world a less sensible mind? . . . Again! He'll give everything away . . . Ah, the double hangman, who's going to spoil everything for me, and who understands nothing, whatever sign one makes!

In *Dépit amoureux*, he is rather less self-confident,[30] displaying a Sganarelle-like cowardice, but he still has his relationship with us, planning future moves in III, i, failing to carry them out according to plan, and complaining to us, as in III, ii, lines 794–5, and III, x, line 1116, because *his* privileged knowledge, concerning the marriage of Valère and Lucile, turns out to be false. He is also capable, in moments of extreme distress, of assuming a mock-tragic air, as at the end of Act IV:

> Malheureux Mascarille! à quels maux aujourd'hui
> Te vois-tu condamné pour le péché d'autrui!   (1135–6)

> Unhappy Mascarille! To what pains are you to be condemned today for another's sin!

Inappropriate registers, 'putting on airs', self-pity and self-deception are characteristics rather of Sganarelle than of Mascarille whose more normal features are collusion with the audience, sharing its superior awareness, at the expense of employers or of other social superiors whose foolishness he underlines for our amusement. He has learned his attitudes from the *commedia dell'arte* servants in Flaminio Scala's sketches, who similarly exploit their masters and mistresses to amuse themselves and their audiences.[31]

Not so Sganarelle: he is without a mask, older, bewildered, truculent, frequently and incurably in the grip of some absurd obsession. He more rarely conspires with us against his fellow characters, or if he does, his plans go awry and leave us laughing at him instead of with him. And when we laugh at him, for whatever reason, he is hurt or indignant. This may happen when his obsession or some other pretext causes him to dress extravagantly. In scene iv of *Le Médecin volant* he appears for the first time dressed as a doctor. Sabine tries to introduce him here to Gorgibus (scene iv), but loses him as he wanders off, preoccupied with his dress and with our laughter at it. In *L'Ecole des maris*, his defiant desire to make 'le bon vieux temps' ('the good old days') live on in his person leads to his attiring himself in a fashion which is two generations out of date, eliciting laughter from the audience when he first appears in Act I, scene i; to which his indignant reaction is: 'Qui me trouve mal n'a qu'à fermer les yeux' (line 74), ('Anyone who doesn't like the look of me has only to close his eyes.')

Perhaps the most impressive example of this extension and complication of dramatic irony is to be found in *L'Ecole des femmes*, where the central character, Arnolphe, is a derivative of the Sganarelle role.

L'Ecole des femmes is a full-length five-act comedy which manages quite comfortably to obey the three classical unities. At the same time, however, it contrives to ignore almost completely the dictates of *vraisemblance* (verisimilitude) and *bienséance* (decorum). Molière's character Arnolphe has to speak over 600 of the play's 1,779 lines, a third of which are either soliloquies or asides of various sorts, containing few indications that they should be addressed anywhere but to the audience. He is also given the sometimes dubious privilege of sharing knowledge or understanding with them, to the exclusion especially of Agnès and Horace. Let us look at some examples.

Act I, scene i is, as you would expect, an exposition scene, a dialogue about principles between Arnolphe and his friend and neighbour Chrysalde. By the end of it, each has become persuaded that the other is mad. Chrysalde finds absurd Arnolphe's hobby of collecting and retailing anecdotes about female infidelity and male gullibility, as well as his intention to marry a sixteen-year-old untutored fool to protect himself from cuckoldry, while Arnolphe finds Chrysalde altogether too tolerant – someone to add to his collection. Molière makes the dialogue biased: we must take sides with Chrysalde because Arnolphe is too unpleasant, too anti-feminine, and cruel to his friend who nevertheless takes the cruelty tolerantly and with good humour. Moreover Arnolphe's attitude towards his young ward is repulsive to us, so that it would be difficult indeed for an audience to sympathize or side with him.

When Chrysalde and Arnolphe get to the end of their conversation and go their separate ways, each speaks his thoughts, as an aside to the audience (195–8):

> CHRYSALDE   Ma foi, je le tiens fou de toutes les manières.
> ARNOLPHE   Il est un peu blessé sur certaines matières.

> CHRYSALDE Good Lord, I think he's absolutely mad. ARNOLPHE He's a bit unhinged about certain things.

Addressing both these speeches to the audience enhances the humour and irony of them. They express successively, in confidence, almost identical opinions, but with in addition, from Arnolphe, the aphorism:

> Chose étrange de voir comme avec passion
> Un chacun est chaussé de son opinion!

It's strange to see how passionately everyone clings to his opinion

as he smugly assumes that we side with him against Chrysalde. We do not, of course: the irony goes against Arnolphe. Unlike a scenario character or one in a prose comedy, he does not have the right or the freedom to react to *our* reaction. But he can, all the same, assume that he has our complicity, at least for so long as all is going well for him. And he can address characters with words which he deliberately intends for our ears as well as theirs, as when he suggests, inviting us to laugh with him, that Chrysalde's marital affairs are not all in order:

> . . . peut-être que chez vous
> Vous trouvez des sujets de craindre pour chez nous;
> Et votre front, je crois, veut que du mariage
> Les cornes soient partout l'infaillible apanage.   (9–12)

Perhaps at home you've got a situation which makes you worry about us; and I believe that your forehead wants horns to be the unfailing privilege of marriage.

Chrysalde can look after himself, of course, but when Arnolphe plays on the innocence of Agnès, his sixteen-year-old ward and potential wife, then our laughter of complicity feels a little uneasy. He digs us in the ribs, as it were, and, for instance, in Act I, scene iii, while underlining Agnès's simplicity, he reveals to us his own lustful intentions regarding this beautiful young person. When Agnès complains of 'les puces, qui m'ont la nuit inquiétée' ('the fleas that have bothered me during the night'), his double-edged 'Ah! vous aurez dans peu quelqu'un pour les chasser' ('Oh! You'll soon have someone to hunt them out for you') has a meaning for her and an extra one for us. Her innocent reply: 'Vous me ferez plaisir' ('You will give me great pleasure') is seized upon joyfully by him to carry on the process: 'Je le puis bien penser'(236–8), ('I can well believe it'). Unless we are misogynists, while laughing at her, we feel sorry for her, and dislike him.

At the end of that scene there is a typical confident Arnolphe monologue (of the sort that he is capable of uttering during the first three acts) addressed to the audience. But it is in fact addressed to only a section of the audience – the ladies. That is to say, he goes over the heads of the *parterre* (the pit), which in seventeenth-century France was populated exclusively by men, and defiantly addresses those ladies who are seated in the *loges* (the boxes) at the back or the sides of the auditorium:

Héroïnes du temps, Mesdames les savantes,
Pousseuses de tendresses et de beaux sentiments,
Je défie à la fois tous vos vers, vos romans,
Vos lettres, billets doux, toute votre science,
De valoir cette honnête et pudique ignorance   (244–8)

Heroines of the hour, learned ladies, who utter fond sentiments and beautiful thoughts, I challenge all your poetry, your novels, your letters and love notes, all your knowledge, to equal in value this honest, modest ignorance.

The speech acknowledges that he does have enemies in the audience, that not everyone out front is his ally, but that he can defy the world, having (he feels) the *parterre* with him, and traditional male-defined morality.

Arnolphe is not always cheerful and confident, however. It is his privilege always to possess knowledge which his young rival Horace does not have, and to share that knowledge with the audience. He is able therefore, in Act I, scene iv, and in subsequent similar scenes which give the play its rhythm, to react to the naïve young man with ironic replies for our benefit. Yet it is in the course of each of these scenes that Arnolphe discovers the progress which Horace is unstoppably making in his seduction of Agnès. We remain privileged with our knowledge, as does Arnolphe, and Horace remains foolishly ignorant, but we are at these moments released from our uncomfortable feelings of helpless complicity, despite the fact that Arnolphe continues from time to time to confide in us, for we also have ironic knowledge at *his* expense which he cannot possess: that the plot will obey the laws of comedy, and that he will be defeated. We are glad to know that we are his false *confidents*.

As the play progresses, then, events and Agnès gradually turn against him, and as this happens, the tone of his monologues changes. They become more Cornelian, more classical. Mock-Cornelian, I should perhaps say, because Arnolphe is no classical hero and, try as he may, does not have a firm grasp of classical eloquence any more than did Mascarille in *Dépit amoureux*. He ceases to address us, and begins instead to introduce into his discourse certain features of classical soliloquy, apostrophizing absent characters, personified objects or abstractions, the heavens, or even parts of his own anatomy ('Patience mon coeur, doucement, doucement', 410 – 'Be patient, my heart, gently, gently'). Thus the role of Arnolphe is a strange mixture: he is able to communicate directly with us, know of our existence when he is confidently believing that he is in charge of events, but cuts himself off from us when anguished and at a loss. And of course, when finally defeated, he is unable to talk at all.

Molière never gave up audience address. It is always there, or available, in his broadest comedies, up to the end of his life. It is available to comic characters who are, or think they are, in charge of events, like Scapin, for instance; or who have, or think they have, right and morality on their side, as does Argan in *Le Malade imaginaire*. But Molière also knows, or learns to appreciate, when and where it is not appropriate. One finds none in *Le Misanthrope* or in *Tartuffe* (except perhaps for the Exempt's speech). There are times when Molière prefers to create a universe as recommended by d'Aubignac, because direct communication with the audience has its limitations. It destroys the theatrical illusion, and can also devalue those characters who are not privileged so to communicate, along with their opinions and what they stand for. Where a serious moral point has to be made seriously, as in *Le Misanthrope* and *Tartuffe*, then audience address is out: classical conventions prevail.

One might go so far as to say that the phenomenon of a character showing familiarity towards an audience is not merely, in Molière's age, unclassical, it is *anti*-classical. It exists, less as a theatrical technique in its own right (as it later does in epic theatre), than as a token sort of defiance of authority, of the authority of the *doctes* (scholars), of Court taste and the Académie Française. At the same time it is a licensed form of defiance, like the antics of the court fool, or the rites of reversal of carnival. It is tolerated in forms of theatre which can safely be regarded in the seventeenth century as 'mere' entertainment, in *commedia dell'arte* sketches and in farces, where it could be said to 'know its place', be as much bound in its own way by convention as the more serious theatre it pretends to subvert. Molière learned this rule the hard way with the 'Querelle de *L'Ecole des femmes*'. He transgressed it once again with the notorious comic double act of Sganarelle and Dom Juan, but, knowing how far to push his luck, made no overt protests when ordered to drop that play for ever. Fraternization between stage and audience remained, during the classical period, a potent source of good-humoured mockery of theatre itself, in the same way that burlesque mocked epic poetry, but somehow it remained compartmentalized. The power and prestige of classicism represented by Corneille and Racine were too strong for it.

Dramatic irony is a rather different matter, of course. It can (it must!) be tolerated in any form of drama, and in fact can only break the illusion when used in conjunction with other meta-theatrical effects. In Act IV, scene v of *Tartuffe*, we have with Elmire the knowledge which Tartuffe does not have, that Orgon is concealed underneath the table. But Elmire speaks with double meaning for Orgon's benefit alone and, being a classical heroine, shares no confidence with us.[32] Context, and the right theatrical conventions which the knowing audience quickly learns to recognize as being appropriate to any given performance, these govern our attitude to dramatic irony, and indeed to soliloquies and to all aspects of the relationship between stage and audience. The 'esprit de géométrie' is at a decided disadvantage in the theatre.

NOTES

1 See *L'Etourdi*, ed. P. Mélèse (Geneva, Droz, 1951), vii–viii.

2 The varieties of 'mediating communication systems' between stage and audience existing in drama in general are enumerated and illustrated in Manfred Pfister's *The Theory and Analysis of Drama* (Cambridge University Press, 1988), section 3.6, 69–84. A less formal approach to the same theme is to be found in Bernard Beckerman, *Theatrical Presentation: Performer, Audience and Act* (New York and London, Routledge, 1990), 110–27.

3 The only play of the period that I have ignored is *Dom Garcie de Navarre* of 1661, labelled a comedy by Molière but, like the play by G.-A. Cicognini of which it is an adaptation, having the characteristics of a tragi-comedy, and containing nothing that remotely resembles a borrowing from the *commedia dell'arte*.

4 On this last play, and on Molière's debt to Nicolo Secchi's *L'Interesse*, see *Dépit amoureux*, ed. Noël Peacock (University of Durham, 1989), Introduction, pp. 13–15, and Appendix II, 144–50.

5 Molière, *Oeuvres complètes*, ed. Georges Couton (Paris, Gallimard, 1971, 2 volumes), II, 95. It is to this edition that I refer throughout. Cf. Gianfranco Folena, 'Les langues de la comédie et la comédie des langues', *Le Théâtre italien et l'Europe: XVe-XVIIe siècles*, ed. Christian Bec and Irène Mamczarz (Paris, PUF, 1983), 23–51.

6 Niccolo Barbieri, quoted by P. Duchartre in *The Italian Comedy*, translated by R.T. Weaver (New York, Dover Publications, 1966), 34.

7 Jacques Copeau, *Registres II: Molière* (Paris, Gallimard, 1976), 77.

8 Francesco Andreini's introductory note, addressed to the 'Gentle Reader', given in *Scenarios of the Commedia dell'arte: Flaminio Scala's 'Il Teatro delle favole rappresentative'*, translated by Henry F. Salerno, foreword by Kenneth McKee

(New York University Press, 1967), xxxi. See also, particularly on 'elastic dialogue' in the *commedia dell'arte* and Molière, 'Arte dialogue structures in the comedies of Molière', *The Commedia dell'arte from the Renaissance to Dario Fo*, ed. Christopher Cairns (Lewiston–Queenston–Lampeter, The Edward Mellen Press, 1989), 142–76.

9 Duchartre, op. cit., 57–8.

10 Ibid, 58–62.

11 Ibid, 58.

12 These examples are all drawn from Mel Gordon, *Lazzi: the comic routines of the Commedia dell'Arte* (New York, Performing Arts Journal Publications, 1983), 13, 41.

13 For a detailed history of the Italian comedy in seventeenth-century France, see Virginia Scott, *The Commedia dell'arte in Paris 1644–1697* (Charlottesville, University Press of Virginia, 1990). See also *Viaggi teatrali dall'Italia a Parigi fra Cinque e Seicento* (Atti del convegno Internazionale Torino 6/8 aprile 1987, Genoa, Costa & Nolan, 1989).

14 Notably by W. G. Moore, *Molière, a New Criticism* (Oxford, Clarendon Press, 1949); Gustave Attinger, *L'Esprit de la Commedia dell'arte dans le théâtre français* (Paris/Neuchâtel, Librairie théâtrale/La Baconnière, 1950); René Bray, *Molière homme de théâtre* (Paris, Mercure de France, 1954); Jean Emelina, *Les Valets et les servantes dans le théâtre de Molière* (Aix-en-Provence, La Pensée Universitaire, 1958); Marcel Gutwirth, *Molière ou l'invention comique* (Paris, Minard, 1966); Cordelia Gundolf, 'Molière and the Commedia dell'arte', *Journal of the Australasian Universities Language and Literature Association*, 39 (1973), 22–34; Philip A. Wadsworth, *Molière and the Italian Theatrical Tradition* (n.p. [Columbia, S. C.], French Literature Publication Company, 1977); David Shaw. 'Theatrical Self-Consciousness in Molière'; *Nottingham French Studies*, Spring, 1991, 1–12

15 *Etudes sur le théâtre français*, II (Paris, Nizet, 1978), 52.

16 See G. Doutrepont, *Les Acteurs masqués et enfarinés du XVIe au XVIIe siècle en France*, Publications de l'Académie royale de Belgique, no. 385 (Brussels, Lamertin, 1928); also C. Cosnier, 'Jodelet: un acteur du XVIIᵉ siècle devenu un type', *Revue d'Histoire littéraire de la France*, 62 (1962), 329–52; and Raymond Lebègue, op. cit., II, 50–68.

17 For a discussion of the complex borrowings made by Molière for *La Jalousie du Barbouillé*, of its relation to his later comedies, and a demonstration that it *is* by Molière, see A. Gill, ' "The Doctor in the Farce" and Molière', *French Studies*, 2 (1948), 101–28.

18 W. G. Moore, op. cit.; see Ch. iii, 'Mask'.

19 See 'Ce que Molière doit à Scaramouche', by H.G.Hall in his *Comedy in Context: essays on Molière* (Jackson, University Press of Mississippi, 1984), 36–55. It should nevertheless be pointed out that playing unmasked does not of itself guarantee a wider range of expression. Jacques Copeau, writing in 1926 (op. cit., 295), protested: 'les écrivains, les érudits et les critiques condamnent le masque comme un instrument sans expression. Ils lui reprochent avec assurance l'immobilité de ses traits. C'est qu'ils ne l'ont jamais vu jouer.' It should also be

borne in mind that the mask generally only covered the upper part of the face, leaving the mouth exposed. Not all commentators close to the profession have liked masks, however. Goldoni was not enthusiastic. See, on him and on the views of other writers, Duchartre, op. cit., 46–9. See also W. D. Howarth, *Molière: a Playwright and his Audience* (Cambridge University Press, 1982), 87–105. For a history of the mask, see *Arte della Maschera nella Commedia dell'Arte*, ed. Donato Sartori and Bruno Lanata (Florence, SES, 1983).

20   For a reproduction of the frontispiece, see H. G. Hall, op. cit., 37.

21   See Scott, op. cit., 30 and 81.

22   See G. Couton's summary of arguments concerning origins and sources in the *Notice* to the sketch in his ed. cit., I, 29–30.

23   One of the most famous portraits of Molière is that by Mignard, dating from 1656–7, showing him as César in *La Mort de Pompée* (Musée de la Comédie Française). Corneille was certainly a firm favourite with the troupe which, once established in Paris, regularly played *Le Cid, Horace, Cinna, Rodogune, Héraclius* and *Nicomède* as well as *Pompée*. The extremely popular *Sertorius* joined the repertoire on 23 June, 1662, and contributed a famous line to *L'Ecole des femmes*, certainly recognized by the Parisian audiences.

24   Gros René was associated with Molière from 1647 until his death in 1664.

25   Or mocked, as when in III, i of *L'Etourdi* Mascarille delivers a 36-line comic parody of a tragic soliloquy which begins:

>   Taisez-vous, ma bonté, cessez votre entretien:
>   Vous êtes une sotte, et je n'en ferai rien.   (901–2)

>   (Be quiet, my kindness, and cease your talk: you're a fool, and I'll do no such thing.)

26   See the edition of Pierre Martino (Algiers–Paris, Carbonel-Champion, 1927), 44 and 140.

27   See H. T. Barnwell's Introduction to Pierre Corneille, *Writings on the Theatre* (Oxford, Blackwell, 1965), xxvi.

28   *L'Art poétique*, Chant III, lines 399–400.

29   See G. Mongrédien, *Dictionnaire biographique des comédiens français du XVIIe siècle* (Paris, CNRS, 1961); on Du Parc, 70; L'Espy, 116–17; Jodelet, p. 93; and, again on the latter, C. Cosnier, *art. cit.*

30   There is doubt as to whether Molière played the part of Mascarille in the original production of *Dépit amoureux*. See N. Peacock's discussion of the problem in his ed. cit., 125–6.

31   On Molière's first two full-length comedies, see K. Bech, 'Le jeune Molière et la *commedia dell'arte*. Thèmes et aspects scéniques dans *L'Etourdi* et *Le Dépit amoureux*', *Revue Romane*, 5 (1970), 1–16. See also Claudia Buratelli, 'L'emigrazione di un testo dell'Arte: da L'Inavertito di Barbieri a L'Etourdi di Molière', in *Viaggi teatrali . . .*, 182–99.

32   Note, however, Jupiter's address to Alcmène in I, iii of *Amphitryon*, when, in reaction to her protests at the absurdity of trying to distinguish between Amphitryon the husband and Amphitryon the lover, he says:

> Ce discours est plus raisonnable,
> Alcmène, que vous ne pensez.

(lines 612–13)

(There is more reason in that remark, Alcmène, than you realize.) Although addressed to her, these words are meaningless to her. Only the audience knows what they mean, and were there no tacit collusion with it on the part of Jupiter, they would not be spoken.

4 Sunset: from *commedia dell'arte* to *comédie italienne*

BRUCE GRIFFITHS

The closure of the Théâtre Italien in Paris in 1697 and the expulsion of the troupe after half a century of performances in the *commedia dell'arte* tradition was followed in 1700 by the publication in six volumes of *Le Théâtre Italien . . .* (etc) by Evaristo Gherardi, the last Arlequin. This invaluable collection of sketches and complete plays, composing the French repertoire of the troupe, enables one to trace an important evolution in the history of the *commedia*.[1]

There had been an Italian troupe permanently established in Paris since 1660, sharing the theatre of the Palais-Royal with Molière's troupe. From 1673 to 1680 it shared the Hôtel Guénégaud with the merged remnants of Molière's company and the Marais troupe. In 1680 it moved to the Hôtel de Bourgogne. Its two most famous comic actors were Scaramouche (Tiberio Fiorilli, 1608–94) and Arlequin (Domenico Biancolelli, 1640–88).[2]

Up to 1680 the repertoire of the troupe had consisted of comedies in Italian in the *commedia dell'arte* tradition, judging by what is virtually the only evidence, a collection of scenarios or *canevas* made by Biancolelli, now extant only in a French translation made by Thomas Gueullette in the eighteenth century.[3] In these *canevas* Biancolelli naturally concentrated on those scenes in which he and the other *zannis* figured, summarizing other scenes in a very cursory manner. This creates the impression that the comedies were much more farcical than perhaps they really were. There is great emphasis on the *lazzis*, the slapstick of the *zannis*.

The troupe was heavily subsidized by the king and performed often at court before an audience of spectators many of whom were cultivated enough to appreciate a performance in Italian. Of ordinary theatregoers few, however, could understand Italian, few could appreciate the strongly localized verbal comedy of the *zannis*, of the

Dottore and the Capitano. The rhymester Jean Loret welcomed the arrival of Locatelli's troupe in 1653 with the significant comments:

> Quoy que la langue Italienne
> Soit pour moy langue Arménienne
> Et que mon esprit soit si sot
> Que je n'y comprends un seul mot,
> Je vais pourtant voir cette troupe
> Aymant mieux manger moins de soupe
> Et boire un petit peu moins de vin
> Que de ne pas voir Trivelin.[4]

A late and perhaps apocryphal anecdote tells how the Italians gained the king's permission to perform in French, in a dispute with Baron who represented the rival (French) troupe. Baron sought to have the Italians banned from using French. Biancolelli asked the king how he should speak: 'As you please', replied the king. 'Sire, I have won my case', said the Italian. Despite Baron's protests, the king refused to alter what he had said and ever since the Italians performed plays in French.[5]

In 1668 the Italians performed *Le Régal des dames*, the first 'Italian' comedy to have been composed in France, with some scenes and a song in French, depicting Paris's greatest fair, the Foire Saint-Germain, with Arlequin as the puppeteer Brioché. After 1680, rather than try to compose French material themselves, the Italians commissioned French authors to write isolated scenes inserted into Italian *canevas*. Gherardi's *recueil*, which prints only French material, suggests that French came to oust Italian almost entirely from the repertoire. From 1681 to 1687 the French scenes amount to perhaps a quarter of each play. Gherardi summarizes 'scenes à l'italienne' only if essential to an understanding of the plot, otherwise omitting them, noting only that they consisted of *lazzis* difficult or impossible to describe.

These omissions make the story-lines of the earlier plays difficult or impossible to follow and give a misleadingly sober impression of these plays.[6]

Before 1687 there had been only one contributor, Anne-Mauduit de Fatouville.[7] Afterwards there were several, most notably Jean-François Regnard (1656–1710) whose comedies may serve to illustrate the changed nature of the Théâtre Italien in the last decade of its existence.[8]

The popularity of the French scenes is shown by the fact that in 1694 Gherardi published a selection of them, and an enlarged edition in 1695. Pirated editions were published in Lyon, Grenoble, Geneva and notably

Amsterdam, where it is most unlikely the readers could have seen performances. The Amsterdam edition of 1697–8 contains material which is, at least in part, verifiably authentic, some probably purloined from Gherardi as he indignantly explains in his preface to the 1700 edition.[9]

Not surprisingly, a comparison of these pirated texts with the 'canonical' text of 1700 shows that the scripts were often revised: but there is little evidence of room for improvisation in the *commedia* tradition. However well the actors might speak French, they had to learn their parts off by heart: they could not improvise in French. In Charles Cotolendi's *Le Livre sans nom* (1695) Arlequin says 'Depuis *La Matrone d'Ephèse* où j'ai été obligé d'apprendre par coeur un rôle français, je suis accablé de mon personnage, d'autant plus que présentement, les auteurs font tomber sur moi tout le poids de la comédie.'[10]

Other actors were handicapped by their inability to speak French, and their roles suffered. In the French scenes the lover Octavio/Octave is conspicuous by his almost total absence. Traditionally his role was not a comic one; but an important part of it was to make the exposition and explain the plot for the audience, as in Regnard's *Les Chinois* (I,ii), an Italian scene merely summarized. Though referred to in *Les Filles errantes*, he does not appear in the French text; in *La Descente de Mezzetin aux Enfers*, the lover Orphée (Aurelio) appears only at the end, to pay a short compliment in Italian. In *La Coquette* he is given a few lines early on, appears in Italian scenes summarized by Gherardi, but does not even figure in the final scene. In *Arlequin homme à bonne fortune* Octave enters as a follower of Arlequin 'Prince des Curieux', and plays Isabelle a compliment in Italian. Her suspicious father asks 'What's he jabbering?' – 'It's a Tonkinese compliment' – 'What! My daughter already knows Tonkinese!' – an obvious borrowing from the *turquerie* at the end of Molière's *Le Bourgeois gentilhomme* but also underlining the fact that Italian was unintelligible.

A little Italian dialogue survives. The exposition of *Le Divorce* is made, oddly, bilingually. The valet Mezzetin speaks in French, and his master Aurelio answers in Italian, though his replies are not essential to an understanding of the scene. In *Les Chinois* (IV.i) Octave admits 'comme tu vois, je parle assez mal François'. By 1695 he had learned enough to be given a short scene with Angélique in *La Foire Saint-Germain* (I,iii) and to appear in two other French scenes (II.ii and III.i).

The most curious example of Franco-Italian dialogue, though this time not because of any inability on the part of the actors, is heard in the opening scene of *Les Momies d'Egypte*. Arlequin and Colombine approach each other speaking parallel lines, beginning in elevated Italian and ending in trivial French, thus:

> ARLEQUIN   Alessandro magno, quel grand filosofo, aveva ragione di dire, che l'amore d'una donna est un sable mouvant, sur lequel on ne peut bâtir que des Châteaux en Espagne.
> COLOMBINE Lucrezia Romana, di castissima memoria, aveva costume di dire, ch'il cuore d'un uomo étoit bien trigaut, et qu'il ne s'y falloit non plus fier qu'à un Almanach' . . .

> ARLEQUIN Alexander the Great, that great philosopher, was right to say, that the love of a lady is a quicksand, on which one can build only castles in Spain. COLOMBINE Lucretia the Roman, of most chaste memory, was wont to say, that the heart of a man was very fickle, and no more to be trusted than an almanac.

The main part of the dialogue is in French, they quarrel, then are reconciled in a mixture of French and Italian. In the same play Scaramouche uses a mixture of French and Italian as the showman L'Epine.

The difficulties of Pasquariel (Joseph Tortoriti) with French are alluded to in *L'Augmentation de la Baguette de Vulcain*. The bluestocking Bélise threatens to harass the Italians, and to prevent them speaking French, till Pasquariel had been accepted into the Académie for his fine language. Arlequin ironically replies 'By then there would be grass growing on the theatre floor'. The actresses playing the important roles of Isabelle (Françoise Biancolelli) and Colombine (Catherine Biancolelli), both daughters of Domenico Biancolelli, and born in France, had no such difficulty.[11]

Gherardi's collection shows that as time went by, the early isolated scenes in French inserted into Italian *canevas* were succeeded by complete comedies entirely in French, such as Regnard's *La Naissance d'Amadis*, *La Foire Saint-Germain*, *La Baguette de Vulcain* and *Les Momies d'Egypte*. However this creates a misleading impression. Only three French plays are listed as having been first performed in 1696, and only two in 1697. In an age when a run of fifteen performances might be regarded as a good run, these plays alone would not have sufficed to keep the troupe in business. It still performed Italian plays from the older repertoire, especially before aristocratic audiences.

Masks and Costumes

Among the most distinctive characteristics of the *commedia* had always been the use of masks and costumes, each linked to a fixed type of character. Italian comic actors were masked; French comic actors put flour on their faces. In the *commedia* only the buffoons were masked as a rule. The lovers wore no masks, but wore costumes as grand and as fashionable as the troupe could afford. The Italian *servetta* was not usually masked. The illustrations to Gherardi's *recueil* do not show Colombine masked, and the practice of having her wear the elegant Venetian half-mask is a relatively recent one. Perrucci states:

> Actuellement les masques sont en carton ou en papier, cirés et teints de couleurs vives, le mieux possible. . . le jeu sous le masque est le partage de ceux qui remplissent les rôles bouffons et comiques; il leur prête un aspect caricatural, un coloris brun, un nez gros ou écrasé, des petits yeux aveugles, un front ridé, un crâne chauve etc . . . [12]

Gherardi shows this tradition in decline, though the company still retained some of the more colourful traditional roles. There was a Punch – Pulcinella or Polichinelle (Michelangelo Fracansani), but Gherardi in his preface says he has omitted the scenes featuring him and the *zanni* Gradelin (Constantino Constantini) as not having been well received. There are thus few traces of him: a hunchback is mentioned in *L'Opéra de campagne* (1692) and one appears in the illustration to *Le Retour de la foire de Bezons* (1695), but neither text gives him any lines. Even in the purely Italian comedies, there is no evidence that his role was other than minor. By 1689 the troupe appears not to have had an actor playing the fixed type of the braggart, the Capitano/Capitan: there are braggarts in Regnard's comedies, but the role was farmed out to the *zannis* or even to Colombine.

The role of Scaramouche had originally been a variety of braggart, but Tiberio Fiorilli had so developed the part that he was more noted for his astonishing versatility, his acrobatics, his mimicry and dumb-show, his singing, dancing and playing of musical instruments. He played without a mask, though his costume did recall that of the Capitano. Pasquariel (Joseph Tortoriti) played a similar type, and in

1694 replaced the aged Scaramouche under the name Scaramouche le jeune. In *La Foire Saint-Germain* (III.iii) he played a drunken braggart, but this was exceptional. He too acted without a mask.

The old magnifico, Pantalone/Pantalon (Giovan-Battista Turri) formed part of the earlier troupes, and of the later troupe between 1686 and 1691, but there are few traces of him in the French plays. There was a Dottore/Docteur (Angelo Agostino Lolli) in Paris from 1653 to 1694, under the stage name Gratiano Baloardo/Grazian Balouard. His dark costume, ruff, and floppy black beret resemble those of Scaramouche, and like Pantalon he wore a half mask. Though allotted substantial roles in many plays in Gherardi's *recueil*, of Regnard's plays only *L'Homme à bonne fortune* features him, as a medical doctor, not the traditional pedant. He was succeeded in 1694 by Cinthio (Marc-Antonio Romagnesi) who since 1688 had played old men, filling in for Pantalon; but he wore no mask. Cinthio probably played the old men in Regnard's comedies; in *La Foire Saint-Germain* he is actually called *le Docteur*, but nothing in his role recalls the prolix and macaronic pedant of the *commedia*. Long-winded doctoral tirades certainly occur in Regnard's plays, but the verbose lawyer in *L'Homme à bonne fortune*, and another in *Le Divorce*, and the babbling author in *La Descente de Mezzetin aux Enfers*, were all played by Colombine.

Of the three important *zannis* of the troupe (Arlequin, Mezzetin and Pierrot), two − Mezzetin and Pierrot − were not usually masked, and both were roles largely or entirely developed in France, and strongly influenced by French comic traditions.

Though in name derived from the Pedrolino of the older *commedia*, a shrewd and energetic clown, the Pierrot of the last decade of the century was quite different. As a lovesick yokel, Pierrot had already featured in the second act of Molière's *Dom Juan* (1665). In the Italian troupe it was Dominique (Domenico Biancolelli) who was credited with changing his own role as Arlequin from that of a stupid second *zanni* into that of an astute first *zanni* and making Pierrot into a naïve second *zanni*. The part of Pierrot was developed by Giuseppe Giaratoni or Jean-Joseph Gératon. He took to wearing a peasant's loose white smock, and followed the French tradition of whitening his face with flour.

Of all the *zannis*, his is the most consistent role. He is the naïve and dim-witted valet of the old man, and his insolence is a sign of his tactlessness; the same naïveté leads him to propose himself to him as a prospective son-in-law, and he is consistently depicted as in love with

Colombine. He is given to inarticulate and incoherent attempts, full of malapropisms, to pay court to her or to explain the facts of life. These earn him beatings from his master and rejection by Colombine. In *La Coquette* he soliloquizes: 'De quoi t'avises-tu d'être amoureux? Tu ne fais plus que quatre repas par jour; tu ne saurois plus t'éveiller qu'à midi sonné. . .' ('What has come over you, to fall in love? Now you eat only four meals a day, you can't wake up till midday . . .') and thinks of suicide. He tells Colombine 'Je me serois déjà jeté vingt fois par la fenêtre de notre grenier, s'il avoit été seulement d'un étage plus bas' ('I would already have thrown myself twenty times out of our attic window, if only it had been one storey lower'). Nevertheless he is treated indulgently by both Colombine and Isabelle. Colombine tells the audience 'La conquête de Pierrot n'est pas bien illustre; je sens néanmoins une secrète joie de voir que rien ne m'échappe. Quelque sévérité qu'affectent les femmes, elles ne sont jamais fâchées de s'entendre dire qu'on les aime.' ('The conquest of Pierrot is no great feat: yet I feel a secret joy at seeing that nothing escapes me. However stern women may pretend to be they are never vexed to hear that they are loved.') Though the other *zannis* play roles as suitors, these are usually assumed to further the intrigue, and the wooing is deliberately offensive and burlesque; whereas Pierrot's advances, comically inept as they may be, are heartfelt. Thus, as the role of lover is so slight in the French texts, we have the curious situation that Pierrot seems to be the main genuinely lovestruck character, and it is not hard to see the potential pathos of the role, developed by later actors. The texts often indicate that Pierrot performs amorous *lazzi*, not specified, being mute by-play. Later, this mutism was to become the main feature of the role.

Mezzetin

The role of the second *zanni*, abettor of Arlequin, was, despite the name (a diminutive of *mezzo*, half, in allusion to the actor's being a small man) created in Paris by Angelo Constantini. He had at first begun his career in the role of Arlequin, but had not gone down well, and so had devised a new role, as a *zanni* without a mask, seconding Domenico Biancolelli, the new Arlequin. When Biancolelli died, Constantini took on the mask and role of Arlequin to fill the gap, but still keeping the name Mezzetin.[13] Hence, but exceptionally, he was the main *zanni* in Regnard's *La Descente de Mezzetin aux Enfers* and Delosme de Montchenay's *Mezzetin Grand Sophy de Perse*. However he does not seem to have been any better received than before, the role of Arlequin passed to Evaristo Gherardi, and Constantini-Mezzetin reverted to being the second *zanni*. However in Regnard's *Le Divorce*, we find Mezzetin apparently as first *zanni*, instructing the gluttonous booby Arlequin, and in the fragmentary *Les Filles errantes* Mezzetin still seems more prominent than Arlequin, who plays a role like that of Pierrot. Even as late as *Les Chinois* we find Mezzetin telling Arlequin what to do to further the plot. In *L'Homme à bonne fortune* he plays valet to Arlequin, but points out that they are both footmen and that there is no real difference between them. Mezzetin often acts as a sort of herald for Arlequin, announcing the other's arrival in some showy and spectacular guise. Mezzetin's musical talents explain the frequent references to his singing, dancing and playing musical instruments. Other roles turn his shortness to comic account, as a female dwarf in *Le Divorce* and as a parrot in *L'Homme à bonne fortune*. His other speciality is as an odd hybrid of braggart and lawyer, affecting a ridiculous mixture of military and legal jargon, as in *Les Filles errantes* and in *La Coquette*.

Broadly speaking, Mezzetin doubled for Arlequin. They could no longer be sharply distinguished as formerly. Perrucci stipulated that the leading zanni should be cunning and witty, and his function was to further the plot; the second zanni was to be utterly stupid.[14]

It was in France, and by Domenico Biancolelli, that Arlequin was changed from being an idiotic second *zanni* to the cunning and protean leading *zanni* familiar to us now. However Regnard's plays show the older concept surviving alongside the newer one. In *Le Divorce* (II,i) we find a childish Arlequin playing 'she loves me, she loves me not' with his buttons and being otherwise puerile, to the annoyance of the astuter Mezzetin. In III, iv, Mezzetin tries to tell him how to plead in court, but Arlequin can grasp only that there will be sausages galore available. In *L'Homme à bonne fortune* he is a naïve booby who consults a lawyer on the topic of marriage, a role at variance with his role as confidence-trickster in the rest of the play. In *Les Filles errantes*, he plays a naïve inn-keeper and is also Mezzetin's gluttonous and incoherent valet; at the end he even plays without his mask.

Though nominally a valet he is in the French text seldom shown in any scenes with any master. In practice he is a free agent, often a criminal one step ahead of the law. In *Le Divorce* he is a thief who was once arrested for forgery and escaped being hanged. In *L'Homme à bonne fortune* he is a confidence-trickster, a bogus Vicomte come to rook the naïve Colombine. In *La Foire Saint-Germain* and in *Les*

Momies d'Egypte he is a shady sideshow keeper, fleecing gullible customers and working hand in glove with Colombine.

Les Chinois concludes with a mock debate on the respective merits of the French and Italian troupes, in which Arlequin, ironically, impersonates a French actor (i.e. was presumably not masked). *Inter alia* he claims that 'Arlequin is always Arlequin . . . whereas a French actor is . . . sometimes soldier, today Caesar and tomorrow Mascarille'. The converse is arguably truer, as the play itself abundantly shows. In it Arlequin has the task of eliminating four suitors for Isabelle's hand, and impersonates all four, as a huntsman, as a major, as a Chinese doctor and as a French actor. Each role has its distinctive costume and verbal comedy, but Arlequin's basic insolence, violence, gluttony and lechery link all the roles, and the illustrations in Gherardi's *recueil* show that his mask and distinctive costume are usually visible beneath the disguises.

Towards women, his insolence takes the form of treating them as if they were mares in a horse fair. In *L'Homme à bonne fortune* he tells Colombine 'raise your head, look straight at me, walk, trot'. He never fails to cast doubts on their virtue: thus in *Le Divorce* he asks Isabelle: 'How long have you been married?' – Isabelle: 'Five or six months' – Arlequin: 'And how many children do you have?'. In *Les Chinois* he insults old Roquillard, calls Colombine 'carogne' (jade) and Isabelle 'une fieffée coquette' (a brazen hussy) whom he promises to consign to a home for fallen women after the marriage. He kicks Roquillard in the belly, and treats him to a stream of insults, asking 'How many daughters have you got for me?' In his recurrent role as burlesque suitor, his lechery is barely veiled. In *La Naissance d'Amadis* he tells Colombine 'How happy I would be if I were the gardener of such a pretty plant as your mistress: I would cultivate her, I would till her and before a year was out I would have a crop from her.'

Arlequin's visually most striking role is that of the bizarre and showy foreign suitor – the Chinese ambassador in *Le Divorce*, the Tonkinese 'Prince des Curieux' in *L'Homme à bonne fortune*, the Chinese doctor in *Les Chinois*, where he presides over a satirical zodiac show, much as he does as 'Empereur du Cap-Verd' in *La Foire Saint-Germain*. These scenes exploit the *zanni*'s talent as singer and dancer, and with their use of decor, costume and stage machinery for effect are certainly in the *commedia* tradition; but the Gherardi *recueil* shows a tendency to make the *zanni* play an ever more static role as master of ceremonies introducing a series of odd characters loosely linked to a very slight plot, in a clear forerunner of the satirical revue and of the music-hall.

Other roles played by Arlequin are clearly derived from the French comedy of manners, but rendered even more caricatural. The comic suitor is often a clodhopping provincial nobleman, recalling Molière's George Dandin and Monsieur de Pourceaugnac. All are characterized by the same blatant cynicism, the same smug parading of their crapulous habits. In *Les Chinois* Arlequin comes courting with a pack of hounds, a turkey perched on his wrist, sounding his horn and complimenting Isabelle in hunting jargon. In *La Coquette* Arlequin plays a similar part as the *baillif du Maine* but is later transformed into another stock part, that of the *marquis ridicule* who enters 'singing and dancing, putting on the airs of a *marquis ridicule*', combing his periwig, and says 'Studied, me, studied? Don't you know I am a gentleman of quality? I can scarcely write my own name!' As a true stage coxcomb he smugly boasts of his boorish behaviour in the theatre (the playboys of the day paid high prices to sit or stand onstage during the performance, and references to their loutish behaviour are frequent in contemporary comedies).

Isabelle

In the final decade the role of *première amoureuse* was taken by Isabelle (Françoise-Marie Apolline Biancolelli, elder daughter of Domenico Biancolelli). Though her acting talent seems not to have been highly admired, she was called on to play a range of parts far beyond that of the demure *ingénue* who traditionally did not play either a comic or very dynamic part in the play. In *Le Divorce*, she is the faithful young wife of old Sotinet, not loving him but unwilling to go through a divorce. She refuses to wear cosmetics and is contrasted with her worldly-wise maid Colombine. Nevertheless she receives a stream of disreputable visitors and the burlesque divorce hearing at the end reveals her to have been something of a *rouée*. As Bradamante in *La Baguette de Vulcain* and Elisène in *La Naissance d'Amadis* Isabelle plays naïve and virtuous heroines.

In *La Descente de Mezzetin aux Enfers* she is the faithful wife of Orphée and resists the cajolery of Mezzetin. In *Les Chinois* she permits the passionate Octave no liberties and bursts into tears when he pretends to faint. In *La Coquette*, though desperate for a husband, she is wary of the coquetry recommended by her cousin Colombine. Isabelle's successor Angélique (Angelica Toscano) who replaced her in 1695, appears in *La Foire Saint-Germain*, where her virtue is emphasized, though the play consists of a series of scenes designed to put her guardian off marrying her, and to this end she plays a range of parts in disguise.

However there is another side to Isabelle, as a brazen hussy, already glimpsed in *Le Divorce*. In *L'Homme à bonne fortune*, as the elder sister of the precocious *ingénue* Colombine, she rails against marriage and children, though anxious to marry first. She is insolent to the father, and to put off an unwelcome suitor dresses as a gallant affecting to be on very intimate terms with Isabelle. In the *Critique* of the play she plays the coarsely-spoken maid Claudine. Again in *Les Filles errantes* she is a coarsely-spoken maid in pursuit of her seducer Cintio, who accuses her of promiscuity.

In short, Isabelle plays no fixed role in the traditional manner: one must rather speak of the virtuosity of the actress. The original, perhaps rather colourless role of the *amoureuse* has been remodelled on that of the more striking Colombine.

Colombine

This important role was played by Catherine Biancolelli, Domenico Biancolelli's younger daughter. The great range of parts she played attests her versatility and popularity. She sings, dances, plays instruments, plays disguised roles and even impersonates men. Following the tradition, she is the wily and cheeky maid of the *amoureuse* in *Le Divorce*, *Les Chinois* and in *La Naissance d'Amadis*; though not a servant, she assists Angélique in *La Foire Saint-Germain*. Her main characteristics are cynicism and insolence, vigorously expressed in racy language. In *Le Divorce* she encourages Isabelle's insolence to her husband and it is she who tells the *zannis* what to do. In *Les Chinois* she seems to have been the old man's mistress; she encourages the coquettish Isabelle to think of marriage; it is she who speaks on behalf of Octave in the disputation she arranges between the two suitors for Isabelle's hand. In *Le Divorce* it is she who arranges the mock hearing at the end. In *La Foire Saint-Germain*, as a freelance *intrigante* prepared to do anything for money, she bribes Arlequin to abet her and dons several disguises to further the plot. In *Les Momies d'Egypte* she helps her lover Arlequin swindle gullible customers, she works for no mistress, there is no Isabelle or Angélique, and this time the plot is managed by Scaramouche.

In nearly all Regnard's plays she shares or takes the lead; in *Les Filles* errantes and *La Coquette*, for instance, Octave is *her* lover, not Isabelle's.

She often plays the *fausse ingénue*, less naïve than she seems, as in her scenes with the lovesick Pierrot in *L'Homme à bonne fortune*: though earlier seen making a bed for two, she affects not to know the facts of life, which the embarrassed Pierrot cannot explain. In *Les Filles errantes* she naïvely describes her own seduction in the scabrous *Scène de la Civilité*. In *La Foire Saint-Germain*, though she does not understand the word *amant*, she is afraid to put her chastity to the test.

Other roles make comic use of her volubility. In *La Descente de Mezzetin aux Enfers*, disguised as an author, she stuns her faithless husband with her long tirades. In *L'Homme à bonne fortune*, as an oracle, she drives Arlequin off the stage with her relentless chatter. She is the leather-lunged advocate Braillardet at the end of *Le Divorce* and she orates on Octave's behalf at the end of *Les Chinois*. She is the voluble bluestocking Bélise in *L'Augmentation de la baguette de Vulcain*; in *Les Momies d'Egypte* she overwhelms Mme Jacquemard with a stream of satirical 'prophecies'.

Can one any longer speak of Colombine as a fixed stage type in the older tradition? Her role as the *ingénue* in *L'Homme à bonne fortune* has nothing in common with her role as a prolix pedant later on in the same play, and neither recalls the wily *servetta*. They testify to the versatility of the *actress*.

The role of the *amoureuse* and that of the *servetta* have visibly converged. The traditional range of fixed types has been replaced by a group of protean *zannis*, male and female, all able to play almost any one of a range of stock *emplois* – the braggart, the pedant, the ridiculous marquis, the comic provincial booby, the bizarre foreigner, the confidence trickster, roles derived from Molière and from more recent French comedies of manners. The older *commedia* was rarely as satirical.

One other *emploi* deserves special notice: that of the comic dame. As in the French comic tradition (cf. Mme Pernelle in Molière's *Le Tartuffe*) the part was usually played by a man. Once only does Colombine play such a part, in the *Critique de l'Homme à bonne fortune*. It is Pierrot who plays the amorous widow in *L'Homme à bonne fortune*, Pasquariel is the comic marquise in *La Coquette*; in *La Foire Saint-Germain* Arlequin is the comic 'dame du bel air' and one of the two comic dames in the *Scène des Carosses* where he fights Mezzetin as another dame. Mezzetin plays a comic dame in *Les Momies* d'Egypte, and Mezzetin and Pasquariel play two dames in *La Coquette*. Thus this role was not attached to any one actor, but had certain constant characteristics. Whether as a coyly amorous widow or burlesque *marquise/comtesse*, the dame is grotesquely fat, gross in appearance and manners, contrasting with an affected prudery and *préciosité*. In the *Critique*, two such dames, one pregnant, return from a performance of *L'Homme à bonne fortune*, and go into paroxysms of disgust at the obscenities of the play, prompting another character to say 'I thought you would serve us your child on the table'. A stock scene is one in which the dames come to blows and manage to half-strip each other. The dramatic function of the role is seldom important, and their appearances are purely gratuitous comic hors d'oeuvre. It is however the clearest surviving link between the Italian comedy and modern British pantomime; the role of the principal boy, played by a girl, is already foreshadowed by Colombine's and Isabelle's playing of male roles.

Conclusion

Of the French authors in Gherardi's *recueil*, perhaps Regnard has best preserved such traditional features of the *commedia* as its brio, slapstick, spectacle, *lazzis*, indecency and broadly caricatural types. His Arlequin and Colombine are not the more refined, graceful or poetic figures made familiar by Marivaux and others. Arlequin's ugly black leather mask still lends colour to the theory of his ancestry as a Germanic demon from the world of the carnival. But there are far fewer masked roles; the change of language virtually eliminated improvisation; more or less fixed scripts replaced the loose outlines of *scenari*; Pierrot and Mezzetin were figures created in France, without masks. The distinction between first and second *zanni* has been blurred, as has the distinction between *servetta* and *amoureuse*. They may play almost any one of a range of stock parts showing the strong influence of Molière and of the French comedy of manners, in broadly caricatural form. These roles come from contemporary French society and comedy, they are not types from the Italian provinces. The comedies are now built almost entirely around the versatile and protean *zannis* and *servetta*, the lover having dwindled to insignificance. Spectacle, song and dance, with whole scenes composed in verse, come to dominate the stage. In the later plays the plot is of the slightest and is a mere pretext for a rather static comedy made up of a series of satirical sketches presided over by Arlequin. Here we see the beginnings of comic operetta, of the cabaret-style revue, of the music-hall. The nearest modern equivalent is probably the British pantomime; the first in this genre were harlequinades early in the reign of Queen Anne. The closure by royal decree of the Théâtre Italien in 1697 dealt it a blow from which it never really recovered. When in 1716 the Italians returned, they soon had to turn once again to authors such as Marivaux for French comedies featuring Arlequin and Colombine; but Marivaux's Arlequin gives only a very faint idea of his traditional character. Though the closure was ostensibly on the grounds that the Italians had staged or intended to stage a comedy *La Finta Matrigna* – or *La Fausse Prude* – alleged to be derogatory of Mme de Maintenon (probably Louis XIV's morganatic wife), one wonders whether this was not a convenient pretext. Since the 1680s all Parisian theatre companies had been tightly controlled by one member or another of the royal family, while Louis himself had long turned his back on the theatre. All criticism of the régime, on French soil, was sternly repressed; satirical works in French often had to be printed in the Low Countries and smuggled in. Might it be that the King saw in the Théâtre Italien the last surviving uncontrolled source of very public satire of his régime, however harmless it might now seem to us?

NOTES

1 Evaristo Gherardi, *Le Théâtre Italien de Ghérardi, ou le Recueil Général de toutes les Comédies et Scènes Françoises jouées par les Comédiens italiens du Roy, pendant tout le temps qu'ils ont été au service*, 6 vols. (Paris, J- B. Cusson and P. Witte, 1700).

2 On this period see also Virginia Scott, *The Commedia dell'arte in Paris 1644 – 1697* (Charlottesville, University Press of Virginia, 1990).

3 See Thomas-Simon Gueullette, *Notes et Souvenirs sur le théâtre italien au XVIIIe siècle* (Paris, E. Droz, 1938) and J. E. Gueullette, *Un magistrat du XVIIIe siècle, Thomas-Simon Guellette* (Paris, E. Droz, 1938).

4 'Though Italian is Armenian to me, and my mind so stupid that I understand not a word, yet I go to see this troupe, preferring to eat less soup and drink a little less wine, than not to see Trivelin'. Cited in G. Attinger, *L'Esprit de la commedia dell'arte dans le théâtre français* (Paris, Librarie théâtrale, 1950), 168.

5 In *Le Calendrier historique des Théâtres pour 1752*, cited in A. Calame, *Regnard, sa vie et son oeuvre* (Paris, PUF, 1960), 54.

6 Thus a play such as Delosme de Montchenay's *La Cause des Femmes* (1687) seems a rather static, wordy, not very amusing comedy, but is shown by allusions in the *Critique de la Cause des Femmes* to have been full of *lazzis* not recorded at all by Gherardi.

7 On Fatouville see V. Scott, op. cit., 280 – 3.

8 Regnard's comedies are most conveniently consulted in: Jean-François Regnard, *Comédies du Théâtre Italien*, ed. A. Calame (Genève, Droz, 1981). But my quotations come from Gherardi's text of 1700. The texts consist of: *Le Divorce* (1688); *La Descente de Mezzetin aux Enfers* (1689); *Arlequin Homme à Bonne Fortune* (1690); *La Critique de l'Homme à Bonne Fortune* (1690); *Les Filles errantes* (1690); *La Coquette* (1691); *La Naissance d'Amadis* (1694) as well as plays written in collaboration with Charles-Rivière Dufresny: *Les Chinois* (1692); *La Baguette de Vulcain* and *L'Augmentation de la baguette de Vulcain* (1693); *La Foire Saint-Germain* (1695) and *Les Momies d'Egypte* (1696).

9 E. Gherardi, *Le Théâtre Italien, ou le Recueil de toutes les Scènes Françoises qui ont esté joüées sur le Théâtre Italien de l'Hostel de Bourgogne* (Paris, G. de Luyne, 1694).

    id. *Le Théâtre Italien, ou le Recueil de toutes les Comédies et Scènes Françoises qui ont été joüées sur le Théâtre Italien. Par la Troupe des Comédiens du Roy de L'Hôtel de Bourgogne á Paris. Troisième* [sic] *édition revuë corrigèe et augmentée*, 3 vols. (Paris, Héritiers de Mabre Cramoisy, 1695–8).

    Pirated texts are found in:

    Suite du Théâtre Italien ou Nouveau Recueil de plusieurs Comédies Françoises: qui ont été jouées sur le Théâtre Italien de l'Hôtel de Bourgogne (n.p. 1697).

    Suplément du Théâtre Italien ou Nouveau Recueil des Comédies et Scènes Françoises qui ont été jouées sur le Théâtre Italien par les Comédiens du Roi de l'Hôtel de Bourgogne à Paris. Tome troisième. Suivant la copie de Paris, 2 vols. (Amsterdam, A. Braakman, 1698).

    La Naissance d'Amadis. Comédie. (Amsterdam, 1697).

    La Foire Saint-Germain. Scènes Françoises de la Comédie Italienne intitulée. La Foire Saint-Germain. Comme elles ont paru dans les premières représentations (Grenoble, 1696).

10 'Since *The Matron of Ephesus* in which I had to learn a French part off by heart, I am overwhelmed by my character, especially now that the authors lay the whole weight of the comedy on me' (Cited in Attinger, op. cit., 10).

11 See Attinger, op. cit., 184.

12 'At present the masks are of cardboard or paper, waxed and as brighly coloured as possible . . . acting with a mask is the lot of those who play farcical and comic roles; the mask lends them a caricatural air, swarthy colouring, a big squashed nose, little blind eyes, a lined forehead, a bald pate etc' – from A. Perrucci; *Dell'arte rappresentativa, premedita ed all'improviso* (Napoli, M. L. Mutio, 1699), cited in Constant Mic, *La Commedia delle'arte* (Paris, J. Schiffrin, 1927).

13 See Ch. Garnier's *Oeuvres complettes de Regnard* (Paris, Duchesne, 1783), Préface, 13–14.

14 Cited in Attinger, op. cit., 40.

5 Lesage and d'Orneval's *théâtre de la foire*, the *commedia dell'arte* and power

GEORGE EVANS

A *foire* play is essentially a mongrel, an 'ingénieux mélange' ('a clever mixture'), as Lesage and d'Orneval put it in the *Préface* they wrote for their anthology.[1] In its background there is a centuries-old European tradition of showmen with all their various forms of entertainments – one-man stand-up comic routines, street singing, puppet shows, animal acts, rope dancing etc. And yet by the start of the eighteenth century, the fair companies which had major seasons from February to Easter (at Saint-Germain) and from July to September (at Saint-Laurent) were in possession of substantial and sophisticated theatres, with scripts provided by teams of writers. And these writers were by no means unsophisticated simple souls merely continuing the showman tradition. To the showman tradition a recent historian of eighteenth-century popular entertainments adds 'the obscene farces of the late Middle Ages, the Comedies of Molière, and *commedia dell'arte* . . . Moreover, the Comique[2] borrowed musical airs, dramatic situations, and the *merveilleux* from its illustrious sister the Opéra . . .'[3] Even this does not exhaust the list of sources of inspiration and material which the fair players and writers drew on. It would be possible to include also *fabliaux*,[4] fairy tales, pastorals and, last but not least, the *Thousand and One Nights* which became such a success through its early eighteenth-century translation.

Lesage and d'Orneval's anthology of fair plays covers the period 1713–34. During this period the fair theatres were at the height of their popularity, and therefore attracted the greatest animosity from the 'official' companies. In response, the fair theatres were, often of necessity, at their most imaginative: in order to circumvent the periodic restrictions imposed upon them by the 'official' companies asserting their rights of monopoly to dialogue or to song, they had to invent new forms (placard plays, monologues) as well as reverting to older forms of fair entertainments such as mime and puppet shows.

Although it is clear that a deal of cross-fertilization had already taken place in the seventeenth century,[5] the emergence of the fair as a real theatrical force in France dates from the 'exile' of the resident Italian company in 1697.[6] This event gave the fair players that vital gap in the market which they were to seize so readily, along with some of the Italians' repertoire and some of their actors, although it remains true that relatively few of the fair players had direct experience of performing in Italian-type plays at the outset. Nevertheless, if we accept what K. and L. Richards say about the early *commedia dell'arte* companies, what the fair companies have in common with them is first and foremost the fact that they were all free commercial theatres who needed to appeal to a wide and diverse audience if they were to make a living and survive.

In the early eighteenth century, however, the fair companies clearly felt they should try to establish a separate identity and therefore sought to stake out their own particular territory. This became especially important for them after the reintroduction of the new 'official' Italian company in 1716. Hence, in those *Prologues* in the Lesage–d'Orneval anthology which deal with the relationships between the existing theatre companies, the emphasis is placed on a clear set of demarcations between the four main parties, the Comédie Française, the Comédie Italienne, the Opéra and the Foire ou Opéra Comique (this latter grouping together a number of different, and occasionally antagonistic,[8] companies). Thus, for example, towards the end of *Le Rappel de la foire à la vie* (1721), the figure representing 'the Public' tries to bring peace between the rival companies by asserting that each one has its own particular appeal: the Comédie Française has tragedy and regular comedy, the Comédie Italienne has the physical stage business of Arlequin's *lazzi*, the Opéra has serious opera and ballet, and the fair has popular song and dance. There is, of course, a good measure of truth in this highly self-conscious set of classifications. There is also, however, a great deal of special pleading and wishful thinking,[9] even if years later Lesage and d'Orneval are still trying to use the same tactics in the *Préface* to their anthology. At the outset these tactics amount to a recognition of the higher status of the fair's rivals and an initial show of respect. For example, in *La Querelle des théâtres* (1718), the figure representing the fair orders Mezzetin to find good seats for the visiting French and Italian figures, explaining that 'ce sont mes supérieures que ces dames-là; je ne suis que leur très humble servante: je ne puis leur marquer trop de respect' (sc. ii) ('these ladies are my betters, I am but

their most humnble servant. I can show no respect too great for them').
These tactics are echoed in the fair's modesty about itself and in the
fulsome praise for the Comédie Française which opens the *Préface*:

> Ce n'est point pour disputer de prix avec les chef-d'oeuvres immortels
> qui mettent le Théâtre français au-dessus de tous les théâtres du
> monde que ce recueil paraît aujourd'hui.

> It is not to compete with the immortal masterpieces which set the
> Théâtre Français above all others in the world that this anthology is
> published.

Such tactics could not work and will soon be abandoned in favour of
more aggressive ones, as we shall see.

The harsh truth is that the commercially competitive environment
which all companies in Paris were part of forced all of them, whether
'official' or 'unofficial', to encroach upon one another's preserves.
Indeed, there seems to have been a constantly shifting pattern of
alliances as the fair sought to achieve status and respectability and the
'official' companies sought an audience. The outcome of *Le Rappel de la
foire à la vie* is that the fair and the Italians join forces, and a year later,
in 1722, the Italians are to be found performing *Le Jeune Vieillard, La
Force de l'amour* and *La Foire des fées* in the fair theatre. And yet, the
Italians are more often than not depicted in other *Prologues* as the allies
of the Comédie Française in the war against the fair companies. On
these occasions it is the Opéra which is presented as the protector or
saviour of the fair companies. Indeed, as in scene vii of *Les Funérailles
de la foire* (1718), it is intimated that the Comédie Française's bitter
hatred of the fair is in reality merely part of a larger-scale conflict
between the Comédie Française and the Opéra.

The measure of these shifting alliances and the scale of the cross-
border raiding come out clearly in the *Avertissement* of *Les Comédiens
corsaires* (1726), that aptly titled *Prologue* which, it is claimed, 'fut fait
peu de temps après *Les Comédiens esclaves,* comédie du Théâtre
Italien, et à l'occasion du goût qui règne depuis quelques années dans les
pièces tant françaises qu'italiennes dans la plupart desquelles on voit le
fond et la forme des divertissements forains' ('was put on not long after
The Slave Players, an Italian comedy, and at a time of the fashion which
lasted from some years in Italian and French plays alike, in most of
which can be witnessed, in both form and content, Fair entertainments.'). And in the playlet itself, the following description is not, as

might first be thought, a description of the Italians' vessel, but that of the Opéra Comique's:

> On voyait du plus haut du mâts
> Un Arlequin sauter en bas,
> Accompagné d'une cohorte
> De Pierrots et de Mezzetins:
> Et pour voltiger de la sorte
> Je ne connais que les Forains.   (sc. iii)

> Up aloft could be seen a Harlequin leaping down, along with a host of Pierrots and Mezzetins. Only the fair players are capable of such aerobatics as that.

Now, this might well remind the audience of the aerobatics of the original rope-dancers and trapeze artists rather that the boisterous physicality of the Italians, but throughout the Lesage–d'Orneval anthology, those figures formerly associated with the Italians – Arlequin, Mezzetin, Scaramouche, Pierrot, Colombine, Polichinelle – are usually the representatives of the fair, whereas the Italians are left with Scapin and Pantalon, and the Comédie Française with Crispin and diverse Romans. All the old Italian characters are fairly protean,[10] although it is Arlequin in particular who can turn up as the Opéra or a Pont Neuf song merchant, depending on whose help the fair company is soliciting or which connection it is trying to make on a given occasion.

Furthermore, when in *Les Comédiens corsaires* Pierrot, 'le chef d'escadre de l'Opéra Comique', is captured and searched, the Arlequin costume which is discovered is taken by a Comédie Française *actress* and the Crispin costume by a Comédie Italienne *actress*. Cross-dressing, along with other forms of disguise, is of course a regular feature of both Italian and fair productions. The following list, with no pretentions to completeness, is illustrative of what can be found in the Lesage–d'Orneval anthology. It ranges from the transvestite Mezzetin–Pierrot duo in *Arlequin roi de Serendib* (1713), and the double change in *Colombine Arlequin ou Arlequin Colombine* (1715), the Pierrot *chanteuse* of *Le Pharaon* (1717) to Arlequin in the role of 'Cybèle en vieille' ('Cybele as an old woman') in the parody *La Grand'mère amoureuse* (1726) and Lisette 'en Arlequin' in *Roger de Sicile* (1731)). However, in *Les Comédiens corsaires* the cross-dressing refers not only to exchanges involving gender, but exchanges involving the identity of the different theatre companies. When the other booty is shared out, the

Comédie Française takes the fair players' song chest, while the Italians seize the cache of parodies claiming that 'cela appartient aux comédiens italiens' ('that belongs to the Italians'), (sc. vii). If we add to this the fact that the same authors could script material for different companies – Lesage had written for the Comédie Française before turning to the fair and the Italians; Piron, on the other hand, would leave the fair for the Comédie Française; Fuzelier wrote for all companies – then it would seem that there is little point in making watertight distinctions.

In the *Préface* that Lesage and d'Orneval wrote for their anthology, they trace an outline history of the fair and its difficulties with the 'official' companies, they try to establish the main characteristics of the fair repertoire – the use of song, extravagant fantasy (even if 'toujours joint à des sentiments naturels et à des portraits satiriques'), a lighthearted treatment of all subjects and an essential simplicity of structure and composition[11] – and they make a bid on behalf of the fair for a modest place of its own in the world of drama. In this final aim, and to avoid stepping on any toes, they admit, most revealingly, what they have excluded from their anthology:

> On y a vu [= aux Foires] tant de mauvaises productions, tant d'obscénités, que les lecteurs pourraient d'abord n'être pas favorables à cet ouvrage . . . Ces productions, qu'on ne peut rappeler que désagréablement pour ce théâtre, n'y sont point employées. Nous n'avons pas même jugé à propos de faire imprimer toutes les pièces qui ont réussi sur la scène de l'Opéra Comique, celles, par exemple, qui ont dû tout leur succès au jeu des acteurs ou à des ballets brillants . . . Nous avons pareillement supprimé celles qui sont tirées des pièces italiennes . . . Ce sont des dépouilles du vieux Théâtre Italien qu'il était juste de restituer au nouveau.

> So many bad pieces and so much obscenity have been seen there that the readers might not at first be favourably disposed to this work . . . We have not included those pieces which can only be recalled unfavourably for this company. We have not even thought fit to publish all those plays which succeeded on the stage of the Opéra Comique, those, for example, which owed their success to the quality of the acting or the brilliant dancing . . . We have also excluded those based on Italian plays . . . which are the legacy of the Old Italian Company which it was right to restore to the New Company.

In other words, the truly obscene, the less scripted and the more Italianate pieces have been edited out. However, like the *Prologues* the

Préface recognizes that the strongest card in the pack, as far as the fair's search for status goes, will be its popularity. For a form of theatre which had no critical theories to conform to and no king to please, but which needed a defence against the threats coming from its 'official' competitors, its main safeguard lay in its appeal to the power of the public. So, while the Comédie Française is depicted as a vicious bitch and the Comédie Italienne as a hypocritical *sournoise* who can easily change sides, it is not by chance that the figure representing the fair is often a kind of coquette. Just as the coquette lives only through and for men, so the fair lives only through and for its public. The fair's public, like the coquette's men, must be wooed and given what it wants. After all,

> Une prude au farouche ton
> Est une très sotte guenon
> Mais une coquette agréable
> C'est un animal raisonnable.   (*Les Animaux raisonnables*, sc. xv)

A sharp-tongued prude is a very foolish monkey, but an attractive coquette is a creature of reason.

The fact that this audience was not a homogeneous or specialized one had, of course, to be taken into account. As Thalie puts it in the *Prologue* to *La Force de l'amour* (1722), 'il faut de la variété dans les mets, pour contenter la diversité des goûts' ('a variety of dishes is needed, in order to satisfy all the different tastes'). Hence the mixture in fair shows of low comedy, with its well loved and well tested routines, and the kind of allusive fun which depends on a degree of cultural awareness, feeding as it does off the successes and magnificent failures of high culture. Attinger makes this mixture another bond between the fair and the *commedia dell'arte*.[12]

In this same *Prologue* Arlequin reveals another key feature of the fair's appeal when he says, 'vous savez qu'il faut des nouveautés à Paris, et surtout à la Foire' ('you are aware that in Paris, and especially in the Fair, novelty is called for'). Novelty meant not only being different from what was on offer elsewhere, but being ever-changing. It did *not* mean being revolutionary or avant-garde to the point of frightening off the audience. The kind of novelty the fair audience demanded was a novelty that involved a subtle combination of the constantly varied with the reassuringly familiar. In short, novelty without bewilderment. Hence the resort to those stock figures who could remain recognizably themselves and yet forever be someone or something else. Similarly, the practice of renewing the lyrics to well known tunes, whether taken from traditional sources or poached from contemporary hits, offered the same effect of endless transformation of seemingly fixed material. In these ways the desire for novelty could be satisfied, without novelty being feared.

As opposed to this kind of novelty, which renews traditions, the fair presents its rivals as companies constantly re-enacting an unchanging tradition or producing new works which do not live up to the quality of the old ones. In this way their status and authority are made to appear no longer justified. In making drama out of their own difficulties, the fair companies use their rapport with the public, and laughter, as their main weapons against their rivals. As Lurcel puts it succinctly, 'dès 1709 ils mettent les rieurs de leur côté' ('from 1709 they got the laughers on their side').[13] And in what is presented as a kind of struggle for power, those familiar elements of the old *commedia dell'arte* tradition which combat power and challenge authority and convention – parody,[14] satire and the fantastic – can be reused, even at the expense of the contemporary Italians!

This obsession with power and its uses is not limited to the relationships between theatre companies. The fair players knew from their own experiences what it was to be relatively weak and what weapons the weak could use. Thus, just as the powerful forces of 'official' culture are treated at first with respect, then with sustained mockery, so it is with representatives of social hierarchies (up to and including monarchy) and with token figures of religious or 'scientific' power. As well as playing the parts of the fair and the other theatre companies, the old Italian stock characters, and especially Arlequin, Pierrot and Mezzetin, can turn up not only as petty crooks, valets and earthy lovers, but in guises ranging from gods, prophets, high priests, kings and princes to, lower down the scale, financiers, *petits-maîtres*, cooks, millkeepers and fishermen, to name but a few. When these stock characters take the lowlier rôles, they are set against the representatives of the higher authorities. In which case, they quake and touch forelocks or insult, ridicule and physically abuse their betters, depending on their relative positions of strength.

From these starting points fantasy can be made to connect with real life, and the stage worlds of antiquity or exotic foreign lands (real or fictional) can co-exist with the contemporary world and with France. Thus a mythological character can easily be found in an eighteenth-century French inn! Even in a play of the most fanciful kind such as *Les Animaux raisonnables* (1718) there is regular reference to the world of actuality. In this play, set on Circe's island where Ulysses' companions have been turned into animals, realities such as the former social positions of the 'animals' (as 'procureur' or 'financier') or the high risks of women dying in childbirth are ever-present.

It would be tedious to list all such references to the contemporary world which are to be found in the *Théâtre de la foire*, but it is worth observing that they range from the most specific allusions to people, places and events to the more general, at times traditional, stereotypical depictions of familiar types of people and behaviour. This range of reference can occur within a single play. In *Le Tombeau de Nostradamus* (1714), for instance, there are one-off allusions to places such as La Salpétrière (sc. viii) along with whole scenes of broader social satire, as in scene v where quarrels about the relative nobility of the petits-maîtres offer an insight into patterns of upward social mobility over a couple of generations (from Meunier to Bailli to Gentilhomme, for example). These references stand alongside effects of supernatural spectacle such as fire-spitting monsters, black magicians and troupes of demons.

More significantly, even a play as unreal as *Les Animaux raisonnables* represents that combination of the realistic recognition of power with release, albeit temporary, from power. This too is one of the hallmarks of the fair. Indeed, the fair provides its audience with the experience of such a release. The enjoyment is the message. The release from power is dependent on the magic of the theatre, just as within a typical fair play such as *Arlequin invisible* (1713) it is the magic element (here invisibility) which gives Arlequin his freedom from the authority of the King of China. In the case of *Les Animaux raisonnables* the release can, in the ultimate wish-fulfilment, be made to endure, through magic, since no 'animal' can be forced to resume his or her former human existence. Free choice becomes a delicious, maybe dangerous, notion.

The fair can, of course, have it both ways if it so wishes. It can mock power, but it can also ridicule the gullibility or servility of those who, out of fear or overreadiness to obey, fall victim to false or baseless powers. This is clearly the case in a play such as *Arlequin Mahomet* (1714), which incidentially gives us a broad range of themes and methods typical of the fair. It opens with the point of contemporary reference: Arlequin is a ruined merchant bemoaning his ill fortune and pursued by creditors. Scientific fantasy enters in the form of a mathematician who, for no good reason, hands over a flying machine to Arlequin. This machine, in the form of a casket, provides both a source of spectacular effects and the immediate solution to Arlequin's problem. Stocking his flying casket not only with the basics of food (the traditional cheese and sausages) and drink but also with that essential instrument of the subversive, the chamber-pot, Arlequin soon finds a use for the latter. From his new 'superior' mid-air position, he tips it over the representatives of law and order, the Watch, who have come to arrest him. After a transformation scene, the love interest is provided in the form of a love-lorn Prince of Persia who is on the point of suicide because his princess has been stolen by a Tartar. Arlequin flies off to the rescue. After a second transformation scene, the disguise element comes into play when, in the gardens of the King of Basra, Arlequin takes on the role of Mahomet, complete with turban and beard. The king and the sixty-year-old fiancé he has forced upon his daughter are duly bombarded with firecrackers from on high, as well as being stunned with blows from the 'prophet's' slapstick. This punishment of abuse of power halts only when it is agreed that the princess may marry her Prince of Persia after all, leaving the 'divine' Arlequin to take as his 'earthly' wife, the servant girl who, in an earlier scene, had already aroused Arlequin's traditional sexuality. A dance of slavegirls and eunuchs brings the show to a close!

This combination of burlesque, vulgarity, and scientific and exotic fantasy is clearly a disruptive force in the lives of those in authority whose desires it frustrates. It sets up a power superior to the powerful and reveals at the same time the common vulnerability of the powerful themselves. That Arlequin should be at the heart of this subversion, indeed, that he is its main vehicle, is only fitting since he embodies in his own person that same combination of elements, thereby coming to represent a kind of revenge of the powerless.

Not that Arlequin provides any model for the proper use of power when he finds himself in a position which gives him the chance to exercise it. His new-found power simply allows him greater opportunities to indulge his traditional desires – until he is brought back to earth with a bump. For example, in *Arlequin roi de Serendib* (1713) Arlequin's immediate reaction to the announcement that he has been made king is conveyed in the following song:

Puisque sur le trône
Vous m'avez placé
Vite, je l'ordonne,
Le buffet dressé;
Sans quoi la couronne
Pour moi vaut moins qu'un fétu.   (I. v)

Since you have installed me on the throne, set up the table, quickly, I command. Without that the crown isn't worth a straw to me.

In the scenes that follow, he gets his portrait painted, dispenses the roughest of rough justice, then turns his thoughts to women:

Oui, vite une maîtresse!
Ma foi, je suis enclin,
Ami, je le confesse,
Au sexe féminin
(. . .)
Ah! Qu'il est doux d'être aujourd'hui
Un homme d'importance!
Mère, époux rampent devant lui;
Et s'il veut voir Hortense
Il n'a qu'à tinter,
Il n'a qu'à compter,
Et la mignonne s'avance.   (II. iv and v)

Yes, a woman quickly now,
God, I do love the ladies, I admit it freely, my friend.
. . .
How great it is to be someone important nowadays! Mothers and husbands kowtow to people like that, and if they want to see Hortense, they have only to ring, they have only to count up to ten and the little darling is there, ready and waiting . . .

Put in power, the lowly simply behave more obviously like the powerful, using/abusing their position in order to 'enjoy life'.

Les Animaux raisonnables and *Le Monde renversé* (both 1718) turn this into a general rule of life. In the former, some animals refuse to take on human form again because their new lives allow them far greater scope to satisfy their desires. Those animals wishing to become men or women again do so only because their new roles prevent them from fulfilling their needs. In Arlequin's case, being a dolphin does not provide him with sufficient chance to be his traditional gluttonous, drunken self. Similarly there are the fish-women who have met a fate worse than death by becoming the victims of a pun when Circe changed them 'en pucelles' ('into Virgins/Shad'). Naturally, 'elles s'ennuyent furieusement de cet état' ('they are desperately unhappy with this state of affairs'), (sc. xiii). The frontispiece of *Le Monde renversé* depicts a scene where Arlequin and Pierrot are seated at table being showered with the food and drink which falls magically from the sky. In the play itself, all the reversals involve having the basics of life (food, drink, sex) served up on a plate and anything disagreeable eliminated. Or again, in *Arlequin roi des ogres* (1720), when the shipwrecked Arlequin is made king of the ogres, his kinship allows him to despatch the royal caterer, who happens to be a giant with seven-league boots, to collect food and drink from Paris, along with some entertainment in the shape of dancers from the Opéra. This is done in the name of 'humanizing' the ogres for whom 'la chair fraîche' ('tender meat') had meant food rather than sex. However, sex is not to be forgotten. King Arlequin provides his friend Scaramouche and others with the pick of the island girls, while he himself, still fearful of the islanders' cannibal tendencies, sends his caterer off with an order for 'quelque beauté asiatique . . . de ces friands morceaux de Sultan' ('some Asian beauty . . . one of those Turkish delights [titbits fit for a Sultan]'), (sc. xviii), thereby exploiting the food–sex running gag.[15] This pun can also be made to serve a satirical purpose, since cannibalism can be equated with other forms of human exploitation. As one of the ogres says to Arlequin when the latter rejects cannibalism for being inhuman,

> Vous qui pensez avoir en partage toute l'humanité, comment en usez-vous les uns avec les autres? Vous vous querellez, vous vous chicanez, vous vous pillez, chez vous le plus fort ôte au plus faible sa subsistence; cela ne s'appelle-t-il pas se manger.   (sc. xii)

> You who think that you are so full of humanity, how do you treat one another? You shout at one another, you cheat one another, you rob one another. In your world the strongest takes the bread from the mouth of the weakest. Isn't that what you call 'having someone for breakfast'!

Even where the sexual roles are reversed, as in *L'Isle des Amazones* (1718), the same general characteristics of humanity prevail. The

Amazon pirates who capture Arlequin and Pierrot simply adopt 'male' behaviour and 'male' language. Pierrot says of one of the Amazons who has taken a fancy to him, 'J'ai entendu une fois qu'elle disait tout bas à l'autre: ce gros garçon est à manger' ('Once I heard her whisper to her friend: I could just eat that big lad.'), (sc. ii). The fearful Arlequin interprets this literally, of course, until wised up by Scaramouche who reveals that a finer fate awaits him – marriage to an 'amazone'. The punning lives on in Arlequin's response: 'Ah! voilà donc ce que c'est que la marinade!', ('So that's what a real basting is!'), (sc. iii). In this perspective Scaramouche holds out the possibility of earthly paradise, to the tune 'Oh! voilà la vie',

> Table bien servie
> Repas toujours longs
> Epouse jolie
> Vin à pleins flacons.
> Oh! voilà la vie.   (sc. iii)

> A well stocked table,
> Endless meals, a pretty wife and free-flowing wine.
> That's the life (for you)!

In all these typical reversals, not being subjected to others and being able to satisfy one's needs and desires is what life is all about. If this is so, then 'la folie' (which comes to mean not some mental aberration or fantasy, but pleasure, fun, entertainment) becomes wisdom. As the 'petit noir et bossu', Torgut, puts it in *Le Jeune Vieillard* (1722),

> Je suis sectateur du grand philosophe qui a fait cette chanson:
> Chers amis, réjouissons-nous,
> Faisons les fous. (*bis*)
> Etre fou et se réjouir,
> C'est être sage;
> Etre sage sans se réjouir
> C'est être fou.   (I. iv)

> I'm a follower of the famous philosopher who wrote this song:
> Dear friends, let's enjoy ourselves, let's go mad. (*repeated*)
> Going mad and enjoying oneself is the wise thing to do.
> Being wise but not enjoying oneself is crazy.

This wisdom is not undermined, even if in the worlds of the plays the reversals or changes of status are not enduring. This is equally true of *Arlequin roi de Serendib* where Arlequin is but a temporary king or of *L'Isle des Amazones* where marriage to the island beauties will only last three months. In one sense, of course, the fair had to take care not to frighten off the audience with advanced social ideas, just as it had to avoid doing so with advanced theatrical ones. As a commercial enterprise it could not go too far beyond the prejudices of its public. The ending of *Arlequin roi de Serendib* is instructive in this context. Arlequin is saved from becoming a human sacrifice by his old accomplices, Mezzetin and Pierrot, and together the three set about looting the island temple. What they intend doing with the stolen jewels does not betray any signs of lessons having been learned:

> Que nous allons boire à Paris
> De flacons de champagne!   (III. viii)

How many bottles of champers we'll down in Paris!

On stage, licence and transgressions may have their limits, and social reversals may be reversed again before the play ends, but men do not change. Only their circumstances change.

This may be interpreted in a number of ways. It can suggest that the fair is fulfilling a popular, carnival mission, allowing but containing subversion,[16] and comforting or distracting the audience for whom radical change seems out of the question in real life. It may reflect a world released from authority and grim convention where old values are being challenged.[17] From this perspective, connections might be made with the atmosphere of the Regency which followed the death of Louis XIV in 1715 and which contrasted so sharply with the sensually drab final years of the Sun King's reign. But it may also represent a vision of a permanently imperfect human world of weak and strong, which, sanely, can only be viewed with ironic amusement. In this case, it is no wonder that the arch-ironist, Lesage, was to feel so at home at the fair. Such irony is both popular and sophisticated. This ambivalent appeal may explain not only why the fair was so successful – until it became too respectable itself – but also why it can be seen both as a liberating force and as a renewal of a tradition of anti-authoritarian, anti-heroic and anti-illusionist spectacle in which stage and audience were in connivence. It is within this tradition that the fair and the *commedia dell'arte* meet.

NOTES

1 All references are to the two-volume 1968 Slatkine reprint of the 1737 ten-volume edition of the *Théâtre de la foire*. Spellings have been modernized. For the *Préface*, see 7–9.

2 Fair shows began to use the name 'l'Opéra Comique' on posters from 1715 onwards.

3 Robert M. Isherwood, *Farce and Fantasy* (Oxford University Press, 1986), p.60.

4 D. Lurcel, *Le Théâtre de la foire* (10/18, Union Générale d'Editions, 1983) makes this connection, 27.

5 Lurcel, op. cit. p.8, quotes Scarron to show that Arlequin was already a presence in the fairs in 1648.

6 For details, see Isherwood, op. cit. 41 ff.

7 K. Richards and L. Richards, *The Commedia dell'Arte: a documentary history* (Oxford, Blackwell, 1990) stresses the diversity of the Italian companies' repertory and acting styles and relates this to commercial factors. They concede however that in other countries the Italians became associated with improvised stage-business of a physical rather than verbal kind.

8 See, for example, the Prologue entitled *La Fausse Foire* (1721) in volume 4 of the Lesage-d'Orneval anthology.

9 K. Richards and L. Richards, op. cit. 258–62, highlight the increased use of music, dance, spectacle and sentiment in the seventeenth-century Italian repertory in France.

10 Virginia Scott, *The Commedia dell'Arte in Paris 1644–1697* (Charlottesville, University Press of Virginia, 1990), 387, notes that already in the Old Italian company in the 1690s 'the *zanni* are interchangeable . . . all without defining characteristics'.

11 This 'simplicity' is usually contrasted with the over-rationalized plotting of classical plays and the prolixity of the Opéra shows.

12 G. Attinger, *L'esprit de la Commedia dell'arte dans le théâtre français* (Geneva, Slatkine, 1981; orig. ed. 1950) 310–11.

13 Lurcel, op. cit., 13.

14 Isherwood, op. cit. and Walter Rex, *The Attraction of the Contrary* (Cambridge UP, 1987) stress the extent of the resort to parody. Rex estimates that there are 'at least seven to eight hundred (parodies), and many others were lost track of . . .' 60.

15 For an extended treatment of the food metaphors, see Roseann Runte, 'A tapestry of sensual metaphors: the vocabulary of Lesage's theatre' in *Eighteenth-century Theatre: aspects and contexts*, ed. M. G. Badir and D. J. Langdon (Edmonton, University of Alberta, 1986) 44–52.

16 On the lack of real transgressions of the social order, in both the fair and Marivaux, see Michelle Venard, *La Foire entre en scène* (Paris, Librairie théâtrale, 1985), 187.

17 See Rex, op. cit. 60 '. . . it is difficult not to interpret the phenomenon as one of the innumerable symptoms of a society that is losing faith in every sort of traditional value – a society turning against itself.' Lurcel, op. cit. 25, goes further in making Arlequin the mouthpiece for new bourgeois values.

6   The servant as master: disguise, role-reversal and social comment in three plays of Marivaux

DEREK F. CONNON

As is pointed out by Norbert Jonard in his study of the *commedia dell'arte*, disguise is one of the principal devices employed in the scenarios of the form.[1] Mel Gordon, in his study of *lazzi*, draws attention to a more specific use of disguise, one which involves not only pretence about the character's identity, but also about his social class: 'Often, the humour grows out of a class reversal, the servant acts like a master and the master becomes confused.'[2] Given the importance of the *théâtre italien* in Marivaux's career, the frequency of his use of the topos of disguise in his plays is hardly surprising, but in only one does he relate it specifically to the notion of social role- or class-reversal, doing so in a context where the device is clearly underlined by the stylized symmetry of the plot: that is to say *Le Jeu de l'amour et du hasard* (1730), where the duplication of the reversal in both male and female characters produces a quartet of individuals all parodying with more or less success their social opposites. Although there is no true use of disguise in the earlier play *L'Ile des esclaves* (1725), since the identity of the various characters is never in doubt either for the audience or for each other, a similarly symmetrical use of role-reversal backed up by costume changes relates it strongly to *Le Jeu*, and in this briefer play the social burden of the device is much more clearly underlined.

Although these are the only plays to use such a symmetrical structure, in a number of others one or other side of the equation is found in isolation. She (or he) stoops to conquer in works like *La Double Inconstance* (1723), *Le Prince travesti* (1724) and *Le Triomphe de l'amour* (1732), and in *La Fausse Suivante* (1724) the result of the trial is the more surprising rejection of the original beloved. But in only one other is there an important use of the situation described by Gordon, in which it is the servant who pretends to be of the class of his master: that is *L'Epreuve* (1740). It is this depiction of the servant as master in these three plays, *L'Ile des esclaves*, *Le Jeu de l'amour et du hasard* and

L'Epreuve that it is my intention to examine here. Whilst there seems little doubt that the Italian theatre was a fundamental influence in Marivaux's frequent use of disguise in his plays, it is a device which is by no means unique to that tradition. By focusing on this one particular aspect, on the other hand, we will be led to a consideration of a much more specifically Italianate aspect of Marivaux's theatre, the development of one facet of his treatment of his most persistently archetypal character, Arlequin.

That costume is an important icon of social status in these plays is in no doubt, otherwise there would be no point in the swapping of clothing specified in *L'Ile des esclaves* when the nobles are cast down to servitude and the servants (or, even more pointedly for the philosophical message, slaves, as they are here) are elevated to higher rank, for here there is no deception involved. Even on this island, where the slaves have realized the injustice and artificiality of social inequality, the symbol of the outward trappings of costume will be one of the most important indicators of the masters' fall from grace and the slaves' elevation.

One anomaly should, however, be noted: the swapping of costumes is specified by Trivelin for both couples: '(*Aux esclaves*) Quant à vous, mes enfants, qui devenez libres et citoyens, Iphicrate habitera cette case avec le nouvel Arlequin, et cette belle fille demeurera dans l'autre; vous aurez soin de changer d'habit ensemble, c'est l'ordre' ('[*To the slaves*] As for you, my children, who are now free citizens, Iphicrate will live in this cabin with the new Arlequin, and this beautiful young lady will live in the other; you will make sure to exchange clothing, that is the rule'), (430–1).[3] Arlequin and Iphicrate exit immediately after this, and at their subsequent re-entry the scene heading specifies 'ARLEQUIN, IPHICRATE, *qui ont changé d'habits*' ('ARLEQUIN, IPHICRATE, *who have exchanged clothing*'), (438). The absence of any similar indication with regard to the female characters, the fact that the continuity of the action prevents them from leaving the stage until after Cléanthis's denunciation of Euphrosine, by which time the exchange has become almost redundant, and the absence of any opportunity for them to resume their original costumes before the final reinstatement of the status quo all point to the fact that Marivaux did not actually envisage any exchange taking place between them in performance. The scene in which the men resume their original clothing (scene ix) is one of the emotional highpoints of the play, and, although the fact that this latter exchange takes place in full view of the audience suggests that it was only some sort of over-costume which was exchanged, with Arlequin retaining his traditional motley, it seems fair to assume that much comic effect would be derived from his inappropriate dress. A remark by Silvia in *Le Jeu de l'amour et du hasard* concerning her disguise as a servant – 'Il ne me faut presque qu'un tablier' ('Virtually all I need is an apron'), (680) – suggests that, on the other hand, as a result of the habitual over-dressing of actors of the time, the costumes of Euphrosine and Cléanthis would have been so similar that the exchange would have made little visual impact;[4] accordingly Marivaux sacrifices it to the fluency of his action. This suggests that, even in *Le Jeu de l'amour et du hasard*, where the women clearly do adopt disguises, the sartorial impression given by Lisette will be both less striking and less inappropriate than that of Arlequin.

The characters' behaviour, though, does not always live up to the costume, and so, in its superficiality, the disguise is shown to have no profound effect on their essence, and it is in the case of Arlequin, where the visual disguise is at its least effective, undermined as it would have been by his traditional trappings of mask and slap-stick as well as clear evidence of his suit of shreds and patches under his assumed garb, that the character also proves least able effectively to fulfil his new role. For if we compare him not only with his female counterparts, but also with Frontin his successor in *L'Epreuve*, who, unencumbered by Arlequin's traditional acessories, would have cut a much more dashing figure in his disguise as master, we will find that it is Arlequin who is least able to provide a convincing impersonation of the ruling classes, and who is in consequence the source of the most broadly parodic humour.

Cléanthis, for example, although not totally devoid of vulgarity – even Trivelin becomes exasperated by her inability to know when to stop at the end of scene iii of *L'Ile des esclaves* – displays a rather subtle sense of satire and observation; indeed, as Haydn Mason has shown,[5] her satirical *tour de force* of scene iii is very closely related to a passage which appears later in *Le Cabinet du philosophe* (1734). And it is she who becomes most obviously exasperated by Arlequin's inability to adjust his behaviour to either his new role or costume:

> CLÉANTHIS   Il fait le plus beau temps du monde; on appelle cela un jour tendre.
> ARLEQUIN   Un jour tendre? Je ressemble donc au jour, Madame.
> CLÉANTHIS   Comment! vous lui ressemblez?
> ARLEQUIN   Eh palsambleu! le moyen de n'être pas tendre, quand on se trouve tête à tête avec vos grâces? (*A ce mot il saute de joie.*) Oh! oh! oh! oh!

CLÉANTHIS   Qu'avez-vous donc? vous défigurez notre conversation!
ARLEQUIN   Oh! ce n'est rien; c'est que je m'applaudis.
CLÉANTHIS   Rayez ces applaudissements, ils nous dérangent.   (442)

CLÉANTHIS   The weather is as beautiful as can be; people call this a tender [i.e. gentle] day.
ARLEQUIN   A tender day? In that case I am like the day, Madam.
CLÉANTHIS   What do you mean, you are like the day?
ARLEQUIN   Sblood! how could I not be tender [i.e. loving], when I am in the company of your charms? (*At this witticism he jumps for joy.*) Ho! ho! ho! ho!
CLÉANTHIS   What is the matter? you are spoiling our conversation!
ARLEQUIN   Oh! it is nothing; I am just applauding myself.
CLÉANTHIS   Cut the applause, it disturbs us.

It is true that the parody of the poetic lover's conceit at the beginning of this extract is almost subtle, but it is clearly only present to permit the inappropriate oath and the naively childlike ebullience, which are much more typical both of the humour produced by Arlequin elsewhere in this particular play and of his usual archetypal self.

Such internal commentaries by the characters on their own and each other's actions as that found in the above extract are of course impossible in *Le Jeu de l'amour et du hasard*, where the disguises must be sustained, but the comedy of Arlequin's role still resides in the inappropriateness of his behaviour:

ARLEQUIN   Un domestique là-bas m'a dit d'entrer ici, et qu'on allait avertir mon beau-père qui était avec ma femme.
SILVIA   Vous voulez dire Monsieur Orgon et sa fille, sans doute, Monsieur!
ARLEQUIN   Eh! oui, mon beau-père et ma femme, autant vaut; je viens pour épouser, et ils m'attendent pour être mariés; cela est convenu; il ne manque plus que la cérémonie, qui est une bagatelle.
SILVIA   C'est une bagatelle qui vaut bien la peine qu'on y pense.
ARLEQUIN   Oui; mais quand on y a pensé, on n'y pense plus.   (688)

ARLEQUIN   A servant down there told me to come in here, and that my father-in-law would be informed that I was with my wife.
SILVIA   No doubt you mean Monsieur Orgon and his daughter, Monsieur!
ARLEQUIN   Yes, my father-in-law and my wife, same difference; marriage is what I am here for, and what they are waiting for; it is all agreed; all we need now is the ceremony, which is a mere trifle.

SILVIA   It is a trifle which it is worth making the effort to remember.
ARLEQUIN   Yes; but once you have remembered it, you do not give it another thought.

Lisette, on the other hand, is used so much by Marivaux as a sort of 'straight-man' for Arlequin's excesses that she provides little humour of her own. As with Cléanthis, her sense of *savoir faire* is sufficiently superior to that of Arlequin for her to react with surprise at his excessive behaviour, as the following extract shows, but it is not developed enough for her ultimately to see through his disguise.

MONSIEUR ORGON   Adieu, mes enfants: je vous laisse ensemble; il est bon que vous vous aimiez un peu avant que de vous marier.
ARLEQUIN   Je ferais bien ces deux besognes-là à la fois, moi.
MONSIEUR ORGON   Point d'impatience; adieu. [*Il sort*].
ARLEQUIN   Madame, il dit que je ne m'impatiente pas; il en parle bien à son aise, le bonhomme!
LISETTE   J'ai de la peine à croire qu'il vous en coûte tant d'attendre, Monsieur; c'est par galanterie que vous faites l'impatient: à peine êtes-vous arrivé! Votre amour ne saurait être bien fort; ce n'est tout au plus qu'un amour naissant.   (693)

MONSIEUR ORGON   Goodbye my children: I will leave you together; it is right that you should have the chance to fall in love a little before you get married.
ARLEQUIN   I would just as soon do the two things at the same time.
MONSIEUR ORGON   Be patient; goodbye. [*He leaves*].
ARLEQUIN   Madam, he tells me to be patient; it is all very well for him to say that, the old dodderer!
LISETTE   It is hard to believe that you find it quite so difficult to wait, Monsieur; it is through pure gallantry that you pretend to be impatient: you have only just arrived! Your love cannot really be very strong; it is no more than beginning.

And again, in the Frontin of *L'Epreuve*, we find that we have almost left the ineptitude of Arlequin behind. True, there is enough Arlequinesque conceit and whimsicality to give away his origins in a comment like 'On s'accoutume aisément à me voir, j'en ai l'expérience' ('I know from experience that people very easily get used to seeing me'), (1326), and his silencing of Madame Argante is much too peremptory to be that of the true master: 'Point de ton d'autorité, sinon je reprends mes bottes et monte à cheval' ('Do not take that authoritarian tone or I will put my boots back on and get back on my horse'), (1331). In general though, Marivaux allows his servant character in this play to achieve an impersonation which is almost credible.

So the costume changes nothing: Silvia and Dorante, Lisette and Arlequin are instinctively drawn to their social equals despite the multiple disguises. Convincing as Frontin's acting may be, he still lacks the nobility which will cause Angélique to love him instead of Lucidor (although in this late play Marivaux again weakens the case against Frontin by the strength of Angélique's fidelity: even a real master, he suggests, would still have failed to win her from Lucidor). Perhaps most interesting is the situation presented in *L'Ile des esclaves*, in which the two slaves, rather than being attracted to each other, are unable to resist the attraction of the nobles, despite the fact that on the island of slaves the latter have become technically their social inferiors. The slaves' sense of their masters' superiority will not easily be modified by mere changes in clothing or arbitrary reversals of the power structure.

The social comment in *L'Ile des esclaves* is quite explicit, although critics who have compared Arlequin's remarks to those of Figaro are perhaps underestimating the significant extent to which the subversive character of comments like the following is mitigated by the tone of reconciliation in which they are spoken: 'Tu veux que je partage ton affliction, et jamais tu n'as partagé la mienne. Eh bien! va, je dois avoir le cœur meilleur que toi; car il y a plus longtemps que je souffre, et que je sais ce que c'est que la peine. Tu m'as battu par amitié: puisque tu le dis, je te le pardonne; je t'ai raillé par bonne humeur, prends-le en bonne part, et fais-en ton profit' ('You want me to share your affliction, and you have never shared mine. Go on then! I must be softer-hearted than you, for I have suffered for longer, and I know what pain is. You beat me out of friendship: because you say so, I forgive you; I mocked you out of good humour, take it in the way it was intended, and learn from it'), (448). Ultimately the play calls for humanity rather than social upheaval.

Similarly, although we may be led by the plight of Silvia and Dorante in *Le Jeu de l'amour et du hasard*, in the most emotional moments of the struggle between love and the reason which tells them they cannot cross the social divide, to question the humanity of a society in which Silvia the mistress would not be allowed to wed Dorante if he really were Bourguignon, and although we may have an amused sympathy for the fact that the plans of Lisette and Arlequin to better themselves socially by marriage are doomed to failure, the play leaves us in no doubt that the mutual attraction of the characters comes not from costume, but from a deeper inherent sense of class and the different outlook on life and love which goes with it, neither of which can be so easily donned or doffed. I have discussed elsewhere, in relation to *La Colonie*, the fact that this situation may be more complex than Marivaux's merely negating his social comment by stressing stereotype and reasserting the status quo, and that the traditional elements provide for the audience a familiar framework through which the philosophical point can be made the more effectively.[6] The main point for the present argument is, however, the way in which all of these plots contain elements of social climbing: the character who assumes the clothing of his social superior begins to think seriously of aspiring to the rank which would usually go with it.

For the two slaves in *L'Ile des esclaves* social elevation is a reality, but only within the mythic confines of the island, a fact which they seem to understand as well as we do, given their disastrous attempts to woo their social superiors from the real world. And, although Cléanthis is admittedly less convinced than Arlequin, their reversion to their original lowly status is self-willed; they realize that their natures are determined by their original roles and that they cannot cope with their new-found responsibility. When Cléanthis asks Arlequin why he has resumed his original costume, the symbol of his servitude, he replies in terms which can be understood on either the literal or the symbolic plane: 'C'est qu'il est trop petit pour mon cher ami, et que le sien est trop grand pour moi' ('It is because it is too small for my dear friend, and his is too big for me'), (449).

The symmetries of *Le Jeu de l'amour et du hasard* make it clear that this is no more an attempt at realistic theatre than *L'Ile des esclaves*. We are a very long way here from the illusionism of Diderot's dramatic theory, or even the specific references to Paris found in *Les Fausses Confidences*. Neither, however, does Marivaux introduce anything like the distancing effect of the Greek setting of *L'Ile des esclaves*: the period is contemporary, and the location sufficiently anonymous to allow Marivaux's audience to identify it with their own milieu. The fact that the costume changes of this play have become true disguise, rather than mere symbolism, means that, despite the title of the play, for Lisette and Arlequin the attempt at social elevation through matrimony is much less of a game than it was for their predecessors in the earlier philosophical piece. Their failure too, although the audience shares with Monsieur Orgon and Mario the knowledge that it is inevitable, is a result of the given circumstances rather than of choice. So in this play we have moved a step closer to social climbing as a true possibility. But only a step: whilst Lisette and Arlequin here lack the self-knowledge of the Arlequin of *L'Ile des esclaves*, which allows him to understand and express the fact that he is happier in his old position, Marivaux shows, through the ease of their acceptance of their disillusionment, that he wishes us to understand that subconsciously they have come to a similar realization, and our sympathy for them is as short-lived as their disappointment:

> LISETTE   Venons au fait. M'aimes-tu?
> ARLEQUIN   Pardi! oui: en changeant de nom tu n'as pas changé de visage, et tu sais bien que nous nous sommes promis fidélité en dépit de toutes les fautes d'orthographe.
> LISETTE   Va, le mal n'est pas grand, consolons-nous.   (719)

> LISETTE   Get to the point. Do you love me?
> ARLEQUIN   Good God, yes: by changing your name you have not changed your face, and you know very well that we promised to be faithful to each other despite all spelling mistakes.
> LISETTE   Come on, it is no great pity, we will get over it together.

By the time Marivaux came to write *L'Epreuve*, he had already completed *Les Fausses Confidences*, a play in which the crossing of the social divide by marriage becomes a reality, for in marrying Dorante, Araminte weds her own servant, as *intendant* a very high-class servant, it is true, but a servant nonetheless. Dorante may have become *intendant* to Araminte as part of Dubois's stratagem to bring about their marriage, but there is no sense in which he has disguised himself as a social inferior, as does the Dorante of *Le Jeu de l'amour et du hasard*: he really has taken the job as Araminte's servant, and such a post is seen to be compatible with the reduced status brought about by the loss of his fortune. His uncle, Monsieur Remy, certainly sees no shame in this position, and even believes the servant Marton to be a fitting bride for his nephew. Araminte, on the other hand, learns from Dubois of Dorante's condition as impoverished son of a good family as early as the first act of the play, but this high social status certainly does not override his position as servant in her house; it is this which makes the psychological struggle so acute as she gradually falls in love with him and is forced to admit her affection both to herself and to her household. And for Madame Argante, her delightfully odious mother, the status of servant negates all other considerations, preventing her ever accepting Dorante as son-in-law; indeed, she is still affirming this at the final curtain: 'Ah! la belle chute! Ah! ce maudit intendant! Qu'il soit votre mari tant qu'il vous plaira; mais il ne sera jamais mon gendre' ('What an unhappy ending! Ah, that confounded steward! He can be your husband as much as you like; but he will never be my son-in-law'), (1235). Despite the mitigating factors of Dorante's high status in both social and domestic terms, Araminte has still taken the very significant step of breaking through the barrier separating her from her servants.

From here we move on to *L'Epreuve*, which is full of the crossing of social barriers, although across a social distance less extreme than that dividing master from servant seen in the earlier plays. Angélique is of a lower class than Lucidor, but they wed. Maître Blaise aspires, however half-heartedly, to his social superior Angélique, and his wealth will eventually represent a step up the social ladder to Lisette, who finally accepts his proposal of marriage.

But what of the disguised character Frontin? Given that the whole point of the plot of this play is that Angélique passes the test which is set for her, perhaps the best measure of Marivaux's intentions concerning the competence of Frontin's impersonation is not his rejection by her, but rather the treatment he receives from Lisette. Whilst her namesake in *Le Jeu de l'amour et du hasard*, although convinced of the social superiority of the disguised Arlequin, is still emboldened to woo him, Frontin, despite being both recognized and loved by his Lisette, nonetheless manages not only to convince her that she is mistaken about his true identity, but also to put any notion that he would be accessible to her out of her mind. So Frontin's disguise succeeds, and we are more inclined to believe his warnings that he may win Angélique away from Lucidor than we are that Arlequin could ever win a true member of the ruling class. But if the servant Dorante is able to win his mistress in *Les Fausses Confidences*, the daring of this conclusion is, as we have seen, at least mitigated not only by his being *intendant* rather than valet, but also by the fact that he is a man who has had both rank and fortune and has been ruined. In *L'Epreuve*, even in a world where both Lucidor and Maître Blaise marry beneath them, the true servant cannot be permitted to find a wife who is of either the nobility or the *haute bourgeoisie*. And the symmetry of the fantasy of the earlier plots has also disappeared, with the result that in this more realistic world there are victims as well as winners: the role he is playing for Lucidor deprives Frontin of Lisette, just as the Marton of *Les Fausses*

Confidences is deprived of the servant who, according to traditional plot-structure, is rightfully hers.

There is a clear development here: as Marivaux moves away from the stock characters and symmetries of traditional *commedia* models, social mobility becomes more of a possibility. And this development is even more pronounced if compared with a well-known seventeenth-century model: the nobles in *Le Bourgeois Gentilhomme* are prepared to trick Monsieur Jourdain out of his money by promises of marriage and of favours, but that these should ever actually be granted is never their intention. In Marivaux's *L'Héritier de village*, on the other hand, the nobles are quite prepared to marry Blaise's children in order to get at his money, the follies and dishonesty of such an alliance being avoided only by the revelations of the *dénouement*.

Clearly this modification has its roots in social reality. It seems likely that contemporary audiences would assume that the Dorante of *Les Fausses Confidences* was ruined in exactly the same way as Marivaux himself, that is in the financial crash caused by John Law. John Lough comments as follows:

> The immediate economic consequences of the *Système* were mixed. On the one hand thousands of people were ruined (it is perhaps to the *Système* that we owe the plays and novels of Marivaux who was driven by his losses in it to seek a living with his pen), and the violent inflation which caused a steep rise in the cost of living brought suffering to the lower classes, especially in the towns . . . Enormous fortunes were made almost overnight; the lackeys of yesterday became the masters of today.[7]

But such social mobility does not imply that members of the ruling class suddenly began forming marital alliances with servants: far from it. Elinor Barber points out that nobles were only likely to marry beneath their status for considerable financial gain, and that even this compromise was far from being universal:

> The poverty-stricken provincial nobility continued to disdain any alliance with the rich bourgeoisie, even though they might be reduced to the status of *hobereaux*. The acceptance by the Court nobility of these marriages may, therefore, be one more indication of its defection from a genuine noble ideology and of its espousal of a way of life no longer congruent with its older functions as a political and military aristocracy.[8]

So the aspirations of Cléanthis and Arlequin in *L'Ile des esclaves* and of Lisette and Arlequin in *Le Jeu de l'amour et du hasard* are unrealistic, and, whilst rightly belonging to the fantasy worlds of these two plays, are, even in that context, inevitably doomed to failure. The slight social mismatch of the marriage of Lucidor to Angélique, on the other hand, may lack some of the fairy-tale extravagance of the earlier plays, but it is perfectly justified in the more realistic atmosphere of *L'Epreuve*, since in terms of contemporary social reality it was actually possible. It is for the same reason that Lisette, although attracted to Frontin, makes no attempt to aspire to the conquest of the master she thinks him to be. Unlike her namesake in *Le Jeu de l'amour et du hasard*, she knows the attempt to be pointless, for she, like the play in which she figures, is more in touch with social reality.

Lionel Gossman comments, however: 'The plain truth seems to be that works of literature do not "reflect" social reality, at least not immediately, so that the relation between the social background and the work of literature is never a simple causal one.'[9] This is certainly true of *Le Jeu de l'amour et du hasard*: there is a degree of reflection of the increased social mobility of the period in the servants' attempts to marry above themselves, but whilst they are not unaware of the difficulty of the attempt, in the real world of the time it would surely have been impossible. Similarly in relation to the masters: although much of the emotional tension of their roles comes from their reluctance even to consider a *mésalliance*, Silvia's eventual manipulation of Dorante to the point that he proposes marriage to a girl whom he believes to be a servant is again the stuff on which dreams and romantic comedies are made, but is not representative of contemporary reality. It is not just, therefore, the symmetricality of this play or the tidiness of its *dénouement* which have an almost fairy-tale quality; the exaggerated aspirations of the servant characters and the extent to which Dorante's love triumphs over the demands of commonsense and social reality come into a similar category. The characters themselves may not feel that they are involved in a game, but through his title Marivaux signals to his audience that the content of this play should be taken none too seriously.

By the time we reach *Les Fausses Confidences* we are in much more plausible territory, for, despite the daring conclusion in which mistress marries not only a servant, but actually her own servant, we can see that the situation is much more closely analogous to that described by Lough and Barber: Araminte is the rich bourgeoise, and Dorante, although ruined, has a social rank which makes him an acceptable partner; Marton too, is quite justified in seeing Dorante as her legitimate partner, since both belong to the servant class. And then, in Marivaux's final play for the Italians, we move ever further from *commedia dell'arte* fantasy, for, as we have seen, *L'Epreuve* depicts a situation which, on the social level at least, is more or less uncontroversial.[10]

But the collapse of Law's system dates from 1720, *L'Ile des esclaves* from 1725, *Le Jeu de l'amour et du hasard* from 1730, *Les Fausses Confidences* from 1737 and *L'Epreuve* from 1740. The plays certainly inhabit post-Law society, but, given this time-scale, they can scarcely be seen as a specific response to the collapse of the *Système*. Should we seek other reasons for the development in Marivaux's approach seen in these plays?

The naming of the characters is not without significance. In *L'Ile des esclaves* names chosen for their relevance to the Greek setting (Iphicrate, Euphrosine, Cléanthis) rub shoulders with the Italianate (Trivelin and Arlequin). It is, of course, the Arlequin archetype who is the most persistently Italian element of Marivaux's theatre, and we note that when he swaps roles and costumes with Iphicrate, even though, as I have suggested, it seems unlikely that the actor playing the part of the noble took over the traditional elements of the costume (the stylized patchwork suit, the mask and the slap-stick), his master does take over his name. This is part of his humiliation: 'Arlequin', as we are told in this play, is little better as an appellation than 'Hé' (428), and we will learn in *Le Jeu de l'amour et du hasard* that one of its principal features is that it rhymes with 'coquin' ('rascal') and 'faquin' ('wretch') (718). In *Le Jeu de l'amour et du hasard*, on the other hand, whilst Silvia in her disguise becomes Lisette and Lisette Silvia, Arlequin even becoming Dorante, Dorante is spared not only Arlequin's traditional costume, but also his name: he becomes Bourguignon. In Marivaux's first important play for the Italians, *Arlequin poli par l'amour*,[11] Silvia had been a fitting partner for Arlequin, but by the time we reach *Le Jeu de l'amour et du hasard* her suitor cannot be expected even to assume his name. Whilst the name Lisette is a traditional enough name for a *soubrette*, it does not have enough archetypal significance to compromise either the dignity or the nature of Silvia's performance as a servant.

Arlequin is another matter: in *L'Ile des esclaves* Iphicrate makes no pretence of actually being Arlequin; all he needs to do is appear offended whenever he is called by this name, and, indeed, the role is so sketchy in the central part of the work that this is virtually all he does do. Dorante, on the other hand, is in disguise, and, in terms of her social status, Silvia has come a long way since her first appearance in a play by Marivaux; there is a sense in which the mere fact of calling himself Arlequin would completely compromise Dorante's wooing of her, for the archetypal force of the name is such that it would be completely inappropriate to the refined servant played by Dorante: 'le galant Bourguignon' (704). The archetypal force of the name also causes it to demand of the actor playing the part, even in disguise, the *lazzi* which are typical of it, and these were not only counter to Marivaux's purpose, they were also, as it were, the property of Thomassin, who was playing the 'real' Arlequin, and not of Luigi (often known as Louis) Riccoboni, who was in the role of Dorante. So the swapping of names demanded by the role-reversal in *L'Ile des esclaves* has disappeared: here roles are still reversed, master pretends to be servant and servant master, but whilst Arlequin still pretends to be Dorante, Dorante emphatically does not pretend to be Arlequin. Arlequin has, in consequence, been marginalized: in *Arlequin poli par l'amour* he is central to the plot. In *L'Ile des esclaves* the servant characters dominate the action and his presence is also, as it were, duplicated by the fact that Iphicrate is given his name. In *Le Jeu de l'amour et du hasard* it is the action involving the masters which is paramount, and when they are on stage we are not even reminded of Arlequin by the disguised Dorante's using his name. And when we reach *L'Epreuve*, Marivaux's last play for the Italians, he has disappeared completely.

When Marivaux calls his female lead in *Les Fausses Confidences* Araminte and in *L'Epreuve* Angélique, it is true that these changes denote a certain change in the type of character, for the former is a rather more emotionally mature woman than the Silvias of the earlier plays, and the latter a little more modest and passive; but these modifications are subtle, the type remains broadly similar and the parts were still played by the actress Silvia. Much the same is true of Riccoboni's Lélios, Dorantes and Lucidor; and if the Marton of *Les Fausses Confidences* is a slightly more serious character than our two Lisettes, the emphasis is surely on 'slightly'. In the case of Arlequin, however, the situation is completely different, for with the name goes the archetype. Indeed, so strong is the archetypal force of the name, that in the scene in *Le Jeu de l'amour et du hasard* in which Arlequin reveals his true identity to Lisette (III. vii) an interesting situation arises: Arlequin confesses to being the servant of Dorante, but does not give his name. Logically, given the symmetry of the plot, Lisette should assume that he is called Bourguignon. But no: a few lines further on, without needing to be told, she calls him Arlequin. That this should occur without causing any sense of incongruity, without giving rise to the feeling that here we have an authorial error, is entirely attributable to the impossibility of dissociating the name from the character-type. The one implies the other, so it would be superfluous for the character to identify himself by name. And so the different name given to Frontin implies a significant difference in character: not for him the traditional trappings of Arlequin's costume. Yves Moraud comments, for instance: 'Arlequin est à peu près le seul personnage qui continue, à la fin du XVII siècle, à porter régulièrement le masque' ('Arlequin is virtually the only character who, at the end of the seventeenth century, still regularly wears a mask').[12] In order to permit the much more convincing portrayal of the master by the disguised Frontin, Marivaux had to make use of such an alternative servant figure: an actor playing Arlequin would have provided the conventional *lazzi*, which the audience would have expected. Not only would the use of the archetypal character without his tomfoolery have disappointed the audience, but the expectations of his name and the conventional trappings of his costume would in any case have ensured that any attempt on Marivaux's part to make the servant's impersonation of the master convincing with him in the role was doomed to failure from the outset.

Kenneth McKee remarks of *L'Epreuve*:

> With its felicitous role for Silvia, *L'Epreuve* was a fitting climax to Marivaux's career as purveyor to the Italian actors. Yet, strangely, the play shows no trace of the old Italian influences. In the twenty years since Marivaux submitted *Arlequin poli par l'amour* to Riccoboni, he drew less and less on the *commedia dell'arte*, and his writing evolved to such a point that none of his last eight plays, except *Les Fausses Confidences*, contain even a minor part for Arlequin.[13]

And that role in *Les Fausses Confidences* has been even more marginalized than the relegation from central character to servant figure that we noted between *Arlequin poli par l'amour* and *Le Jeu de l'amour et du hasard*, for in this play he has even become a secondary servant, the dolt who amuses us with his *lazzi* in a few cameo-like scenes, and has but minor importance for the plot; the main function is reserved for the Machiavellian first servant and *meneur du jeu*, Dubois.

Arlequin was for Marivaux, to a large extent, not merely an archetype, but an actor: Tommaso Visenti, known as Thomassin. There seems no doubt that, at the height of his powers, he played the part very well, but, in the few years before his death in 1739, 'après une longue maladie' ('after a long illness') as the *Mercure* stated,[14] his failing health must have made him a less acrobatic and lively *zanni* and possibly even a less reliable colleague. After his death, the Italians replaced him with Carlo Bertaggi, but Marivaux had already written his final Arlequin; his loss of interest in the role coincides with Thomassin's decline. But is the playwright being controlled by the archetype, or the archetype by the playwright? Does Marivaux stop writing roles for Arlequin because he loses Thomassin, or is it through loyalty for the actor that he goes on writing them for as long as he does? Is the development in Marivaux's theatre a result of the disappearance of Arlequin, or is he dropped because he is incompatible with the new direction that Marivaux is pursuing?

There is no clear or certain answer to these questions, and it would be misguided to claim that one alternative were true to the exclusion of the other, but certain trends related to the concerns we have already examined suggest that the second of each pair of alternatives may represent the dominant force in Marivaux's development. We have seen that Arlequin dominates the plot in *Arlequin poli par l'amour*. *La Double Inconstance* (1723) has a similarly artificial symmetricality to our first two comedies of role-reversal, but the work is constructed in such a way that in each part of the plot one of the *commedia* characters (Arlequin and Silvia, who at this point is still seen as his legitimate partner) is paired with one of the courtly characters, thus spreading the *commedia* influence evenly through the texture of the play. By the time of *L'Ile des esclaves* and *Le Jeu de l'amour et du hasard* the servants are paired together as are the masters, but if in the former the servants dominate the plot, in the latter it is the masters who hold centre stage. In *Les Fausses Confidences* and *L'Epreuve* the symmetry has disappeared and it is the masters who are at the centre of the plot-line, the *commedia* archetypes having been first marginalized and then banished. This development marks a gradual abandonment of the *commedia dell'arte* models which Marivaux adopted at the beginning of his career, in favour of a more emotional and sentimental form of drama represented by the dominance of the higher-born characters, a form which is more typical of later currents in eighteenth-century French theatre.[15] And along with this move towards the dominance of a more serious form of comedy we find a tendency for both settings and social attitudes to become more realistic; the latter trend we have already examined, the former can be seen in the move from the fantasy worlds of *Arlequin poli par l'amour* and *L'Ile des esclaves* to the anonymously contemporary setting of *Le Jeu de l'amour et du hasard* and further to the specific references to Paris found in *Les Fausses Confidences* and *L'Epreuve*; the Madame Dorman for whom Frontin has worked, for instance, lives, 'du côté de la place Maubert, chez un marchand de café, au second' ('by the Place Maubert, at a coffee merchant's, on the second floor'), (1327). There are certainly exceptions to this trend, *La Dispute* (1744), for example, which, although written after *L'Epreuve*, inhabits a world every bit as fantastic as the three island comedies,[16] but the general trend seems clear enough. Indeed, *Les Fausses Confidences* and *L'Epreuve* inhabit very similar milieux to Marivaux's two great novels, *La Vie de Marianne* and *Le Paysan parvenu*, both of which were undertaken during the period between *Le Jeu de l'amour et du hasard* and *Les Fausses Confidences*, and both of which are much concerned with the theme of social climbing which we have also observed in our comedies of disguise and role-reversal.

So the issue of disguise and role-reversal and Arlequin's relationship to this theme turn out to be related to the central development of Marivaux's theatre away from its *commedia dell'arte* origins. Arlequin's inability to change his nature is central to the philosophy of *L'Ile des esclaves*, and adds to the comedy in a play like *Le Jeu de l'amour et du hasard*, where the basic artificiality of the plot structure makes it clear that we should not take lapses in credibility too seriously. A play like *L'Epreuve*, in which our response to Angélique's emotional crisis depends on our ability to believe that she is taken in by Frontin's disguise, would be impossible with Arlequin in the role of disguised servant. For Arlequin cannot ever truly be disguised; Marivaux may polish him, he may become Sauvage, Deucalion or Roi de Serendib,[17] but fundamentally he is always immutably himself.

NOTES

1 *La Commedia dell'arte* (Lyon, L'Hermès, 1982), 71.
2 *'Lazzi': The comic routines of the 'Commedia dell'Arte'* (New York, Performing Arts Journal Publications, 1983), 37.

3 All references to Marivaux's plays are from *Théâtre complet*, ed. Marcel Arland (Paris, Gallimard, 1949).

4 Jean Emelina comments too: 'Les frontispices de l'edition de 1701 [du *Théâtre italien* de Gherardi] en six volumes ne permettent pratiquement pas de distinguer d'après l'habit, Colombine de sa maîtresse' ('The frontispieces of the six-volume 1701 edition [of Gherardi's *Italian Theatre*] hardly allow us, in terms of costume, to distinguish at all between Colombine and her mistress'), *Les Valets et les servantes dans le théâtre comique en France de 1610 à 1700* (Grenoble, PUG, 1975), 398.

5 'Women in Marivaux: Journalist to Dramatist', in *Women and Society in Eighteenth-Century France: Essays in Honour of J.S. Spink*, ed. E. Jacobs, et al. (London, Athlone Press, 1979), 42–54, (49–50).

6 'Old dogs and new tricks: Tradition and revolt in Marivaux's *La Colonie*', in *The British Journal for Eighteenth-Century Studies*, XI (1988), 173–84.

7 *An Introduction to Eighteenth-Century France* (London, Longmans, Green, 1960), 146.

8 *The Bourgeoisie in 18th-Century France* (Princeton University Press, 1955), 102.

9 French Society and Culture: Background for 18th-Century Literature (New Jersey, Prentice-Hall, 1972), 113.

10 There is, of course, Frontin's suggestion in the first scene that he may win Angélique from Lucidor, but, in the event, this comes to nothing. The controversial aspects of this play reside rather in the morality of Lucidor's treatment of Angélique, and perhaps also the fact that Lucidor's manipulations lose for Frontin his rightful bride.

11 The brief allegorical *L'Amour et la Vérité* had been given by the Italians on 3 March 1720. *Arlequin poli par l'amour* followed on 17 October of the same year.

12 *Masques et jeux dans le théâtre comique en France entre 1685 et 1730* (Lille, Atelier Reproduction des Thèses, Université de Lille III, 1977), 393, n. 22.

13 *The Theater of Marivaux* (New York University Press, 1958), 231.

14 See *Théâtre complet*, ed. F. Deloffre, 2 vols. (Paris, Garnier Frères, 1968), II, 341.

15 Although, mercifully, even in his most sentimental plays, *La Mère Confidente* (1735) and *La Femme fidèle* (1755), Marivaux never approaches the humourlessness of Nivelle de La Chaussée at his most larmoyant, of Madame de Graffigny or of Diderot's *drame*. Arlequin may have disappeared from *L'Epreuve* and Frontin's role may be quite restricted, but Maître Blaise is the source of much low comedy. However, whilst the figure of the dialect-speaking peasant may have his roots in similar *commedia dell'arte* characters, Maître Blaise is so French in both his attitudes and accent that he has left any hint of the Italian far behind.

16 *L'Ile des esclaves*, *L'Ile de la raison* and *La Colonie*.

17 See the plays by Delisle de La Drevetière, Piron and Lesage.

7   Ernest Dowson's 'full Pierrot'

GLYN PURSGLOVE

Aubrey Beardsley described his extraordinary novel *Under the Hill* as 'his own little variations on the Tannhäuser theme'.[1] Work after work by the English poets of the 1890s, as well as by their French exemplars, takes the form of a 'variation' (or a series of variations) on one or other 'myth'. Thus, for all its startling individuality Laforgue's *Moralités légendaires* is at least characteristic of its age insofar as it is a set of such 'variations'. The best known works of Ernest Dowson are his shorter lyrical poems, and in reading them one is often conscious of this sense of variations being played upon the inherited 'myths' of poetry. Sometimes – as in 'Libera Me', 'Potnia Thea' or the 'Villanelle of Acheron' – these are the materials of classical mythology itself; sometimes – as in many of Dowson's best lyrics – the poems are peopled by figures from the poems of Horace and Propertius, works which made up a personal mythology for Dowson. In, for example, '*Non sum qualis eram bonae sub regno Cynarae*' and 'Amor Profanus' the Cynara and Lalage of Horace's Odes achieve a status which, while it draws profoundly on their origins, is not limited by them. In Dowson's single dramatic work, *The Pierrot of the Minute*, such techniques of allusion and variation are carried to a new complexity and employed with a striking purposefulness. Since the text is not generally familiar, I shall quote from it at some length in the following account.

Dowson's play was written late in 1892, having been commissioned by the American poet William Theodore Peters, a fellow member of the Rhymers Club. Dowson was normally a dilatory worker, but *Pierrot* was completed in less than three weeks, under considerable pressure. The first performance was scheduled for 22 November at the Chelsea Town Hall. In late October Dowson was writing to Victor Plarr: 'Your letter should have been answered before this: but I have been frightfully busy, having rashly undertaken to make a little Pierrot play, in verse, for Peters . . . the article to be delivered in a fortnight. So until this period of severe mental agony be past, I can go nowhere.'[2] At about the same time (the letter is undated but was probably written on 24 October) Dowson told Peters (whom he sometimes addressed as 'Cher Pierrot' or, as on this occasion, 'My dear Pierrot') 'I am starting on the play, & will push on with it *quam celerime*. But I find it excessively difficult and fear that with a limitation of two characters I can not attempt any dramatic effect. Is this required? Or will you be satisfied with a *folium rosae* which must depend entirely on its verses and the speaking of these to carry it through, with the help of the Pierrot's tradition?'[3] He continued to find the work hard; he had never written under the pressure of such a deadline. As he confided – only half-jokingly – to Plarr, there were other worries associated with its composition too: 'I would this play were done: half of it is completed & I have seven days more, but the second half is mightily oppressing me. And I am horribly afraid that when it is written I may be worried with rehearsals and enforced company with terrible South Kensington young ladies and fashionable Chelsea Mesdames.'[4] Work continued; he acknowledged helpful criticism from Peters and from Lionel Johnson. A letter to Arthur Moore (probably written on 10 November) wittily (although inaccurately – the passage he has in mind is to be found in The Book of Job XXXI, 35 – not in Solomon) expresses his 'sufferings': 'I am beginning to realize, that the Hebrew word which has been translated "book" in the wish of Solomon, that his "enemy had written one" should have been rendered "play". Oh, that mine enemy would write one, or that I had never been foolish enough to try . . . The performance is fixed for the 22nd. next at Chelsea Town Hall . . . I am so awfully sick of it that I feel inclined to take a week at Brighton until it is done.'[5] At other times his enthusiasm was greater and he took a very lively interest in the details of his play. On 2 November he was writing again to Peters:

The play is done, I think, save only the song to your formula, which I will try & make before Saturday. I hope you will like my ending; but I am not quite sure about it. Will you not write an epilogue? I think that should be, after the excellent XVIIIth custom by a different hand to the play. My notion is that the birds twitter, Pierrot sinks back on his couch, She calls up music to be his mandragore; he sleeps. Then she says a speech over him, & retires: Pierrot is left sleeping; her escort of moonbeams sing the song as yet unwritten, and the curtain falls, Pierrot lying asleep. A moment or two afterwards it goes up again, &

Pierrot comes forward with his epilogue to the ladies, which I hope you will write.[6]

Dowson speaks of his play's effect being dependent on 'the help of the Pierrot's tradition'. By now a number of historians have traced the development of that tradition – from Pierrot's emergence from the Pedrolino of the *commedia dell'arte*, acquiring his familiar name and costume late in the seventeenth century in France, to his innumerable later transformations on the stage and on canvas, in verse and in music.[7] Dowson's generation of English poets was heavily influenced by their immediate predecessors amongst the French poets; Dowson himself had spent a good deal of his childhood in France and was especially well read in French poetry. For him 'the Pierrot's tradition' certainly included the poems of, for example, Giraud, Verlaine and Laforgue. It also included more trivial incarnations, such as Michael Carré's very popular *L'enfant prodigue*, which Dowson saw and enjoyed in 1891, or the versions on the stages of the London music-halls of which Dowson was so fond. Dowson was not, of course, alone in the London of the 1890s in his interest in Pierrot – it was a figure to be found everywhere. Indeed Arthur Symons could insist that 'Pierrot is one of the types of our century, of the moment in which we live or of the moment, perhaps, out of which we are just passing.'[8] Certainly Dowson's play suggests that he found in Pierrot a figure of profound typicality, both personal and general. Most who employed the figure of Pierrot did so as the embodiment of a stance, an attitude towards the pains and joys of life. Symons, for instance, describes the Pierrot in terms of just such a complex of attitudes:

He feels himself to be sickening with a fever, or else perilously convalescent; for love is a disease, which he is too weak to resist or endure. He has worn his heart on his sleeve so long, that it has hardened in the cold air. He knows that his face is powdered, and if he sobs, it is without tears; and it is hard to distinguish, under the chalk, if the grimace which twists his mouth awry is more laughter or mockery. He knows that he is condemned to be always in public, that emotion would be supremely out of keeping with his costume, that he must remember to be fantastic if he would not be merely ridiculous. And so he becomes exquisitely false, dreading above all things that 'one touch of nature' which would ruffle his disguise, and leave him defenceless. Simplicity, in him, being the most laughable thing in the world, he becomes learned, perverse, intellectualising his pleasure, brutalising his intellect; his mournful contemplation of things becoming a kind of grotesque joy, which he expresses in the only symbols at his command, tracing his Giotto's O with the elegance of his pirouette.[9]

Such a Pierrot embodies a condition; Dowson's concern, on the other hand, is with a process, with the origins of that condition about which Symons writes so eloquently. His Pierrot is part of an explanatory myth.

The Pierrot of the Minute is set in a glade of the Petit Trianon, by a Doric temple. It is twilight and a little Cupid upon a pedestal is visible. Pierrot enters, carrying lilies. He is presented to us – through his opening speech – as a kind of questing knight:

> My journey's end! This surely is the glade
> Which I was promised: I have well obeyed!
> A clue of lilies was I bid to find,
> Where the green alleys most obscurely wind;
> Where tall oaks darkliest canopy o'erhead,
> And moss and violet make the softest bed;
> Where the path ends, and leagues behind me lie
> The gleaming courts and gardens of Versailles;
> The lilies streamed before me, green and white;
> I gathered, following: they led me right,
> To the bright temple and the sacred grove:
> This is, in truth, the very shrine of Love!   (1–12)

This Pierrot is in that tradition of dreaming and enchanted travellers who include the Lady in Milton's *Comus* and the shipwrecked courtiers of *The Tempest* – Dowson's text later contains clear echoes of both works. We do not yet know who or what Pierrot has 'obeyed' in pursuing his quest. The language alludes lightly, but unmistakably, to myths of quest and test; even the world of the traditional ballads is evoked in a phrase such as 'leagues behind me lie'. In describing the beautiful 'clue' of lilies Pierrot uses a verb – 'streamed' – whose full significance will only become clear later. The lilies, of course, are a recurrent symbolic prop in the work of the 'decadent' poets. Theodore Wratislaw writes of 'the silver lips of lilies virginal' and in 'White Lilies' uses the flowers to judge the 'cultured vice' of a 'frail spirit',[10] while Arthur Symons, in 'Morbidezza', demonstrates the familiar connection of lily and moon:

White girl, your flesh is lilies
Grown 'neath a frozen moon,
So still is
The rapture of your swoon
Of whiteness, snow or lilies.

The virginal revealment,
Your bosom's wavering slope,
Concealment,
'Neath fainting heliotrope,
Of whitest white's revealment,

Is like a bed of lilies,
A jealous-guarded row,
Whose will is
Simply chaste dreams: – but oh,
The alluring scent of lilies![11]

In his most famous lyric – 'Non sum qualis' – Dowson opposes the
riotously flung roses to Cynara's 'pale, lost lilies' (the poem merits
quotation in full, since its central tensions have an obvious bearing on
Dowson's working out of his themes in his Pierrot-play):

Non sum qualis eram bonae sub regno Cynarae

Last night, ah, yesternight, betwixt her lips and mine
There fell thy shadow, Cynara! thy breath was shed
Upon my soul between the kisses and the wine;
And I was desolate and sick of an old passion,
    Yea, I was desolate and bowed my head:
I have been faithful to thee, Cynara! in my fashion.

All night upon mine heart I felt her warm heart beat,
Night-long within mine arms in love and sleep she lay;
Surely the kisses of her bought red mouth were sweet;
But I was desolate and sick of an old passion,
    When I awoke and found the dawn was gray:
I have been faithful to thee, Cynara! in my fashion.

I have forgot much, Cynara! gone with the wind,
Flung roses, roses riotously with the throng,
Dancing, to put thy pale, lost lilies out of mind;
But I was desolate and sick of an old passion,
    Yea, all the time, because the dance was long:
I have been faithful to thee, Cynara! in my fashion.

> I cried for madder music and for stronger wine,
> But when the feast is finished and the lamps expire,
> Then falls thy shadow, Cynara! the night is thine;
> And I am desolate and sick of an old passion,
>   Yea hungry for the lips of my desire:
> I have been faithful to thee, Cynara! in my fashion.

Associated with all that is chaste, coldly virginal and unattainable, the lilies are hardly a promising 'clue' for one who seeks love, for one whose quest is to be conducted in the grove of Venus. The lilies which streamed before Pierrot were 'green and white'. Richard Le Gallienne tells us that 'innocence has but two colours, white or green'.[12] Led by the stream of white and green, Dowson's Pierrot has completed the first stage of his quest. Like any good questing knight of romance, Pierrot's search is in part a search for lessons about his own identity. He 'timidly' approaches the temple:

> It is so solitary, I grow afraid.
> Is there no priest here, no devoted maid?
> Is there no oracle, no voice to speak,
> Interpreting to me the word I seek?

> (*A very gentle music of lutes floats out from the temple. Pierrot starts back; he shows extreme surprise; then he returns to the foreground, and crouches down in rapt attention until the music ceases. His face grows puzzled and petulant.*)

> Too soon! too soon! in that enchanting strain,
> Days yet unlived, I almost lived again:
> It almost taught me that I most would know –
> Why am I here, and why am I Pierrot?   (13–20)

As he takes a scroll from his bosom we learn of the 'commandment' he has obeyed in making his journey here:

> '*He loves to-night who never loved before;*
> *Who ever loved, tonight shall love once more.*'
> *I* never loved! I know not what love is.
> I am so ignorant – but what is this?

> (*Reads*)

> '*Who would adventure to Encounter Love*
> *Must rest one night within this hallowed grove.*

Cast down thy lilies, which have led thee on,
Before the tender feet of Cupidon.'
Thus much is done, the night remains to me.
Well, Cupidon, be my security!
Here is more writing, but too faint to read.

(*He puzzles for a moment, then casts the scroll down.*)

Hence vain old parchment. I have learnt thy rede.   (28–39)

His magical scroll has invited him to 'adventure'. The scroll's initial
pronouncement is, of course, an adaptation of the refrain of the
Pervigilium Veneris – 'cras amet qui nunquam amavit quique amavit
cras amet'.[13] The echo is heavily ironic. The *Pervigilium Veneris* is a
festive poem (its specific occasion the *trinoctium* of Venus), a
celebration of vitality, of freshness and life, in a land and a time where:

ver novum, ver iam canorum, ver renatus orbis est;
vere concordant amores, vere nubunt alites,
et nemus comam resolvit de maritis imbribus

and from which 'the maid of Delos' is urged to retire. The pleasures of
love pulse through both society and nature:

rura fecundat voluptas: rura Venerem sentiunt:
ipse Amor puer Dionae rure natus creditur:
hunc ager cum parturiret ipsa suscepit sinu,
ipsa florum delicatis educavit osculis.

cras amet qui nunquam amavit quique amavit cras amet.

ecce iam super genestas explicant tauri latus,
quisque coetus continetur coniugali foedere:
subter umbras cum maritis ecce balantum gregem,
et canoras non tacere diva iussit alites.

cras amet qui nunquam amavit quique amavit cras amet.

Pierrot's experience, on the other hand, is of solitariness. Where the
Latin poem celebrates man and his part in love's annual renewal of the
world, Pierrot's presence in the garden, not on a spring morning but in
the gathering gloom of twilight, teaches him only the lesson of his own
solitude:

1. Aubrey Beardsley's frontispiece to *The Pierrot of the Minute*, 1897 (see p. 156).

Ah me! how pitiful to be alone.
My brown birds told me much, but in mine ear
They never whispered this – I learned it here:
The soft wood sounds, the rustlings in the breeze,
Are but the stealthy kisses of the trees.
Each flower and fern in this enchanted wood
Leans to her fellow, and is understood;
The eglantine, in loftier station set,
Stoops down to woo the maidly violet.
In gracile pairs the very lilies grow:
None is companionless except Pierrot.   (61–71)

Pierrot sleeps and from the temple there 'streams' (the earlier 'stream'
of lilies is, as it were, refined a further degree) 'a bright radiance, white
and cold', which falls upon his sleeping face. The whiteness of
moonlight meets Pierrot's own whiteness. This is decidedly not the
landscape of the *Pervigilium Veneris*, and Diana has not withdrawn.
Rather it is with her, or at least with one of her surrogates, that Pierrot is
to 'prove . . . what is this thing called love' (77). From the temple there
descends a Moon Maiden who stands and considers the sleeping figure.
Her initial words make it clear that Dowson is now concerned with
variations upon an additional myth – that of Diana and Endymion:

    Who is this mortal
        Who ventures to-night
    To woo an immortal,
        Cold, cold the moon's light,
    For sleep at this portal,
        Bold lover of night.
    Fair is the mortal
        In soft, silken white,
    Who seeks an immortal.
        Ah, lover of night,
    Be warned at the portal,
        And save thee in flight!   (78–89)

Many a poet, English and otherwise, has told, like John Fletcher,

    How the pale *Phœbe*, hunting in a grove,
    First saw the boy *Endimion*, from whose eyes,
    She took eternall fire, that never dies,
    How she convaid him softly in a sleepe,

His temples bound with poppy to the steep
Head of old *Latmus*, where she stoopes each night,
Gilding the mountaine with her brothers light
To kisse her sweetest.[14]

For Michael Drayton, in his neoplatonic *Endimion and Phoebe* of 1595, the human lover is a type of both the philosopher and of the aspiring human soul; for Keats, in *Endymion: a Poetic Romance*, the story occasions an exploration of ideas about the nature of poetry and the poet, about the search for ideal beauty (Dowson perhaps remembers the business of the scroll in Book III of Keats's poem). In the poems of both Drayton and Keats, Endymion is a figure of some grandeur. Some Victorians still viewed the figure that way. Coventry Patmore, in an essay called 'Dreams' which was first published in the *St James's Gazette* in 1887, alludes to the myth as an allegory of human 'experiences of the realities of spiritual perception' and insists that,

> To refuse to give to dreams the weight they deserve as being often among the most impressive and even life-affecting parts of man's experience, is stupidity too great to be argued with. If to dream is to dwell in unrealities, not knowing them for such, what is the life of many but an uninterrupted dream? The wise, however, will own with Goethe, 'They are not shadows which produce a dream. I know they are eternal, for they ARE'. He who has known, even once in his life, the *somnus Endymionis*, in which the Queen of Purity has visited him as being also the Queen of Love, lifting his ideal, if not his way of life, for ever after, and convincing him that the felicity of the spirit and its senses is as far above the best of the waking life of the body as the electric light is above that of a smoking torch, will have discarded the ignorant distinction between realities and dreams, and will understand how
>
> > Real are the dreams of gods, and smoothly pass
> > Their pleasures in a long immortal dream.[15]

Lacking the obvious grandeur of most of his predecessors, Dowson's 'Endymion' is a figure 'burdened with a little basket' who moves 'timidly' and 'starts at his shadow' – but his experiences serve to present an examination of issues no less important. The Endymion of myth travelled the heavens and acquired immortality. Dowson's is but a Pierrot (and an Endymion) 'of the minute' and when he proclaims similar aspirations he is readily persuaded to settle for something rather less obviously sublime:

THE LADY
  What wouldst thou of the maiden of the moon?
  Until the cock crow I may grant thy boon.

PIERROT
  Then, sweet Moon Maiden, in some magic car,
  Wrought wondrously of many a homeless star –
  Such must attend thy journeys through the skies, –
  Drawn by a team of milk-white butterflies,
  Whom, with soft voice and music of thy maids,
  Thou urgest gently through the heavenly glades;
  Mount me beside thee, bear me far away
  From the low regions of the solar day;
  Over the rainbow, up into the moon,
  Where is thy palace and thine opal throne;
  There on thy bosom –

THE LADY
  Too ambitious boy!
  I did but promise thee one hour of joy.
  This tour thou plannest, with a heart so light,
  Could hardly be completed in a night.
  Hast thou no craving less remote than this?

PIERROT
  Would it be impudent to beg a kiss?   (178–96)

We are offered plentiful reasons to think that this desire, also, is 'too
ambitious'. It too is a desire for forbidden knowledge. His failure to
read to the end of his scroll, and his hubristic dismissal of it as a 'vain
old parchment' have already struck an ominous note. As the Moon
Maiden first stoops – Diana-like – over the sleeping Pierrot she calls him
'unwitting boy' and muses 'What Pierrot ever has escaped his fate?' (92–
3). As she looks at him she finds him still 'arrayed in innocence' (104)
and resolves

    Well, I will warn him, though, I fear, too late –
    What Pierrot ever has escaped his fate? (106–7)

On his awakening she does, indeed, warn him clearly enough:

    PIERROT   (*In ecstasy, throwing himself at her feet*)
      Then have I ventured and encountered Love?

> *THE LADY*
>   Not yet, rash boy! and, if thou wouldst be wise,
>   Return unknowing; he is safe who flies.   (119–21)

He is advised to 'Return unknowing' – but Pierrot, in the garden, inevitably will not choose to leave without acquiring the promised 'knowledge', however dangerous. He will plead with the Lady:

> Unveil thyself, although thy beauty be
> Too luminous for my mortality.   (126–7)

There is a beautiful naïvety to Pierrot's intrepidity. The Lady asks him if he did not read the scroll's warning, and he tells her that he read it all 'save where it was illegible and hard'. She reads him the warning:

> '*Au Petit Trianon*, at night's full noon,
> Mortal, beware the kisses of the moon!
> Whoso seeks her she gathers like a flower –
> He gives a life, and only gains an hour.'

> *PIERROT   (Laughing recklessly)*
>   Bear me away to thine enchanted bower,
>   All of my life I venture for an hour.

> *THE LADY*
>   Take up thy destiny of short delight;
>   I am thy lady for a summer's night.
>   Lift up your viols, maidens of my train,
>   And work such havoc on this mortal's brain
>   That for a moment he may touch and know
>   Immortal things, and be full Pierrot.   (138–49)

In his 'moment' of contact with the immortal, Pierrot may, indeed, become 'full Pierrot', achieve a new wholeness of life and identity. But he will do so only at the price of knowing, for ever after, how far he is from that fullness of life. No longer will he be 'arrayed in innocence'. Not for him the eternal sleep of the immortal Endymion. Whether he wishes it or not, he is now the servant of the moon, once he has kissed the Moon Maiden. It is with good reason that when they kiss 'he withdraws with a petulant shiver. She utters a peal of clear laughter.' The coldness and sweetness of the Maiden's lips brings a new knowledge to Pierrot – she is a Keatsian *belle dame sans merci*, even a type of Graves's 'White Goddess'[16]:

Cold are thy lips, more cold than I can tell;
Yet would I hang on them, thine icicle!
Cold is thy kiss, more cold than I could dream
Arctus sits, watching the Boreal stream:
But with its frost such sweetness did conspire
That all my veins are filled with running fire;
Never I knew that life contained such bliss
As the divine completeness of a kiss.

In that 'completeness' is all his future sense of his own and life's
incompleteness, the awareness of his exile from 'fullness'. Unlike
Endymion he must return to live in the mortal, fallen world, now
unprotected by his previous innocence. He, along with 'dreamers all,
and all who sing and love', must acknowledge the moon's power over
his heart. He has joined the company of 'the lunatic, the lover and the
poet'.[17] The Lady's final speech, once again over a sleeping Pierrot,
makes clear the future effects of this experience:

I leave thee, sleeper! Yea, I leave thee now,
Yet take my legacy upon thy brow:
Remember me, who was compassionate,
And opened for thee once, the ivory gate.
I come no more, thou shalt not see my face
When I am gone to mine exalted place:
Yet all thy days are mine, dreamer of dreams,
All silvered over with the moon's pale beams:
Go forth and seek in each fair face in vain,
To find the image of thy love again.
All maids are kind to thee, yet never one
Shall hold thy truant heart till day be done.
Whom once the moon has kissed, loves long and late,
Yet never finds the maid to be his mate.
Farewell, dear sleeper, follow out thy fate.   (477–91)

Through his variations on mythical themes, Dowson discovered in
the figure of the Pierrot a personal 'myth' which seems to underlie, and
explain, much that is most typical of his work, and which has an
interesting relationship with the events of his own life.

It was in 1891, the year before the composition of *The Pierrot of the
Minute*, that Dowson met, and fell in love with, Adelaide Foltinowicz,
daughter of the impoverished Polish proprietors of a restaurant in
Soho. Dowson was twenty-two; Adelaide Foltinowicz was just twelve.

It was to her innocence and simple charm that Dowson was attracted. She was no more attainable than the Moon Maiden was attainable for Pierrot. By the time that he was writing his play, the tensions and difficulties of his feelings towards Adelaide were making themselves felt. To an old Oxford friend, Sam Smith, Dowson wrote:

> I go on in precisely the same situation in Poland. I can't somehow screw myself up to making a declaration of myself to *Madame*, although I am convinced that it is the most reasonable course . . . She herself is sometimes very charming, sometimes not! But in the latter case it is merely my own abominably irritable temper which is to blame. I have had an interview of abnormal length with Lionel [Johnson], in which he argued with me most strenuously all night. He had been dining at my Uncle's (the Hoole's), and apparently this infatuation of mine was openly discussed the whole of dinner-time *par tous ces gens*. So I do not see how it can go on very much longer without an understanding or a *fracas* – the latter I suppose will be inevitable first – with my people. Altogether *Je m'embête horriblement*; and my only consolation is that if it is so obvious to all my friends and relatives it ought to be equally so to the Poles as well . . . Another year of the stress and tension and uncertainty of these last 6 months will leave me without a nerve in my composition and I am not sure whether I have any now.[18]

Writing to Smith in April 1893, Dowson tried to take a positive view of things:

> It is a very odd history – Heaven knows how it will end. In my more rational moments however, I am inclined to consider that that is of quite secondary importance; the important thing is that one should have, just once, experienced the mystery, an absolute absorption in one particular person. It reconciles all inconsistencies in the order of things, and above all it seems once and for all to reduce to utter absurdity any material explanation of itself or of the world.[19]

Of course, life could scarcely be lived always as it occasionally appeared in 'rational moments'.

The situation had its affinities with Dowson's favourite 'myths' in Horace. It must have seemed like a strange reminiscence of one of the 'Lalage' poems – Ode Five of the Second Book (complete with another reminder of lunar purity):

Nondum subacta ferre iugum valet
cervice, nondum munia comparis
	aequare nec tauri ruentis
	in venerem tolerare pondus.

circa virentis est animus tuae
campos iuvencae, nunc fluviis gravem
	solantis aestum, nunc in udo
	ludere cum vitulis salicto

praegestientis, tolle cupidinem
inmitis uvae: iam tibi lividos
	distinguet Autumnus racemos
	purpureo varius colore.

iam te sequetur:(currit enim ferox
aetas, et illi, quos tibi dempserit
	apponet annos), iam proterva
	fronte petet Lalage maritum,

dilecta, quantum non Pholoë fugax,
non Chloris, albo sic umero nitens,
	ut pura nocturno renidet
	luna mari Cnidiusve Gyges,

quem si puellarum insereres choro,
mire sagacis falleret hospites
	discrimen obscurum solutis
	crinibus ambiguoque voltu.[20]

Whether Dowson ever wanted his 'Lalage' to grow up is doubtful; he probably preferred her childish innocence, more readily idealized and less threatening. Indeed, reading the account of their relationship in Mark Longaker's biography of Dowson,[21] it is hard not to feel that he was attracted to Adelaide by the very fact that she was unattainable, and that differences of age and class were likely to keep her that way. Poems such as the seven 'Sonnets of a Little Girl' or 'Ad Domnulam Suam' suggest that his feelings were not of a sort to find fulfilment in a relationship with a mature woman (though these poems were not written with Adelaide in mind):

Little lady of my heart!
	Just a little longer,
Love me: we will pass and part,
	Ere this love grow stronger.

. . .

> Little lady of my heart!
>   Just a little longer,
> Be a child: then, we will part,
>   Ere this love grow stronger.

When Adelaide did, like Horace's Lalage, 'seek a husband', it was not to be Dowson. In 1897 she married Auguste, her father's waiter.

The Pierrot of the Minute establishes a myth by which to account for the unattainability of human love, for the transience of human joy, for the characteristic decadent tension between an ideal once known but now lost and an inferior actuality. One English Renaissance allegorizer of myths tells us (amongst other things) that 'every man may be called *Endymion*, for we are all in love with air and empty clouds, with toys and vanities'.[22] Dowson's Pierrot can now love only 'air and empty clouds' but will, to his pain, never forget that he has known a 'dear Immortal':

PIERROT
> Since I know thee, dear Immortal,
> Is my heart become a blossom,
> To be worn upon thy bosom.
> When thou turn me from this portal,
> Whither shall I, hapless mortal,
> Seek love out and win again
> Heart of me that thou retain?

THE LADY
> In and out the woods and valleys,
> Circling, soaring like a swallow,
> Love shall flee and thou shalt follow:
> Though he stops awhile and dallies,
> Never shalt thou stay his malice!
> Moon-kissed mortals seek in vain
> To possess their hearts again!

PIERROT
> Tell me, Lady, shall I never
> Rid me of this grievous burden!
> Follow Love and find his guerdon
> In no maiden whatsoever?
> Wilt thou hold my heart for ever?

2. Aubrey Beardsley's cul-de-lampe to *The Pierrot of the Minute*, 1897 (see p. 157).

Rather would I thine forget,
In some earthly Pierrette!

THE LADY
   Thus thy fate, whate'er thy will is!
Moon-struck child, go seek my traces
Vainly in all mortal faces!
In and out among the lilies,
Court each rural Amaryllis:
Seek the signet of Love's hand
In each courtly Corisande!   (281–308)

The Moon Maiden and Cynara alike are symbols of an innocent joy
which is forever lost but which can never be forgotten, to which the
lover and the poet must remain faithful in their fashion – in the very act
of betrayal. In its widest sense Dowson's play is his 'variation' on the
Fall. Pierrot may be Endymion and Everyman; he is also, in the simplest
and grandest sense, Man. In this garden he has had his time with the
immortal, and now he must be turned from the garden's portals,
expelled after his 'minute' in Eden. The image of the paradisal garden
from which the poet-lover is excluded occurs on many occasions in
Dowson's lyrical poems. It underlies 'Nuns of the Perpetual Adora-
tion', whose nuns are 'calm' and 'secure' in their garden 'behind high
convent walls'. It is given explicit expression in 'Terre Promise' which
remembers 'minutes' of happiness and records the 'always' of later
knowledge:

Even now the fragrant darkness of her hair
Had brushed my cheek; and once, in passing by,
Her hand upon my hand lay tranquilly:
What things unspoken trembled in the air!

Always I know, how little severs me
From mine heart's country, that is yet so far;
And must I lean and long across a bar,
That half a word would shatter utterly?

Ah might it be, that just by touch of hand,
Or speaking silence, shall the barrier fall;
And she shall pass, with no vain words at all,
But droop into mine arms, and understand!

The measure of Pierrot's loss is wonderfully captured in two of the
illustrations which Aubrey Beardsley prepared for the publication of

Dowson's play in 1897. In the frontispiece a charming and youthful Pierrot, deep in a heavily flowered garden, looks out at the reader. Beardsley is at his most Watteau-esque; there is a distinct resemblance to the Gilles-Pierrot of paintings such as the *Italian Comedians* in the National Gallery of Art in Washington, or *Gilles and Four Other Characters of the Commedia dell'Arte* in the Louvre. In the book's cul-de-lampe, however, a Pierrot with a skull-like head looks back over his shoulder as he leaves the garden. The knowledge of death is most certainly upon his face. There is no reminiscence of Watteau here; we are more likely to think of a Renaissance *Expulsion from Paradise* – save that Pierrot does not even have an Eve who has shared his experience to keep him company. His isolation is even greater, his misery the more profound. There is no sense in Beardsley's picture – or in Dowson's text – that Pierrot has the world all before him, or that he can be confident that providence will be his guide. His is, indeed, a 'solitary way'. It seems right and proper that we should be reminded of *Paradise Lost*; in its own much smaller way, in a thoroughly non-epic age, Dowson's 'Dramatic Phantasy in One Act' has found means to articulate both a personal and a historical unease in terms of one of the grandest myths of all. In doing so he has certainly found a way of showing us 'full Pierrot'.

NOTES

All quotations from *The Pierrot of the Minute* and from other poems by Ernest Dowson are taken from *The Poetical Works of Ernest Dowson*, edited by Desmond Flower, 1934 (3rd edition, London, Cassell, 1967). Quotations from *The Pierrot of the Minute* are followed by the appropriate line numbers.

1 Quoted thus (p.245) in Annette Lavers, 'Aubrey Beardsley, Man of Letters', in I. Fletcher (ed.) *Romantic Mythologies* (London, Routledge & Kegan Paul, 1967), 243–70.
2 *The Letters of Ernest Dowson*, Collected and edited by Desmond Flower and Henry Maas (London, Cassell, 1967), 246.
3 Ibid., 245.
4 Ibid., 247.
5 Ibid., 252.
6 Ibid., 249–50.
7 Amongst the most useful accounts are those by Robert F. Storey, *Pierrot, A Critical History of a Mask* (Princeton University Press, 1978); Constant Mic, *La Commedia dell'Arte, ou le théâtre des comédiens italiens des XVIᵉ, XVIIᵉ &*

XVIIIe siècles (Paris, J. Schiffrin, 1927); Georges Doutrepont, *L'Evolution du type de pierrot dans la littérature française* (Brussels, Académie Royale de Langue et de Littérature Françaises, 1925) and *Les types populaires de la Littérature Française* (Brussels, M. Lamertin, 1928); Paul Hugounet, *Mimes et Pierrots: Notes et documents inédits pour servir à l'histoire de la pantomime* (Paris, Fischbacher, 1889); A. G. Lehmann, 'Pierrot and *fin de siècle*' in *Romantic Mythologies*, ed. I. Fletcher, 209–23.

8 *Studies in Seven Arts* (London, M. Secker 1924), 96; the essay is dated 1898.
9 Ibid., 96–7.
10 'Hothouse Flowers' and 'White Lilies' in *Orchids* (London, L. Smithers, 1896), 23 and 10.
11 'Morbidezza', *Silhouettes*, 2nd edition (London, L. Smithers, 1896), 13.
12 '*The Boom in Yellow*', in *Prose Fancies*, Second series, (London, J. Lane, 1896), 79–89; the quotation occurs on p.79.
13 All quotations from the *Pervigilium Veneris* are taken from the Loeb Classics edition, *Catullus, Tibullus and Pervigilium Veneris*, ed. F. W. Cornish (Cambridge (Mass) and London, Heinemann 1924).
14 *The Faithful Shepherdess*, I.iii.36–43, quoted from *The Dramatic Works of the Beaumont and Fletcher Canon*, ed. F. Bowers (Cambridge University Press, 1976) III, 513. Useful information on some of the many English poets to have treated the theme can be found in E. S. Le Comte, *Endymion in England* (New York, King's Crown Press, 1944) and E. C. Guild, *A List of Poems Illustrating Greek Mythology in the English Poetry of the Nineteenth Century* (Brunswick ME, Bowdoin College, 1891). An interesting comparison is with Symons's 'Pierrot in half-Mourning', a poem added to *Silhouettes* in 1896:

> I that am Pierrot, pray you pity me!
> To be so young, so old in misery:
> See me, and how the winter of my grief
> Wastes me, and how I whiten like a leaf,
> And how, like a lost child, lost and afraid,
> I seek the shadow, I that am a shade,
> I that have loved a moonbeam, nor have won
> Any Diana to Endymion.
> Pity me, for I have but loved too well
> The hope of the too fair impossible.
> Ah, it is she, she. Columbine: again
> I see her, and I woo her, and in vain.
> She lures me with her beckoning finger-tips;
> How her eyes shine for me, and how her lips
> Bloom for me, roses, roses red and rich!
> She waves to me the white arms of a witch
> Over the world: I follow, I forget
> All, but she'll love me yet, she'll love me yet!   (*Silhouettes*, 1896, 90)

15 Coventry Patmore, *Courage in Politics and Other Essays, 1885–1896* (Oxford University Press, 1921), 100–101. The lines quoted are from Keats's *Lamia* (I.127–8).

16 'La Belle Dame Sans Merci', of whose poet-lover the 'narrator' remarks 'I see a lily on thy brow' (l.9), is obviously connected with Keats's feelings towards Fanny Brawne. Interestingly, Dowson himself apparently compared his relationship with Adelaide Foltinowicz with that between Keats and Fanny Brawne (see Mark Longaker, *Ernest Dowson*, 3rd edition (Philadelphia, University of Pennsylvania Press, 1967), 246.

17 *A Midsummer Night's Dream*, V.i.7.

18 *Letters*, ed.cit., 231.

19 Ibid., 279.

20 *The Odes and Epodes*, Loeb edition, ed. C.E.Bennett (Cambridge (Mass) and London, Heinemann, 1919), 118.

21 Op. cit.

22 Alexander Ross, *Mystagogus Poeticus or The Muses interpreter* (London, 1648), 107.

8   *Commedia dell'arte* in Rubén Darío and Leopoldo Lugones

DAVID GEORGE

Spain is different from France or Italy in that prior to the late nineteenth century, there are relatively few recorded instances of *commedia dell'arte* in either its popular culture or its literature and art. Those that there are are almost invariably associated with the Lent carnival. The company of the Italian actor, Alberto Ganassa, who enjoyed a considerable reputation in Spain in the late sixteenth century, so caught the imagination of the organizers of the Valencia carnival that in 1592 *ganassas* are found in a carnival procession in Valencia.[1] In the late eighteenth century too there is evidence that *commedia dell'arte* characters appeared as part of the repertoires of Italian troupes who were in Spain at the time. These troupes also performed pantomime, acrobatics and puppet shows and so a phenomenon somewhat similar to that of the French *théâtres de la foire* seems to have existed in Spain. The *commedia dell'arte* is also once more linked with carnival in eighteenth-century Spain, as J. E. Varey explains:

> La acción de una de las pantomimas de 1774 se localizó en un molino . . . el cartel de este año la llama 'una mui lucida diversión nueva, que será una Comedia Inglesa, que han hecho en Paris la Quaresma pasada: el título es, las Desgracias de Arlinquin, y las Picardías del Molinero, volando al aire Casas, Ventanas, Molinero y Arlinquin todo junto, adornado de Tramoyas, todas de buen gusto.'[2]

> The action of one of the pantomimes in 1774 is set in a mill . . . the billboard of that year calls it 'a splendid new entertainment, which will be an English play, which they put on in Paris during Lent last year: the title is, The Misfortunes of Harliquin, and the mischievous acts of the miller, with houses, windows, Miller Harliquin and all flying through the air, decorated with stage machinery, all in good taste.'

The carnival is indicated by the reference to Quaresma, of which the Arlinquin forms a part.

A new kind of interest in the *commedia* emerges in the late nineteenth and early twentieth centuries, due almost entirely to French influences on the Hispanic literature, particularly poetry, of the period. Literature written in Spanish was transformed in the period from the late 1880s to the First World War by a movement known as *modernismo*, although the movement began in prose.

I say 'literature written in Spanish' rather than 'Spanish literature', because *modernismo* was essentially a Latin American phenomenon, although, naturally, it did influence Spanish writers, and overlaps to an extent with the literary movement in Spain known as the Generation of 1898. D. L. Shaw, however, stresses the differences between the two movements and highlights some of the essential features of *modernismo*:

> In contrast to the writers of the '98 group in Spain, who were basically preoccupied with the national problem, the *modernistas* were self-consciously cosmopolitan in outlook. Like Pater and Wilde in Britain and the Parnassians in France, the *modernistas* were aggressively devoted to conscious aestheticism, to Art as the supreme absolute, to Beauty as the overriding ideal, and to radical formal innovation in prose-writing and poetry as the means of its achievement. They exalted creative imagination and fantasy as opposed to realist observation and to the accepted canons of high nineteenth-century bourgeois literature.[3]

Modernista literature is characterized by interest in what was viewed as eternal rather than in contemporary issues, in classical and Germanic myths and in eighteenth-century France. *Modernista* poems are often set in far-away or imaginary lands, and populated by pale princesses wearing exquisite jewellery who stroll in elegant gardens where splendid peacocks show their tails, or by rivers where beautiful swans float gently by. To some extent this is, of course, a caricature of *modernismo*, and is an oversimplification. It does, though, help to give the flavour at least of the early years of the movement.

Later *modernismo*, however, belonging roughly to the period after 1905, tends to be more ironic and detached, and concerned to blend the poetic with images of the prosaic and the everyday. The poets in question considered that *modernismo* itself had degenerated into cliché, and that poetry had to be renewed once more. Clearly, the question is much more complex than this, but there is a general tendency from idealism to scepticism. The critic José Olivio Jiménez sums up the change; he characterizes early *modernismo* in the following way:

> . . . el respeto a la belleza; la búsqueda de una palabra armoniosa y pura, que reflejara la armonía secreta de la creación tan añorada por el artista de la época . . . la confianza en el poder salvador y por ello sagrado del arte . . . fe en la palabra artística, conciencia de arte . . . se aventuraron por los ámbitos de lo que no tenían: el lujo y el placer, siempre asociados en el decadente al dolor y a la muerte. O se evadieron a realidades igualmente lejanas: al brillo cosmopolita de París o al refinamiento de la Francia del siglo XVIII, al repertorio rutilante y prestigioso de las mitologías (clásica y nórdica), a países exóticos como la China y el Japón.[4]

> . . . respect for beauty; the search for the harmonious, pure word, which would reflect the secret harmony of creation for which the artist at that period so yearned . . . the confidence in the saving and therefore sacred power of art . . . faith in the artistic word, consciousness of art . . . they set out in search of what they did not have: luxury and pleasure, always associated in the case of the decadent writer with pain and death. Or they escaped to equally distant realities: to the cosmopolitan glitter of Paris or to the refinement of eighteenth-century France, to the shining, prestigious repertoire of mythology (be it classical or Nordic), to exotic countries like China and Japan.

Later *modernismo*, explains Olivio Jiménez, turns against its own clichés:

> . . . por los caminos de la ironía y la distancia crítica, prepararán al cabo esa negación del modernismo . . . usarán sin embargo el lenguaje como un ya acerado instrumento de esa actitud irónica que les sostiene. Y de aquí los resultados expresivos esperables: el humor, el socavamiento paródico, la burla, y hasta la caricatura de aquellas entidades supremas de la belleza que sus antecesores profesaban como artículo de fe.[5]

> . . . through the paths of irony and critical distance they [i.e. later *modernistas*] were to prepare finally a negation of *modernismo* . . . nevertheless, they were to use language as a by now sharp instrument of that ironical attitude which sustained them. And this gave rise, predictably, to: humour, parodic undermining, joking, and even caricature of those supreme entities of beauty which their predecessors professed as an article of faith.

The present chapter aims to analyse two very different treatments of the *commedia dell'arte* in two Latin American *modernista* poets, the Nicaraguan Rubén Darío (1867–1916), and the Argentinian Leopoldo Lugones (1874–1938), and by so doing to show how this reflects the changes in *modernismo* observed by Olivio Jiménez. Darío may be considered a representative of earlier *modernismo*, particularly in his collections of poetry *Azul (Blue)* (1888) and *Prosas profanas (Profane Verses)* (1896), and Lugones a typical example of the more ironic *modernista*, especially in his highly influential *Lunario sentimental* (which could be translated either as *Sentimental Calendar* [lit. *Lunar Calendar*] or as *Crazy Sentimentalist*) (1909). Although there is a certain amount of overlap between the two poets (they were, in fact, good friends, and respected each other's work), a comparative study of their treatment of the *commedia* will reveal fundamental differences between them. It will also highlight a shift in how the commedia was seen by Hispanic poets. Limitation of space does not permit me to consider other *modernista* manifestations of *commedia* in writers like Benavente, Manuel Machado and Valle-Inclán, but a comparative study of the theme in Darío and Lugones will serve to indicate the general trends, while at the same time illustrating the transformation of *modernismo* effected by such poets as Lugones.

On analysing Darío we shall examine four basic issues: the question of escapism; Pierrot as Romantic lover; the *commedia* as an intermediary between material and spiritual worlds; and a Latin American dimension of the *commedia*. Three aspects of the Lugones *commedia* will most concern us: the blend of the sentimental and the grotesque, and the predominance of the latter over the former; the mocking of the Romantic Pierrot and other *commedia* characters through theatricality and the use of often startling imagery; and the town/country question.

The *commedia dell'arte* is generally part of an escapist modernista fantasy in Darío. This is best illustrated in the poem 'Canción de carnaval' ('Carnival song'), from *Prosas profanas*. It is headed with a quotation from Banville: 'le carnaval s'amuse!/Viens le chanter, ma Muse . . . '. The whole poem is an apostrophe to Talía, the muse of drama, and colour, rhythm and smell dominate: 'mueve tu espléndido torso/por las calles pintorescas,/y juega y adorna el Corso/con rosas frescas'[6] ('move your splendid torso through the colourful streets, and play and adorn the Corso with fresh roses'). Darío urges us to treat the carnival as an opportunity to forget our worries: 'penas y duelos olvida,/canta deleites y amores' (562), ('forget your woes and suffering, sing about joys and loves'). Melancholy has no part in the carnival: 'lleva un látigo de plata/ para el spleen' (562), ('carry a silver whip to combat spleen'). Neither is there any suggestion of sadness beneath the false mask that one finds in other writers, or indeed elsewhere in Darío's work. The emphasis is on surface gaiety: 'sus gritos y sus canciones,/ sus comparsas y sus trajes,/ sus perlas, tintes y encajes/ y pompones' (563), ('its shouts and its songs, its masquerades and its costumes, its pearls, shades, lace and pom-poms'). There is no time for reflection in the hectic carnival: 'pirueta, baila, inspira/ versos locos y joviales;/ celebre la alegre lira/ los carnavales' (562), ('pirouette, dance, inspire mad, jovial poetry; let the joyful lyre celebrate the carnivals').

The carnival, of course, was an unusual or abnormal period, in which respectable people could let their hair down, their identities hidden behind their mask. Bakhtin and his followers have explored the subversive, anti-establishment aspects of such manifestations of popular culture as the carnival,[7] and indeed Julio Caro Baroja has a full-length study of the carnival phenomenon in Spain.[8] Darío, however, does not attempt to explore the possibilities of carnival and mask in 'Canción de carnaval', being content to describe and convey the colourful atmosphere, into which the characters of the *commedia* masks fit. Darío gives only brief thumbnail sketches of some of them in the poem, as, for example, when he evokes the diamond-patterned costume of Harlequin and the hump of Pulcinella or Punch: 'mientras Arlequin revela/ que al prisma sus tintes roba/ y aparece Pulchinela/ con su joroba' (561), ('while Harlequin reveals that he steals his colouring from the prism and Pulcinella appears with his hump . . . '). There are shades of the Verlaine Colombine in Darío's description of her as 'la bella' ('the *belle*'), although there are no hints in 'Canción de carnaval' that Colombine is 'méchante'. Darío's Pierrot is also reminiscent of the Pierrot who appears in 'Pantomime', the lines: 'y descorcha una botella/ para Pierrot' (561) ('uncork a bottle for Pierrot'), recalling Verlaine's Pierrot, who 'vide un flacon sans plus attendre,/ Et pratique, entame un pâté' ('empties a bottle without delay, and, ever practical, starts his pâté').[9] There are suggestions of the Deburau Pierrot in both these descriptions, as in the following stanza from 'Canción de carnaval', in which Pierrot represents a combination of poetry and pantomime: 'que él te cuente cómo rima/ sus amores con la luna/ y te haga un poema en una/ pantomima' (562), ('let him tell you how he rhymes his loves with the moon, and let him make you a poem in a pantomime').[10]

Pierrot as poet is, of course, a commonplace in French Symbolist poetry, and is found in another poem from *Prosas profanas*, 'El faisán' ('The pheasant'). Once again the setting is that of the Lent carnival ('aquella noche de Carnestolendas') (565), but this time the poet/ Pierrot, suffering sadness due to unrequited love, is unable to participate in it. The frivolous games of the *fêtes galantes* are recalled, as is the traditional disguising of one's identity behind the carnival mask:

La careta negra se quitó la niña,
y tras el preludio de una alegre riña
apuró mi boca vino de su viña.

Vino de la viña de la boca loca,
que hace arder el beso, que el mordisco invoca.
¡Oh los blancos dientes de la boca loca!

En su boca ardiente yo bebí los vinos,
y, pinzas rosadas, sus dedos divinos
me dieron las fresas y los langostinos   (565)

The girl took off her black mask, and, after the prelude of a light-hearted banter, my mouth tasted wine from her vine. Wine from the vine of the crazy mouth, which makes the kiss burn, which begs for the bite. Oh the white teeth of the crazy mouth! I drank the wines from her burning mouth, and like pink pincers, her divine fingers gave me strawberries and lobsters.

As the above lines indicate, the atmosphere is extremely *décadente*, but the frivolity masks the sadness of the poet/Pierrot: 'yo la vestimenta de Pierrot tenía,/ y aunque me alegraba y aunque me reía,/ moraba en mi alma la melancolía' (565), ('I was wearing a Pierrot costume, and although I was joyful and although I laughed, my heart was filled with melancholy'). These lines are a clear expression of the surface colour and gaiety of the *commedia* merely masking a melancholy state, which is, of course, heightened by the repeated use of the 'm' sound in the final line. The suffering of the poet/Pierrot is caused by the fact that the girl has a new lover, a 'peregrino pálido de un país distante' (566), ('pale pilgrim from a distant land').

The poet mentions to his casual carnival pick-up ('amada de un día' – 'lover of one day') that the moon has been covered by a cloud, which is commented upon by the golden pheasant of the title in the concluding lines of the poem: '«¡Pierrot, ten por cierto/ que tu fiel amada, que la Luna, ha muerto!»' (566), ('Pierrot, you can be certain that your faithful love, the Moon, is dead!'). Although the moon as the faithful lover of Pierrot is clearly contrasted with the carnival pick-up, Darío's tone seems to be somewhat mocking, perhaps even self-deflating. It is almost as if he is trying to get the *décadence* into some sort of perspective. 'El faisán' is an interesting poem, which explores to an albeit limited extent the possibilities of the mask, and marvellously evokes a *décadent* carnival atmosphere, only for the poet to deflate it somewhat at the end.

In the two Darío poems so far examined, we have seen a contrasting approach to the *commedia*, especially to the figure of Pierrot. Duality is also the characteristic of Darío's clown figure. Darío was particularly fascinated by the English clown Frank Brown, who entertained three generations of Argentinians in the Teatro San Martín in Buenos Aires. Darío devotes a number of pages of his autobiography to Brown, and writes of him: 'Hay que tener en cuenta que el arte del «clown» confina, en lo grotesco y en lo funambulesco, con lo trágico del delirio, con el ensueño y con las vaguedades y explosiones hilarantes de la alienación.'[11]('You have to remember that the art of the clown, in its grotesque and *funambulesque* aspects, borders on tragic delirium, dream and the vagueness and hilarious explosions of madness.')

Darío recognizes that the art of the clown combines such seemingly incompatible qualities as the grotesque, tragedy, delirium and dream, although he does not explore the potential of these so-called comic characters for combining sentimentality and the grotesque as, for example, the Spanish dramatist Valle-Inclán does with his *commedia* figures in *La marquesa Rosalinda* (1912).

Frank Brown makes another appearance in the carnival of 'Canción de carnaval': 'únete a la mascarada,/ y mientras muequea un clown/ con la faz pintarrajeada/ como Frank Brown . . .' (561), ('join in the masquerade, and while a clown grimaces with his face daubed like Frank Brown . . .'). Darío is not interested in the tragic side of the clown in this poem, however, unlike another poem entitled simply 'Frank Brown': 'Frank Brown, como los Hanlon Lee,/ sabe lo trágico de un paso/ de payaso, y es, para mí,/ un buen jinete de Pegaso.' (978) ('Frank Brown, like the Hanlon Lees, knows how tragic a clown's walk is, and he is, for me, a good horseman of Pegasus.')

Darío's Frank Brown, like Banville's clown, provides a link between the circus spectator and an imaginary ideal world. He 'salta del circo hasta el Parnaso./ Banville le hubiera amado así' (978), ('leaps from the circus to Parnassus. Banville would have loved him like this'), and 'el niño mira a su payaso/ de la gran risa carmesí,/ saltar del circo al cielo raso' (979), ('the child watches his clown with the big crimson smile leap from the circus ring to the ceiling'). Here is perhaps the main reason for Darío's interest in the circus, pantomime and the *commedia*: their ability to transcend the poet's immediate surroundings and suggest to us an ideal existence far removed from our own humdrum one. They are clearly derived from what Russell S. King has called the ' "vertical" aspirations' of Banville as poet-clown, 'from reality to ideality, from the physical to the spiritual'.[12]

Another example of these ' "vertical" aspirations' is found in Darío's prologue to *Teatro de ensueño* (*Dream Theatre*), written by the Spanish *modernista* dramatist, Martinez Sierra. The prologue is entitled 'Melancólica sinfonía' ('Melancholy symphony'), and in it Darío presents an unashamedly idealistic apology for the magical qualities of these art forms:

> Nosotros sabemos lo trágico del clown, lo lírico de una danzarina de cuerda, lo ideal del circo; el hechizo oculto de la pantomima. Siempre es la influencia de las máscaras la que nos hace rememorar o prever una existencia aparte de lo que conocemos por nuestros sentidos actuales; de ahí proviene la revelación mallarmeana del arcano prestigio del ballet, ciertos aspectos de las fiestas galantes, el misterio del Gilles de Watteau, la incomparable magia gráfica del enigmático y prodigioso Aubrey Beardsley.[13]

> We know how tragic is the clown, how poetic is a rope dancer, how ideal is the circus; we know too the secret magic of the pantomime. It is always the influence of the masks which makes us recall or foresee an existence which is apart from what we know through our human senses; and from this comes the Mallarmean revelation of the enigmatic prestige of the ballet, certain aspects of the *fêtes galantes*, the mystery of Watteau's Gilles, the incomparable graphic magic of the enigmatic and prodigious Aubrey Beardsley.

The passage underlines the symbolic significance of the pantomime, the circus, the *commedia* and ballet in that they are intermediaries between our world and another one which is beyond our own perception. The key phrases in the above passage are 'ideal', 'secret magic', 'an existence which is apart from what we know through our human senses', 'enigmatic prestige', and 'mystery'. These phrases also, of course, underline the *modernista* interest in the occult.[14]

The ' "vertical" aspirations' are once more associated with the Watteau Gilles in a Darío poem entitled 'Balada en loor del ' "Gilles" de Watteau', which was written in Paris in 1911. In this poem Darío evokes the 'melancolía nocturna' ('nocturnal melancholy') with which Gilles passes by, and he is linked with a world of mystery and dream:

> un supraterrestre violín
> en sueño terrestre encantó.
> Y un ensueño he tenido yo,
> pasado, bello, extraordinario:
> en la grupa de un Sagitario,
> raptado, el Gilles de Watteau.   (1057)

> an other-worldly violin cast a spell on a worldly dream. And I have had a dream, faded, beautiful, extraordinary: on the rump of a Sagittarius, kidnapped, Watteau's Gilles.

The interplay between the human and the mythological, the 'worldy' and the 'other-worldly', is typical of Darío. As in French poetry from Banville to Apollinaire,[15] a *commedia* figure is the intermediary between the two worlds, and the launching-pad for the poet's evocation of a poetic dream-world beyond our prosaic, limited and limiting human existence. He belongs to the familiar *modernista* 'distant land': 'lejos en un país que adoro,/ vi a Gil, a eco de serenata,/ cortar margaritas de plata/ en unas montañas de oro' (1057), ('far away in a land I adore, I saw Gil, to the echo of a serenade, cutting silver daisies on mountains of gold'). The Gilles of the 'Balada' possesses the spiritual qualities which French poets saw in the Watteau portrayal of this *forain* character: he is 'más espíritu que materia' (1057) ('more spirit than matter').

A similar spirituality characterizes the Parisian Pierrot evoked by Darío in his autobiography, where, as in 'El faisán', Pierrot is the typically Symbolist/*modernista* melancholy loner, an externalization of the poet's soul:

> Luego será un recuerdo galante en el escenario del siempre deseado París. Pierrot, el blanco poeta, encarna el amor lunar, vago y melancólico, de los líricos sensitivos. Es el carnaval. La alegría ruidosa de la gran ciudad se extiende en calles y bulevares. El poeta y su ilusión, encarnada en una fugitiva y harto amorosa parisién, certifica, por la fatalidad de la vida, la tristeza de la desilusión y el desvanecimiento de los mejores encantos.[16]

> Later it will be a gallant memory on the stage of the always longed-for Paris. Pierrot, the white poet, embodies the lunar love, vague and

melancholy, of sensitive poets. It's carnival time. The noisy gaiety of the great city spreads through streets and boulevards. The poet and his illusion, embodied in a fugitive, amorous Parisian girl, bears witness, through life's chance, to the sadness of disillusion and the dissipation of the finest moments of magic.

As in 'Canción de carnaval' and 'El faisán' Pierrot is a 'poet', and the relationship between him and the moon is the stereotyped Romantic one, very different, as we shall see, from that evoked by Lugones. The atmosphere, as in 'El faisán', is one of vague *modernista* melancholy caused by unrequited love, and Pierrot is the loner who is unable to relate to the hectic carnival atmosphere of which all the *commedia* characters are a part in 'Canción de carnaval'. Disillusion with love is responsible for the breaking of the illusion, but this theme is treated completely seriously, and without any of the cynical humour that is characteristic of Lugones's portrayal of the *commedia*. He is the stereotyped 'poor' Pierrot.

The above passage is similar in many ways to one from *El teatro de Pierrot* (*Pierrot Theatre*), which is a personal history of the Parisian Pierrot written by another Latin American *modernista*, the Guatemalan poet Enrique Gómez Carrillo:

> Porque Pierrot, en Montmartre, se ha convertido en un muchacho sentimental, tierno, alocado, artista y amoroso. Fuera de Colombina, lo único que le interesa es el Arte – cualquier arte. A veces se hace arquitecto y sueña en edificar altas torres de nieve para encerrarse a llorar. Otras veces la Escultura lo tienta y con el pulgar modela en el espacio formas ondulantes. También le gusta la Poesía a causa del madrigal. Pero lo que más le entusiasma es la Música y la Pintura, que son las artes más adecuadas para la seducción. Cuando no tañe la guitarra bajo el balconcillo florido, escribe esquelas ofreciendo a su amada que va a pintarle su retrato. Y Colombina, ante esta tentadora promesa, acude. Colombina es coqueta, y como conoce la inflexible monotonía de los espejos, desea verse en un lienzo. Pero Colombina, a la larga, no quiere a Pierrot, puesto que Pierrot es pobre y triste.[17]

> For Pierrot, in Montmartre, has become a sentimental lad, tender, crazy, an artist, and in love. Apart from Columbine, all that interests him is Art – any art. Sometimes he becomes an architect and dreams of building high towers of snow so that he can shut himself up and weep. On other occasions he is tempted by sculpture and draws undulating shapes in the air with his thumb. He also likes Poetry because of the

madrigal. But what excites him most is Music and Painting, which are the art forms most suited to seduction. When he is not strumming his guitar beneath the flower-filled balcony, he is writing love letters offering to paint his beloved's portrait. And Columbine gives in to this tempting promise. Columbine is a coquette, and since she knows all about the inflexible monotony of mirrors, longs to see herself painted on a canvas. But Columbine, in the long run, does not love Pierrot, because Pierrot is poor and sad.

Here Pierrot is painter rather than poet, but the sensitive artistic temperament which leads to his suffering and loneliness is the familiar Symbolist and *modernista* one.[18] The phrase 'Pierrot is poor and sad' sums up the Darío–Gómez Carrillo approach to the figure. It was Gómez Carrillo who introduced Darío to Paris, which was to a large extent the spiritual home of Latin American *modernismo*. To quote Suárez Miramón on Darío's love of Paris: 'París era para él "la ciudad del arte, de la belleza, de la gloria y, sobretodo, la capital del amor, la reina del ensueño".'[19] ('Paris was for him "the city of art, beauty, glory and, above all, the capital of love, the queen of fantasy and illusion".')

Those familiar with Latin American literature since the mid-nineteenth century will be aware of a tension between Europeanism and *indigenismo*, or attachment to native cultures. Following independence from Spain, there was a debate in many Latin American countries as to how closely tied to the old country and continent their futures should be. In Argentina there was a particularly fierce political struggle in the nineteenth century between the unionists, who were strongly pro-European and city-based, and the federalists, who favoured traditional rural values. A work entitled *Facundo* (1845), by the unionist writer Domingo Sarmiento, contains the staunchest defence of Europeanism, which is equated with civilization, and is contrasted with the barbaric customs of the cowboys or gauchos of the pampas. *Facundo* is a thinly veiled attack on the Argentinian dictator Juan Manuel de Rosas, and receives its best-known riposte in *Martín Fierro* (1872), an epic poem on gaucho life by Sarmiento's political opponent José Hernández, who denounced the exploitation of the gaucho and called for a reappraisal of his so-called barbarism.

The question of Europeanism versus native traditions, or *indigenismo*, continued into the twentieth century. Following the First World War, the witnessing by Latin American intellectuals of what they saw as European barbarism led many of them to reject European values and turn more to their own native traditions. Two famous novels of the 1920s, *Don Segundo Sombra* (1926) by the Argentinian Ricardo Güiraldes and *Doña Bárbara* (1929) by the Venezuelan Rómulo Gallegos suggest that the best future for their respective countries lay in a compromise between Europeanism and *indigenismo* or between civilization and barbarism.

Although the source of much *modernista* writing was European, particularly French, the European–Latin American tension was evident in some of their work. José Rodó's *Ariel* (1900), for instance, contrasts the barbarous spirit of 'northern' nations, epitomized by the United States, with a more civilized, essentially Mediterranean spirit which characterized Latin America.

Darío's own work written after the publication of *Ariel* reflected this tension, particularly *Cantos de vida y esperanza* (1905) and *El canto errante* (1907), where in some poems Darío clearly accepts Rodó's thesis. He also perhaps reluctantly accepts that contemporary reality should form a part of his work, something he had specifically rejected in *Prosas profanas*. For example, in the prologue to *Prosas* he wrote: 'Veréis en mis versos princesas, reyes, cosas imperiales, visiones de países lejanos o imposibles: ¡qué queréis!, yo detesto la vida y el tiempo en que me tocó nacer.' (546) ('In my poems you will see princesses, kings, imperial things, visions of distant or impossible lands: what do you expect! I detest the life and the time in which it has been my misfortune to be born.') Art is clearly superior to life, and Darío notes a lack of knowledge of Art on the part of the younger writers of Latin America: 'La obra colectiva de los nuevos de América es aún vana, estando muchos de los mejores talentos en el limbo de un completo desconocimiento del mismo Arte a que se consagran.' (545) ('The collective work of the new American writers is as yet empty, since many of the finest talents are in a limbo of a total lack of knowledge of the very Art to which they devote themselves.')

Naturally, the *commedia*, as has already been mentioned, is an integral part of this artistic, superior world, with its mystery, colour, exoticism, but also the dual function of the Pierrot/clown. Nevertheless, even in *Prosas profanas*, a Latin American setting is suggested for the carnival in both 'Canción de carnaval' and 'El faisán'. In 'Canción de carnaval', Darío seeks to introduce a Latin American, and more specifically an Argentinian element into the Banvillian carnival, in the reference to the 'abeja porteña' ('the Buenos Aires bee') in stanza 4, and in the lines 'sé . . . / . . gaucha, con la guitarra/ de Santos Vega' (562), ('be . . . gaucho, with the guitar of Santos Vega'). The Banvillian ('funambulesca') and the Argentinian are combined in the final stanza, which portrays the triumphant victory of the joyful carnival: '... y lleve la rauda brisa,/ sonora, argentina, fresca,/ la victoria de tu risa/ funambulesca.' (563) ('. . . and let the rushing breeze, noisy, Argentinian, fresh, carry the victory of your funambulesque laughter.')

Also, in 'El faisán' the Parisian setting is modified: the lines 'se despedían de sus azahares/ miles de purezas en los bulevares' (566), ('thousands of pure aromas are given off by the orange-blossoms in the boulevards') are more reminiscent of a Mediterranean or perhaps a subtropical atmosphere than of a northern European one. I would not want to overstate the importance of the setting, since geography in *modernista* writing is usually impressionistic, and the poets are more concerned with creating an exotic atmosphere than with precision.

The setting of one other poem from *Prosas profanas* is, however, quite specifically the countryside near Buenos Aires, and the poem deals with *indigenismo*, albeit in a fairly light and non-polemical way. This is 'Del campo', where 'la amada de Pierrot' ('Pierrot's sweetheart', presumably Colombina) inhabits an idealized country setting away from the hustle and bustle of modern urban life in Buenos Aires, along with fantastic Shakespearean figures such as Puck, Titania and Oberon. The country setting, however, is merely an artificial escape, and the last two stanzas of the poem evoke the death of poetry in Argentina, in an image of the gaucho, setting off into the wilderness for the last time, an image which seems to anticipate the ending of *Don Segundo Sombra*:

> De pronto se oye el eco del grito de la pampa;
> brilla como una puesta del argentino sol;
> y un espectral jinete, como una sombra cruza,
> sobre su espalda un poncho, sobre su faz dolor.

> —«¿Quién eres, solitario viajero de la noche?»
> —«Yo soy la Poesía que un tiempo aquí reinó:
> ¡yo soy el postrer gaucho que parte para siempre,
> de nuestra vieja patria llevando el corazón!»   (559–60)

Suddenly the echo of the cry of the pampa is heard; it shines like an Argentinian sunset; and a ghostly rider crosses the scene like a shadow, a poncho on his back, grief on his face. "Who are you, lonely traveller of the night?" "I am Poetry who once ruled here: I am the last of the gauchos who is leaving our old fatherland for ever, taking his heart with him."

Although Gordon Brotherston is correct to say that 'rural Argentina is addressed playfully' in the poem,[20] the last two stanzas are strongly sentimental.

This sentimentality – a feature, as we have seen, of Darío's *commedia*, carnival, circus and pantomime – contrasts markedly with the position taken towards *commedia* characters by Leopoldo Lugones. Lugones is much less sentimental and more detached than Darío, and more concerned with creative language than with beauty and emotion. Nevertheless, as Benítez says: 'Al final Lugones siempre deja latente cierta benevolencia indulgente para con los tipos que retrata; debajo de las caretas carnavalescas, llenas de fuertes colores y con rasgos exagerados, podemos adivinar casi siempre la presencia de un autor sentimentalmente conmovido.'[21] ('When all is said and done, beneath the surface of Lugones' portrayal of his types there is always a certain indulgent benevolence; beneath the carnival masks, which are full of vivid colours and exaggerated features, we can almost always detect the presence of an author who is moved sentimentally.') One may contrast this view with the following observation of Allen W. Phillips: 'Todo el mundo ha advertido en Lugones una falta de intimidad . . . muchas veces se repite que Lugones queda lejos de su obra, sin poder establecer ese vínculo amistoso y afectivo con el lector.'[22] ('Everyone has noticed a lack of intimacy in Lugones . . . it has often been repeated that Lugones maintains a distance from his work, and is unable to establish an emotional link with his readers.') We shall observe instances of both sentimentality and cynical detachment in Lugones, although, as we shall see, it is the latter which predominates.

We shall, however, begin with an untypical example, in which, although familiar Lugonian humour is present, the sentimental eventually triumphs over the grotesque. This is *El Pierrot negro*, a pantomime in four scenes, or *cuadros*, based on the traditional cuckolding of Pierrot by Columbine with Harlequin, and Pierrot's subsequent frustration and anger. This is clearly conceived by Lugones as a 'set-piece' situation, as for instance in the following description of Pierrot in scene i: 'a esa hora llorará furioso el nuevo desvío de Colombina' (303), ('at this moment he will be lamenting furiously Colombina's latest rebuff'): the future tense in the Spanish is here a future of probability, or inevitability, and has the effect in this context of highlighting the ritualistic nature of the action.

The first sign that Pierrot's frustration is, at least in part, to be comically treated comes when the 'white character' falls into a bowl of black dye having heard Colombina's mocking laughter from the street, and turns completely black. The rest of the pantomime revolves around Pierrot's attempts to return to his state of whiteness, through various magic devices, and a trip to the moon, that home of whiteness!

One of the most striking features of *El Pierrot negro* is the way in which Lugones satirizes *modernista* commonplaces by moving them into an incongruous setting. In the first scene, for instance, which is set in a dyer's, the twilight setting is conveyed through typically *modernista* impressionism, but this seems out of place in a modern urban environment where nature is dehumanized: 'A los fondos de una tintorería, en el crepúsculo. Vagas construcciones de arrabal. Barracas, viviendas de tabla, dos o tres árboles raquíticos. Todo ello fundido en la suave tinta violeta de la hora.' (303) ('At the back of a dyer's, at twilight. Unclear lines of buildings on the outskirts of the town. Huts, shacks, two or three stunted trees. The whole scene is blended into the soft violet light of the twilight hour.')[23]

Another *modernista* cliché which is satirized in this pantomime is the interest in the occult and magic, which we observed in Darío's essay 'Melancólica sinfonía'.[24] Scene ii is set in an alchemist's, and the owner unsuccessfully tries various magic tricks in order to help Pierrot regain his whiteness. These include conjuring up mermaids and land nymphs to perform ritualistic dances around Pierrot, and offer him precious metals. When these devices fail, Pierrot insists on his trip to the moon, and once more Lugones uses juxtaposition to turn a serious situation (Pierrot's frustration) into a comic one. The alchemist gives Pierrot a broomstick, but refuses to provide him with the talisman until he has been paid. The Romantic association of Pierrot with the moon is thereby made prosaic, and the urgent soul-baring of Pierrot, so familiar in Romantic and Symbolist poetry, is the butt of humour. Likewise, all the magic (including the trip to the moon) fails to remove Pierrot's blackness: this is achieved by his passing through a common or garden raincloud on his return to earth. It is as if Lugones is parodying the ' "vertical" aspirations' of the Banville–Darío poet-clown, as Pierrot ascends to the moon in search of happiness, but finds it only when he comes back down to earth with a bump.

However, unlike some of the poems in the *Taburete de máscaras* section of *Lunario sentimental*, in *El Pierrot negro* Lugones' attitude to the frustrated Pierrot is by no means completely cynical. There are moments when he seems to be genuinely tragic, in particular when the mermaids dance around him: 'Danzan en torno de Pierrot, ofreciéndole los dones acuáticos que las adornan: sartas de corales y de perlas; nácares, madréporas, pececillos de colores, algas extrañas. Pierrot permanece inmóvil y mudo.' (306) ('They dance around Pierrot, offering him the aquatic gifts with which they are adorned: strings of corals and pearls; mother-of-pearl, coloured little fish, strange seaweeds. Pierrot remains motionless and dumb.') This 'motionless and dumb' Pierrot clearly recalls the Watteau Gilles. Through movement and gesture Lugones conveys the Symbolist/ *modernista* theme of the lonely Pierrot, but there is no suggestion that the scene is comic or grotesque.

The same applies to the following description at the end of scene i: '¡Un viaje a la luna! Pierrot, desesperado, implora al astro, mientras Polichinela se mofa de él a su espalda; hasta que, convencido de su impotencia y de su irreparable destino, el triste amante estalla en lágrimas.' (305) ('A trip to the moon! Pierrot in desperation begs the star, while Pulcinella mocks him behind his back; until, convinced of his impotence and his irreparable destiny, the sad lover bursts into tears.') Here as elsewhere in this pantomime the serious Pierrot is contrasted with the other *commedia* characters who are mocking and cynical.

However, mocking cynicism does not triumph over seriousness in *El Pierrot negro*. On the contrary, it is love that triumphs over materialism at the end of the play. The only proof Pierrot has of his trip to the moon is a handful of stones in his pocket. They turn out to be precious, he hands them to Colombina, but she flings them behind her, and while the onlookers hurl themselves at the treasure, she 'busca amorosa los labios de Pierrot' (311), ('amorously searches out Pierrot's lips'). Pierrot has won over the unfaithful Colombina, who sees that however serious a character he may be, he is preferable to the cowardly and cynical Arlequín and Polichinela.

Pierrot's impotence leading to frustration is at the heart of one of the poems from *Taburete de máscaras*, 'Cantilena a Pierrot' 'Ballad to Pierrot'). However, this time, the frustration is absurd, and Lugones applies the irony that is his hallmark to his portrayal of the figure. Several striking images are employed in the poem to convey Pierrot's impotence and frustration.[25] He is like the bad bell-ringer who cannot reach the clapper ('como mal campanero/ que no alcanza la badaja' – 172), and the fox who never catches the ripe grapes ('como el zorro en la viña/ jamás la ve madura' – 172).

However, it is through his depiction of the Pierrot–moon relationship that Lugones most fully illustrates his point. Allen W. Phillips, for example, analyses how Lugones converts the Romantic and Symbolist moon into an essentially prosaic symbol, and treats it with familiar mocking humour.[26] This point is well illustrated in 'Cantilena'. The moon mocks Pierrot through failing to turn up for a date because of her high orbit; Pierrot's patience in waiting for her is likened to a fisherman waiting for his catch, only to be given the slip by his target. Lugones uses an extremely complicated image of a game of billiards to suggest the moon playing with Pierrot: 'cual si armara a tu flaco/ desgaire de palote,/ su disco mondo el bote/ Que junta al mingo el taco', ('as if she were arming your skinny stick-like awkwardness, her plain, bare disc is the thrust which joins the cue ball to the cue'). ('Bote' is very hard to translate: it could mean 'thrust' or 'bounce', but 'el tonto del bote' means 'prize idiot').

The final two stanzas of the poem suggest a futile remedy should his frustrations continue and should the moon prolong his absurd existence by continuing to trick him. He is advised: 'espérala sedienta/ y atrápala en tu aljibe' ('sit down and wait for her, and catch her in your water cistern'). Pierrot, it seems, is capable of capturing the reflection, but not the essence. Here is Pierrot the fool, mocked and reviled by the moon.

In 'Cantilena' Pierrot emerges as both simpleton and deceiver. We have seen a number of examples of the former, and the latter is highlighted through the exposure of his pretentious affectation. The pomposity with which he addresses the moon is ridiculed by ordinary people: 'la platitud plebeya/ con imbécil apodo,/ clasifica el gran modo/ de tu prosopopeya', ('the common people in their simplicity give an imbecile nickname to your pompous grandiloquence'). Pierrot's penchant for writing poetry to his beloved is referred to as the 'lírico embuste/ con que la llamas linda' (the lyrical fraud with which you call her beautiful'), while the lines 'escríbele una resma/ de epitalamios y odas ('write her a ream of wedding songs and odes') are sarcastic in tone.

The Pierrot of 'Odeleta a Colombina' ('Mini ode to Columbine') is even more absurd than his counterpart in 'Cantilena'. The pantomime he performs for Colombina is the direct result of his drunken state: this is a poem in which, as we shall see, the grotesque predominates over the sentimental. As in 'Cantilena' Pierrot is satirized chiefly through the juxtaposition of his pretensions with the absurdity of the figure he cuts. For example, in the sixth stanza he groans and calls Colombina 'Clori', 'plagiando una oda vieja' (176) ('plagiarizing an ancient ode'). The poetic name and form are clearly inappropriate to the whining pantomime with its foolish jumble of words ('necio mixtifori' – 176), while a little later his love is referred to as 'unskilled in poetic verbiage' ('poco ducho/ del poético ripio' – 176).

So far we have seen a dual attitude to Pierrot in Lugones's work. His love eventually wins through in *El Pierrot negro*, but his pretentious seriousness is ridiculed in 'Cantilena a Pierrot' and 'Odeleta a Colombina'. 'A las máscaras' ('To masks'), another poem from *Taburete de máscaras*, contains a Laforguian mixture of the sublime and the mundane in the following depiction of depersonalized Pierrots:[27] 'pobres Pierrots sin luna,/ que en erótico albur,/ desdeñan la fortuna/ papando un bol de azur' ('poor moonless Pierrots who scorn fortune in an erotic game of chance by gulping down a bowl of the azure').

One is reminded of lines from 'Odeleta a Colombina':

En la sombra infinita
Donde su luz extingue,
La luna echará un pringue
Vivaz, de carpa frita;

Y amagará la hartura,
Cuando en torno a esa carpa,
Trinando como un arpa
Pulule la fritura   (179)

In the infinite shadow when its light is extinguished, the moon will cover the fried carp in boiling oil; and it will threaten satiation, when the fried fish swarms around that carp, trilling like a harp.

Here, the prosaic description of fish frying is juxtaposed with poetic images like 'infinite shadow' and 'trilling like a harp' to produce, as in the description of the Pierrots in 'A las máscaras', a comic effect.

In the sixteen-line poem 'El Pierrotillo', the poet's attitude to his Pierrot is not so obviously mocking as it is in 'Cantilena a Pierrot', 'Odeleta a Colombina' and 'A las máscaras'. For example, it is not clear whether the diminutive of the title is mocking or endearing. Pierrot tries to turn the tables on his unfaithful mistress the moon by cocking a snook at her. She then responds by kicking him up the backside and sending him into space: the poem ends with the following lines: 'un puntapié/ le manda allá/ y se/ va . . . ' (166) ('a kick sends him there, and he disappears . . . '). Nonetheless, although the poet's attitude is ambiguous, the 'pierrotillo' belongs clearly to the line of pathetic clowns which are often found in Symbolist and post-Symbolist poetry. A frequently noted feature of Lugones's poetry is the urban setting he employs. In some of his *commedia* works he deliberately juxtaposes this with the idealized country scenes associated with Darío and earlier *modernismo*. The final scene of *El Pierrot negro* for instance takes place in a Watteau-like country gathering in which Arlequín, Colombina and Polichinela are entertainers, in contrast with the description of the slum-dwellings which in their turn are set against a *modernista* sunset in the first scene.

'A las máscaras' is a blend of the Watteau *fêtes galantes* and the urban carnival, and is a satire of both. The satire is achieved through the juxtaposition of an elegant country setting and a sordid urban environment. One can contrast, for instance, the following two stanzas: 'máscaras blancas, únicas/ joyas del dominó,/ bajo lunares túnicas/ o chaponas Watteau' (154), ('white masks, unique jewels of the carnival costumes, beneath lunar tunics or Watteau-style blouses); and: 'Colombinas en crisis/ bajo turbio farol,/ asoleando sus tisis/ con barato arrebol' (155), ('Columbines in crisis beneath the dim street lamp, sunning their tuberculosis with cheap rouge'). The sensuality of the country gathering ('nucas gusto a champaña,/senos al new-mown-hay' (155), ('necks which taste of champagne, breasts of new-mown hay'), is counterbalanced by the cacophony of 'divergentes oboes/ sin sombra de compás;/ bizarros cacatoes/ bajo cosmos de gas' (155) ('divergent oboes without the shadow of a beat, strange cockatoos beneath gas cosmos').

Lugones has here subverted the harmony of music one normally associates with *modernismo*, and inserted a twentieth-century urban landscape into the idealized country settings associated with Watteau's paintings and imitated by the early *modernistas*, subverting the latter. His picture of the city environment contrasts sharply with that of Darío in his carnival poems; for Lugones, that very prosaic element so despised by earlier *modernistas* is an integral part of poetry.[28]

The love which characterizes Lugones's presentation of the *fêtes galantes* and the carnival in 'A las máscaras' is ritualistic and theatrical: 'Corazones galantes,/ que en comedia de amor/ pierden (*agítese antes/ de usarse*) su candor.' (156) ('Gallant hearts, which in love's comedy lose (*shake before using*) their candour.') The italicized 'stage direction', which emphasizes the ritualistic element, typifies Lugones' cynical humour. Love is also essentially deceitful, and the carnival frivolous, a point once more made by Lugones in an earlier stanza with his cynical, elegant humour: 'beso que en fútil salsa/ condimenta el desliz,/ precio de perla falsa/ por una hora feliz.' (155) ('a kiss which flavours the indiscretion with a futile sauce, the price of a false pearl for one hour of happiness.') Here the theme of the one-night carnival stand, treated with sentimentality by Darío in 'El faisán, is witheringly satirized by Lugones: the image of the 'futile sauce' adding spice to the affair anticipates the extension of the image to satirize ritual in the 'shake before using' image.

Expectations of a primitive carnival spontaneity *à la* Bakhtin in 'A las máscaras' are dashed when the primitiveness too is artificial: 'berrea una comparsa/ su epilepsia común,/ en primitiva farsa/ de cafres de betún.' (156) ('a masquerade bellows its common epilepsy, in a primitive farce of shoe-blacked negroes.')

The characters of the *commedia* with their usual adaptability and malleability, move between country and urban settings, suffering a crisis of identity in the process. Pierrot, in particular, loses his purity though not his innocence. His posturings are often pathetic, and his gestures empty, as in the following description from 'Odeleta a Colombina': 'esbozan sus afanes/ mímicas morondangas/ que amplían en sus mangas/ alados ademanes.' (175) ('His yearning sketches out a mimed nonsense, which puffs out winged gestures in his sleeves.') The empty gesture and word are features of Lugones's portrayal of the *commedia*, particularly in 'Odeleta a Colombina', where several characters are parodied. Arlequín is an empty posturer, Lugones emphasizing his hand and arm gestures: 'arlequín mequetrefe,/ con su mano afable y luenga,/ te subraya su arenga/ finchado como un jefe' (175), ('good for nothing Harlequin, with his long, affable hand, emphasizes his harangue, puffed up like a boss'). In the following stanza, Lugones seems to anticipate the Spanish dramatist and novelist Valle-Inclán, who developed an aesthetic of the grotesque in which he often brilliantly satirized the traditional honour code of Spain:[29] 'Arlequín, con remedos/ de militar sainete,/ para un lance a florete/ se ensortija los dedos.'(178) ('Harlequin, in a parody of a military farce, puts rings on his fingers in preparation for a fencing foil.')

The most grotesque of the *commedia* characters is Polichinela, whose traditional function as a violent, drunken lecher is treated with Lugonian humour. Again from 'Odeleta a Colombina':

Y el gran Polichinela,
Rojo como una antorcha,
A tu salud descorcha
Su frasco de mistela.

Como un hechizo corre
Su erótico menjurje,
Y su joroba surge
Bella como una torre   (177)

And the great Pulcinella, red as a torch, uncorks his bottle of *mistela*
and drinks to your health. His erotic brew flows like a magic spell, and
his hump rises, as beautiful as a tower.

One may contrast Polichinela's actions here with the innocent deeds of
Darío's *commedia* figures in 'Carnival song'. The eroticism hinted at in
the final phrase is continued in the following stanza: 'que asiéndote a su
cuello/ con audacias modernas,/ le oprimes con tus piernas/ como a un
feliz camello.' (177) ('he holds you to his neck with modern audacity,
and you squeeze him with your legs as if he were a cheerful camel.')
Lugones's Polichinela is a far more daring creation than his briefly
sketched counterpart in Darío's 'Carnival Song', in terms both of his
actions and of the language with which he is evoked.

Both Darío and Lugones belong to the nineteenth-century French
poetic tradition of the *commedia*, since Pierrot, the central *commedia*
character, is essentially a sad and lonely clown. Their approaches to
Pierrot are, however, very different from one another, Darío accentuating pathos, and Lugones ridicule. These differences carry over into
practically all other aspects associated with their portrayal of the
commedia, such as innocence, spirituality, love, the town/country
question, and, above all, the function of language. For Darío language
is musical, sensuous and sometimes gently humorous. Lugones sees it as
sharp, even wounding, striking and unexpected. It is this vision of
language which shapes their respective concepts of *commedia*.
Through our comparative study of these two Latin American poets, we
have discovered within the *modernista* convention a most varied and
rich portrayal of a stock theme.

NOTES

1 See, for example, N. D. Shergold, 'Ganassa and the *Commedia dell'arte*', *Modern Language Review*, 51 (1956), 359–68.

2 *Los títeres y otras diversiones populares de Madrid: 1758–1840* (London, Támesis, 1972), 25.

3 *The Generation of 1898 in Spain* (London, Ernest Benn, 1975), 5.

4 *Antologia critica de la poesía modernista* (Madrid, Hiperión, 1985), 20, 24.

5 Ibid., 34.

6 Rubén Darío, *Obras completas*, 11th edn. (Madrid, Aguilar, 1968), 562. Further quotations from Darío's poetry are taken from this edition, and the corresponding page references are given in the body of the text of the article. One should note in 'Carnival Song' the presence of the carnavalesque full rhyme.

7 See, for example, Mikhail Bakhtin, *Rabelais and his World*, translated by Helene Iswolsky (Cambridge, Mass., MIT, 1968).

8 Julio Caro Baroja, *El carnaval* (Madrid, Taurus, 1979).

9 Paul Verlaine, *Oeuvres poétiques complètes* (Paris, Gallimard, 1962), 107.

10 The blend of comic pantomime and poetry is a feature of Banville's evocation of *commedia dell'arte*, for instance in the playlet 'Les Folies-Nouvelles', which is part of *Odes funambulesques* (1857); and the essay 'Le Clown et le poète' (1879), in *Critiques*, edited by Victor Barrucand (Paris, 1917), 421–2.

11 *La vida de Rubén Darío escrita por él mismo* (Barcelona, Maucci, 1915), 207.

12 'The Poet as Clown: Variations on a Theme in Nineteenth-Century French Poetry', *Orbis Litterarum*, 33 (1978), 238–52 (240).

13 G. Martinez Sierra, *Teatro de ensueño*, 3rd edn. (Madrid, Renacimiento 1911), 14.

14 See, for example, Cathy Login Jrade, *Rubén Darío and the Romantic Search for Unity* (Austin, University of Texas Press, 1983).

15 See, for example, Russell S. King, 'The Poet as Clown'. See also Susan Harrow's chapter on Apollinaire.

16 *La vida de Rubén Darío escrita por él mismo*, 182–3.

17 *La mujer y la moda. El teatro de Pierrot* (Madrid, 1921), 224–5.

18 See, for example, Ana Suárez Miramón, *Modernismo y 98* (Madrid, Cincel, 1980), 31.

19 Ibid., 57. The fascination with Paris clearly reflects the *topos* of Bohemia.

20 Gordon Brotherston, *Latin American Poetry* (Cambridge University Press, 1975), 64.

21 Introduction to Leopoldo Lugones, *Lunario sentimental*, edited by Jesús Benítez (Madrid, Cátedra, 1988), 75. All quotations from Lugones' poetry are taken from this edition, and the corresponding page references are given in the body of the text of the article.

22 'Notas para un estudio comparativo de Lugones y Valle-Inclán (*Lunario sentimental* y *La pipa de Kif*)', *Boletín-Biblioteca Menéndez Pelayo*, 56 (1980), 315–45 (321).

23 The town/country question will be examined in more detail later in the chapter.

24 See p. 168.

25 In the prologue to the first edition of *Lunario sentimental*, Lugones emphasizes

the role of imaginative imagery in the work: 'Hallar imágenes nuevas y hermosas, expresándolas con claridad y concisión, es enriquecer el idioma, renovándolo a la vez . . . el lugar común es malo, a causa de que acaba perdiendo toda significación expresiva por exceso de uso; y la originalidad remedia este inconveniente, pensando conceptos nuevos que requieren expresiones nuevas.' (Cited in Benítez ed., 92) ('By finding new and beautiful images, and expressing them with clarity and concision, one enriches the language and renews it at the same time . . . the commonplace is bad, because it ends up by losing all expressive meaning by being over-used; originality solves this problem, through thinking of new concepts which require new expressions.') Critics often refer to Lugones' original use of imagery, in particular metaphor. Lugones's famous fellow-Argentine, the poet and short-story writer Borges, is full of praise for Lugones's use of metaphor, and was influenced by it, (see Jorge Luís Borges, *Leopoldo Lugones* (Buenos Aires, Pleamar, 1965), 33).

26 'Aquel símbolo sagrado de los románticos está para siempre desterrado, y se ha convertido en un astro domesticado o urbanizado. Objeto y blanco de la ironía de Lugones es el planeta muerto, sin vida y sin sentimiento.' ('That sacred symbol of the Romantics has been banished for ever, and has become a domesticated, urbanised star. The dead planet, lifeless and without feelings, is the object of Lugones's irony.') ('Notas para un estudio comparativo', 327). Benítez, however, believes that the Lugones moon has a slightly different purpose: 'Lugones ha pretendido hacer belleza (que para él era sinónimo de «bien») utilizando símbolos del mal – como la luna – en una especie de conjuro neutralizador con el que aspira a conseguir una meta tan deseada como es la unión de opuestos.' (Benítez ed., 58) ('Lugones aimed to produce beauty (which for him was a synonym of "good") by using symbols of evil – such as the moon – in a kind of neutralizing spell with which he aspired to achieve his highly treasured goal of the union of opposites).'

27 For similarities between Laforgue and Lugones, see Raquel Halty Ferguson, *Laforgue y Lugones: dos poetas de la luna* (London, Támesis, 1981).

28 The Mexican critic and poet Octavio Paz sees the Lugonian presentation of an urban environment as a characteristic of later *modernismo*: 'El modernismo había poblado el mar de tritones y sirenas, los nuevos poetas viajan en barcos comerciales y desembarcan, no en Citera, sino en Liverpool; los poemas ya no son cantos a las cosmópolis pasadas o presentes, sino descripciones más bien amargas y reticentes de barrios de la clase media; el campo no es selva ni desierto, sino el pueblo de las afueras . . . ironía y prosaísmo: la conquista de lo cotidiano maravilloso.' ('*Modernismo* had filled the sea with Tritons and mermaids, the new poets travel in commercial boats and land, not in Cythere, but in Liverpool; the poems are no longer songs to past or present cities, but rather bitter and ironical descriptions of middle-class suburbs; the countryside is not jungle or desert, but an outlying town . . . irony and the commonplace: the conquest of the wonder of everyday reality.') (reproduced in Lily Litvak, *El modernismo*, 2nd edn., (Madrid, Taurus, 1981), 97–117 (114)).

29 As for example, in *Los cuernos de don Friolera* (1921).

9   *Commedia dell'arte:* Blok and Meyerhold, 1905–1917

W. GARETH JONES

In 1906 Aleksandr Blok, the greatest poet to emerge from Russian Symbolism, was commissioned by Fakely (Torches), a new publishing venture, to write a play based on a poem he had produced the previous year, 'The Puppet Booth' ('Balaganchik'). Fakely was an enterprise of Russia's 'mystical anarchists' whose visionary programme of Symbolist individualism yoked with collective, communal action was to be developed by their own theatre.[1] Its director was to be Vsevolod Meyerhold who, already in the Studio established alongside Stanislavsky's Moscow Art Theatre, had dreams of reviving the Dionysian mystery play with direct, and even ritualistic, audience participation.[2]

Blok's attitude to the commission was mixed. Too much rational debate about mystery irritated him and he explained to Valery Bryusov in a letter of 25 April 1906: 'Mystical anarchism also will not produce mystery plays, at least I don't think it will: I feel it has neither lightness nor laughter'. And he went on to write that for him 'the modern Mystery is essentially a little puppet-like: it is suffused with laughter and turns somersaults.'[3] In dedicating his *Puppet Booth* to Meyerhold, Blok was at least presenting the young director with a marionette Mystery which depended greatly on exploiting the stylized figures of the *commedia dell'arte*, Colombine, Pierrot and Harlequin.

From where had these figures come to St Petersburg in 1906? There is no evidence that they had come directly from Italy through study of the traditions of the *commedia dell'arte*. It is more likely that they had come to Russia by way of the eighteenth-century canvases of Watteau, Lancret and Fragonard as interpreted by the French Parnassian poets and in particular by Verlaine whose influence was at its height with the third edition of his *Fêtes galantes* recently published in 1891. Aleksandr Blok himself, however, was never prepared to admit Verlaine's influence. In this, he allied himself with the Russian generation of poets who insisted that their symbolism sprang from Russian sources and was not a product of Western decadence. In his first reference to Russia's 'new poetry' in the autumn of 1901, Blok denied that it had come into being under the influence of the verse of Western Europe.[4] Much later, in his autobiography, Blok stressed how he had rejected Verlaine's advice in his *Art poétique* to 'throttle eloquence'. Within his family, he recalled, the dominant literary values were of an old-fashioned kind: 'In vulgar parlance, as Verlaine would have it, the predominant position was held here by *éloquence* . . . And it is to that dear, old-fashioned *éloquence* that I shall be obliged to my dying day that, for me, literature did not begin with Verlaine, nor with any form of decadence (VII, 12).' Verlaine even appeared, portrayed unflatteringly as a muttering old drunkard in the sleazy tavern of the opening scene of Blok's play *The Stranger*, which was one of the trilogy of plays of which *The Puppet Booth* was the first. Blok may well have been attempting to conceal his debt to the French poets when, in the draft to *The Puppet Booth*, the figure of Colombine, who was to head the cast list, was given the simple Russian name of Masha.[5]

It is the portrayal of Colombine, perhaps, that suggests that Blok, despite his protestations, was heavily prompted by the French poets of the previous generation. Blok's Colombine is not the laughing, flighty but innocent little creature of the original *commedia dell'arte* tradition,[6] but owes more to Verlaine's picture of malicious menace:

> Une belle enfant
>   Méchante
>
> Dont les yeux pervers
> Comme les yeux verts
>   Des chattes . . .

In *The Puppet Booth* Pierrot's first reference to her is: 'Unfaithful girl! Where are you? . . .' (IV, 10), and she is mistaken by the Mystics for Death (IV, 12).

However much Blok shunned the influence of his French predecessors, the latter's use of the *commedia dell'arte* figures had made them stock characters in the general European culture of the turn of the century. Consequently many saw *The Puppet Booth* as a pleasant theatrical detour, rather than the beginning of a new road. Konstantin Mochulsky gives us a glimpse of the way in which Blok's young friends reacted to the first reading of the play in January 1906 and suggests the reasons for the play's initial popularity: 'Those who first heard the play and then its audience were charmed by the incomparable delight of this *commedia dell'arte*. No more poetic, musical or lightwinged work was created by Russian twentieth-century neo-romanticism than this melancholic, mocking harlequinade.'[7] With its characters Pierrot, Harlequin and Colombine, with its stylized form of acting dictated by ample stage directions and with its setting in a fairground booth, the play clearly drew on the tradition of the *commedia dell'arte*, even if in its later transformations of the harlequinade, pantomime and marionette theatre. Yet at the time of its first production, the full significance of this attempt to infiltrate the traditions of the *commedia dell'arte*, debased by the fairground, music-hall and circus, into the theatre of the Russian intelligentsia was not generally recognized. Valery Bryusov's positive reaction to the formal experiments of *Balaganchik* was not typical of his fellow poets and contributors to the liberal journal *Vesy*. Bryusov wrote of Blok's *Puppet Booth*:

> It is written in the conventional manner of a marionette theatre or pantomime. His characters have wooden gestures like puppets, and their speech is like the fistula in Petrushka shows. But this rejection of our artistic complexity, this new form of simplification, open up unexpected depths. Blok's drama indicates new artistic means, points out a truly new path in art . . .[8]

Another, and most violent, reaction, was the rage of those who felt that they themselves were the target of the mocking harlequinade. Its conventions were seen as a deliberate attempt by Blok to subvert the new theatre of the Symbolists. *The Puppet Booth* was blasphemous. If the *commedia dell'arte* had been employed traditionally to undermine high culture, then Blok certainly exploited that tradition to good effect. Not surprisingly, a conservative journal – Suvorin's *Novoye Vremya* – understood that the play made mockery of the audience for conventional theatre.[9] Even Blok's allies were disturbed. In the eyes of Andrey Bely, his erstwhile friend, Blok, had deliberately turned their 'temple of arts' into a low, fairground booth. In his memoirs Bely complained that '. . . the enormous 'bluebird' had perished; the *Fair Lady* had been transformed into Colombine, and her knights into the 'mystics'; the rose-pink atmosphere turned out to be flimsy paper torn by somebody; there was nothing beyond the paper. All that was shown by *The Puppet Booth*.'[10]

The Puppet Booth was indeed seen by Bely and the other Symbolists as a direct attack on their ideals by a man who had until then shared their views. For the play undermined the poetry that Blok had already written. And for his part Blok did not conceal the fact that his play was a response to his being cast as a mystical babbler on the evidence of his early poetry, his *Verses about the Fair Lady*, which sang the praises of the Eternal Feminine revealed in Vladimir Solovyev's religious philosophy. His 'cruel harlequinade' mercilessly mocked the apocalyptic visions and eschatological yearnings of his erstwhile friends and of his own younger self.

The Puppet Booth opens with 'mystics of both sexes in frock-coats and fashionable gowns' sitting around a table in 'an ordinary stage room with three walls, window and door'. By the window sits Pierrot in a white overall with pale make-up, 'like all Pierrots', as Blok's direction stresses. A third character who soon makes an appearance is the Author, who significantly disclaims responsibility for the Pierrot:

> What is he saying? Most honourable audience! I hasten to assure you that this actor is making a cruel mockery of my copyright. The action takes place in Petersburg in Winter. Where has he got this window and guitar from? I have not written my drama for a fairground booth . . . I assure you . . . (IV, 10)

The appearance of the Author throws into relief the original *commedia dell'arte* tradition of mime and improvisation which is outside the control of a literary playwright. 'I never decked out my heroes in clown's costume! They are playing out an old legend without my knowledge' (IV, 14), the Author complains. Meanwhile the ample stage directions offered great possibilities for Meyerhold's stylized direction of *commedia dell'arte* movements.

As *The Puppet Booth* opens, mystics, who seem to have come from a Maeterlinck play,[11] await the coming of a mysterious lady from a distant country, a woman in white carrying the symbolic scythe of death. Who comes in but Colombine; in her simple, earthly beauty she is taken by the mystics for the Eternal Feminine and image of Death for whom they have been waiting and listening. Pierrot with his common-sense disabuses them: 'It's Colombine, my sweetheart!' Despite the entreaties of the mystics, Colombine declares that she will never leave Pierrot. At that moment a lithesome Harlequin in cap-of-bells appears and in a mime throws Pierrot down, takes Colombine away and she gives him a smile. The mystics lose their hands and faces, leaving empty frock coats behind. Again the protesting Author appears, aghast at the characters dressed up as clowns playing out some old legend.

The scene changes to a masked ball with ladies, knights and clowns. The disconsolate Pierrot sits 'on the bench where Venus and Tannhäuser usually kiss' (IV, 14). Three pairs of lovers then appear. The first are dressed in blue for the boy and pink for the girl and gaze upwards, imagining themselves to be in a church. The second are a diabolic pair: she wears a black mask and swirling red cloak, while he has a red mask and black cloak. The stage direction specifies 'a whirl of cloaks' (IV, 17). The third pair of lovers are a medieval lady and her knight. He wears a cardboard helmet and carries a wooden sword. Suddenly a clown rushes out of the crowd, sticks his tongue out at the knight and is hit over the head by the wooden sword. The clown hangs over the footlights with blood flowing from his head wound, and he cries 'I am bleeding to death from cranberry juice!' (IV, 19).

A torchlight procession appears and the masked actors crowd together. Harlequin steps forward out of the chorus and proclaims his wish to leave this society which does not understand spring or love for the world where his young breast can breathe freely. He leaps through the open window but the expanse beyond turns out to be a painted paper hoop and his legs stick out through it. Through the hole in the paper hoop, the female figure of Death with her scythe is seen. The forgotten Pierrot now approaches this figure and, as he nears her, she turns again into the girl Colombine. As their hands reach out to each other, the triumphant Author jumps between them, declaring that his copyright has been restored: 'Most honourable Audience! My cause is not lost! My copyright is restored! You can see that the boundaries have collapsed. This gentleman has fallen through the window. All that remains is for you to bear witness to the happy rendezvous of two lovers after a long parting!' (IV, 20). But the conventional happy ending is frustrated when all the decor is whisked away and the masked actors and Colombine disappear. Pierrot, left all alone, bewails the loss of his 'cardboard sweetheart', takes out a pipe and strikes up a tune 'about his pale face, his burdensome life and his sweetheart Colombine' (IV, 21).

The ingredients of the play which derive from the *commedia dell'arte* are plain. So obvious are they that critics have accepted their presence without considering why Blok had assembled those ingredients and for what purpose.

Blok's biography gives us one clue to the source of the concept of using the puppet booth. During 1905 Blok and his closest friend

Yevgeni Ivanov developed the habit of relieving the intensity of their conversations with humorous self-parody. Ivanov saw himself as a ginger-haired, blob-nosed circus clown while Blok cast himself in the role of the classic, pale Pierrot. It was during this companionable clowning, it has been suggested, that Blok 'hit upon the idea of the mystics of the puppet-booth, for the two saw all mystical frauds (and sometimes even themselves) as puppets without real, inward being: clowns stuffed with sawdust and bleeding cranberry juice, empty dummies, faceless above immaculate stiff collars.'[12]

The immediate source of the play, however, was the poem of the same name 'Balaganchik', written in July 1905, which Chulkov had invited Blok to use as a base for his play.

The Puppet Booth

Look, the puppet booth is open
For merry and splendid children,
A boy and girl are looking at
Ladies, kings and devils.
And that hellish music rings out,
The wail of a despondent fiddle bow.
A frightful devil has seized the babe,
And the cranberry juice runs down.

The Boy

He will be saved from black anger
By the wave of a white hand.
Look over there: lights
Are approaching from the left . . .
Do you see the torches? the wisps of smoke?
It must be the Queen herself . . .

The Girl

Oh, no, why do you tease me so?
That is the devil's own entourage . . .
The Queen walks abroad in broad daylight,
Entwined with garlands of roses,
And her train is carried, with ringing swords
By her entourage of lovelorn knights

Suddenly the clown has hung over stagefront
And is screaming: 'Help me!
I am bleeding to death from cranberry juice!

Bandaged with rags!
My head wears a cardboard helmet!
And in my hand a wooden sword!'

The boy and girl burst out in tears,
And the merry puppet booth was shut.   (II, 67–8)

But the play had been foreshadowed in an earlier poem of Blok dated
6 August 1902 which had been sent to Zinaida Gippius on 14 September
with the note: 'Meanwhile I am cutting through this thick, thunderous
atmosphere with a cruel harlequinade whose poetic expression I am
sending to you' (I, 609). In that poem, Harlequin appeared in his
costume in a masked ball and his wooden sword traced characters for
his lady. A jingling Harlequin appears again in a poem of 7 October
1902 to seduce a pale Colombine at a masked ball and leave behind a
trembling, deceived Pierrot (I, 227). In July 1903 his poem 'The Double'
('Dvoynik') introduced Colombine and the two Harlequins, young and
old, who were pursuing her (I, 287 – 8). On 14 May 1904 a poem states
that when he dies, the moon will emerge like a heavenly Pierrot and a
red clown will arise (II, 37). Harlequin and the clown appear in a lyric
dated 26 May 1904, 'At the hour when daffodils are tipsy' (I, 322).

Although we have seen that the French Parnassian and Symbolist
poets had revivified the *commedia dell'arte* characters and ensured that
they retained a prominent position in common European culture, and
while we can point to those *commedia* figures in Blok's early verse that
anticipate the *Puppet Show*, it is not possible to explain why they
should have impressed themselves on his imagination. By looking at the
totality of Blok's work, it is, of course, possible to see that the pairing of
Harlequin and Colombine fits in well with the pairs of traditional
European literary figures established by the systems of thought and art
of the past. Central to the poetry of the early Blok is the figure of the
medieval Fair Lady accompanied by her Knight servitor. Hamlet and
Ophelia, Don Juan and Donna Anna, Carmen and Jose are other sexual
pairings – archetypal in European literature – who play a dominant role
in Blok's poetic universe.

Blok turned to these standard, fixed and traditional character types,
not for lack of imaginative power but because he wished to illuminate
his own subjective experiences in the light of established representations of common humanity. If he cast himself in the role of the patiently
waiting chivalrous knight paying homage to an idealized Fair Lady,
another side of his own experience was to see that Fair Lady

192 STUDIES IN THE *COMMEDIA DELL'ARTE*

transformed into the cardboard Colombine with himself a jingling Harlequin or pale Pierrot. The feminine characters came also to embody social reality for Blok. If the apocalyptic yearnings of the Russian intelligentsia had seen the revolutionary spirit of the early twentieth century and the 1905 Revolution as the coming of their eternal feminine, the failure of that Revolution led it to be seen in the sordid reaction of 1906 as the cardboard Colombine of *The Puppet Show*.

It is by poetic intuition rather than by literary planning, therefore, that the elements of the *commedia dell'arte* found their way into Blok's *Puppet Show*, but those common, general images acquired in his verse and dramas a depth and significance, since they carried the force and immediacy of his own spiritual experience. If it remains impossible to trace the channels through which the *commedia* elements were assimilated into Blok's world, it is possible to see how they were brilliantly exploited by him. They enabled him, in the first place, to exteriorize in a dramatic form the bitterness, self-hatred, irony and anger that had been building up, as he himself recalled much later, 'in the police department files' of his soul (VII, 301). He too, like Verlaine, could manifest his feelings 'costumés en personnages de la comédie italienne et de féeries à la Watteau . . .'[13]

His personal experiences in 1905, the collapse of his marriage to Lyubov Mendeleeva, his nausea at seeing his wife treated as the embodiment of the mystical Fair Lady by the literary coterie around him, the failure of the Revolution and the reaction that followed – all this was reflected in *The Puppet Booth* in which he attempted to uncover the duality of life, its instability and its proximity to the mysterious and unattainable. Everything is false, shifting, unreliable. Life is play-acting; all the world is not even a stage, but a puppet booth; people are clowns; the standard stage set of the St Petersburg room turns into a dream-like medieval masked ball; the Eternal Feminine is a cardboard doll; the chivalrous knight is armed with a wooden sword; high emotion switches to farce; suffering is feigned and inconsequential; human blood turns out to be cranberry juice; the firmament itself turns out to be a flimsy paper hoop.

The Puppet Booth was Blok's farewell to his previous world of dream and illusions, but a world that had been generally stable. The play signalled his acceptance of the earthly reality around him, but a reality that was shifting, elusive and disturbing, and had to be expressed in his 'cruel harlequinade'.

But why the harlequinade? It has been claimed that Blok came to his *Puppet Booth* as an innocent. 'The perfection of the piece', wrote Pyman, 'was beginner's luck. Blok, when he wrote it, had no experience of writing for the stage. Neither did the form he found spring from discussions with Meyerhold and Vyacheslav Ivanov, who at that time were dreaming of a revival of the Dionysian mystery play with immediate audience participation. Almost certainly, Blok did not think of himself as an innovator.'[14]

However, those discussions with Meyerhold and Vyacheslav Ivanov were indicative of Blok's close involvement in the debates on the nature of the theatre that were a feature of the first decade of the twentieth century. He had been an amateur actor who had performed monologues and scenes from *Romeo and Juliet, Hamlet, Woe from Wit, Boris Godunov, The Covetous Knight*.[15] Although the apparent contrast between his intimate lyrical poetry and his liking for performing heroic, tragic roles has been noticed,[16] it is nevertheless true that his main lyrical themes had often found their expression in theatrical images. His experience was often 'scenically' expressed and the reader of his poems is invited to visualize these scenes and their *dramatis personae*. Very occasionally, as we have already seen, the pairings of Harlequin and Colombine, Pierrot and Colombine, perform in his poetry, but they appear as passing disturbances in his first volume of lyrical poetry *Verses about the Fair Lady*. The Fair Lady and her devoted knight are sharply delineated dramatic types, generalized and conventional, and in the stylized medieval drama of their relations Blok seemed to find a resolution of his own alarms and doubts.

In choosing to make an apparently sudden switch in his theatrical taste and sympathies with *The Puppet Booth*, Blok used the *commedia dell'arte* to break the conventions of the heroic Shakespearian theatre. His deliberation here was later expressed in his poem 'Balagan' (November 1906) with its epigraph taken from Dumas' play on Kean, 'Well, old nag, let's go to smash our Shakespeare' (II, 123). The pictured scene in the poem is of a poor, worn-out cart carrying the strolling players, Harlequin, Pierrot and Colombine. Blok urges them to 'ply their trade, so that all should be illuminated and pained by truth personified.'

In what ways were the *commedia dell'arte* personae more capable of personifying truth than the existing conventional theatre?

Their primary characteristic was the flexible range of their inherent duality which Blok showed that he had recognized in his poem 'The

Double' ('Dvoynik') of July 1903 where the Harlequin costume concealed a young and old suitor who were, despite the great gap in their ages, the same man (I, 287 – 8). A similar paradox is found in *The Puppet Booth* where the fixed external appearances of the *dramatis personae* do not reveal a fixed character. Pierrot, in an exchange with the President of the mystics over the true nature of Colombine (is she a mystical embodiment of Death or a down-to-earth sweetheart?) is able to say 'Either you are right and I am an unfortunate madman. Or you are mad – and I am a lonely, misunderstood lovelorn swain' (IV, 13).

A mark of the *commedia dell'arte* was the autonomy of the professional actors, uncontrolled by the tyranny of the dictatorial author, and this is brought out in *The Puppet Booth* by the failure of the distraught Author to control his copyright. The Author may invade the stage to inveigh against the headstrong wilfulness of the actors, but his protests are ignored by the *commedia* figures who work out their own destiny. The stage direction for Pierrot after the Author's exit is eloquent: '*He did not pay any attention to the Author*' (IV, 10).

At the end of Blok's original poem the boy and girl are bitterly disappointed by the fiction and sham of what they have seen. Blok exploits to the full the alienation effect which was to become a feature of twentieth-century, avant-garde theatre. The clown disabuses the children in the poem by declaring that his blood is in reality cranberry juice. In the play version of *The Puppet Booth* the theatricality is increased by the way in which the spectacle ruins the Author's intention of presenting a well-made play, set in a Petersburg room, with a conventional plot of the frustrations to young love, their removal and a happy ending. The interruptions of the Author himself destroy any attempt at suspension of disbelief and his final attempt to regain control of the drama is frustrated by the sudden removal of all the stage set and machinery. Alone on a bare stage with his pipe, Pierrot is left to conclude the comedy by addressing the audience.

The Puppet Booth is remarkable too for the weighting in favour of spectacle as against words. Stage directions abound to specify the lighting, costume, movement, gesture, expression, setting and stage properties required to animate the play. The appeal was more to the eye than the ear. It was an attempt to provide material for the folk or popular theatre which Blok, in his articles after 1905, saw as the way of revitalizing drama which had fallen into an atrophied and bourgeois phase.

Its potential was immediately apparent to the director, Meyerhold, to whom Blok dedicated the play and who also played the crucial part of Pierrot. Blok certainly did not see the play as an attempt to restore the traditions of the *commedia dell'arte* to twentieth-century drama but rather, as he explained to his director, 'a moment of catharsis for me; an escape from lyrical isolation' (VIII, 170). Meyerhold, however, looking back on his career in 1912 in the foreword to his book *On the Theatre*, pointed to the significance of the play for his development. While his work in producing Molière's *Don Juan*, and *Colombine's Scarf*, his own adaptation of a Schnitzler pantomime, had been particularly significant, he acknowledged that 'The first impetus to lend my art definite direction was given, however, by the happy invention of my plans for A. Blok's wonderful *Puppet Booth*.'[17] He revealed the extent of his debt in the third part of his book *On the Theatre* which he entitled 'Balagan' ('Fairground Booth').[18]

Many of the axioms Meyerhold now propounded for the new theatre, which would be a restoration of the old theatre, could have stemmed from his experience with *The Puppet Booth*. Directors now preferred mime to words because mime could reveal 'all the power of the original elements of Theatre: the power of the mask, gesture, movement and plot'.[19]

Much of the lost power could be rediscovered by a study of old forms of theatre, and the Harlequinade produced by Meyerhold in 1911, unlike *The Puppet Booth*, had as its main aim the reconstruction of the true *commedia dell'arte* achieved by a study of original scenarios. The 'author' in this case was 'the reconstructor of the old stage, gave the *mise en scène*, movements, poses and gestures as he found them described in the scenarios of the improvised comedy'.[20]

The Actors in *The Puppet Booth* who had shown their autonomy from the Author won favour from Meyerhold who saw the restoration of old theatrical forms as emancipating the actor and giving him the right to perform *ex improviso*. The modern dramatist should content himself with the apparently easy but in fact complicated task of composing scenarios for the actor.

The primary aim of the new restored theatre would be to amuse rather than to instruct. 'The new *Theatre of Masks*', wrote Meyerhold, 'will learn from the Spanish and Italians of the seventeenth century to build their repertoire on the laws of the Fairground Booth [Balagan] where "to amuse" always precedes "to teach" and where movements are given greater value than the word.'[21]

In his *Puppet Booth* Blok had shown that he had understood the power of a masked figure such as Harlequin in the theatre. Such a figure could throw off the shackles of a naturalistic, imitative performance by putting on his mask, his costume of many colours and flaunting his technique as dancer, acrobat, jester and juggler. If Blok had come to understand this power of a masked figure by intuition, then Meyerhold, after his initiation as the Pierrot and director of *The Puppet Booth*, came to understand the peculiar power of the *commedia dell'arte* by study. In his *On the Theatre* Meyerhold recommended a careful perusal of the forgotten scenarios of Flaminia Scala (1611) in order to comprehend 'the magical power of the mask'. Harlequin's mask concealed, he suggested, a simple servant, an inveterate joker: at the same time the mask hid a contradictory 'potent magus, wizard and magician', 'a representative of infernal powers'.[22] Between these two poles an infinite range of variations was possible and it was the actor's art, by movement and gesture, to suggest who was behind the mask at any one time, whether it be the Bergamo peasant or devil. He argued strongly for seeing the source of the strength of Molière's comedies in the heritage of the *commedia dell'arte*.[23]

As he expounded his view that the theatre of the future should be reanimated by assimilating the mask, movement and gesture of the *commedia dell'arte*, Meyerhold was disturbed by the rise of the cinema. The cinema's threat in 1912 was its reliance on extreme naturalism, the ability of the movie-camera to capture life by news-reel photography.[24] In retrospect we know, of course, that Meyerhold's fears were unfounded. One of the ways in which Eisenstein describes his *Battleship Potemkin* is in terms of the *commedia dell'arte*, which is often alluded to in his theoretical writings on the cinema. Eisenstein's association with Meyerhold, of course, may explain the former's interest in the *commedia dell'arte*. Certainly his camera never took up the position of a recording news-reel device, but was used to distort perspective and present a series of dazzling 'turns' in a scenario. The mask, too, was a central component of Eisenstein's cinema, his notion of 'tipazh' purporting to be a cinematic variant of the mask and stereotyped role of the *commedia dell'arte*.

Aleksandr Blok's *The Puppet Booth* may have been for its author primarily a lyrical drama. It was, however, unintentionally a piece of theatre that gave new force to the traditions of *commedia dell'arte*. Not only did it inspire Meyerhold, but also formed an unexpected link between artists as distinctive as Watteau and Eisenstein.

NOTES

1 See James West, *Russian Symbolism. A Study of Vyacheslav Ivanov and the Russian symbolist aesthetic* (London, Methuen, 1970), 132–4.
2 Ibid., 141–3.
3 Aleksandr Blok, *Sobranie sochineniy v vos'mi tomakh*, edited by V. N. Orlov, A. A. Surkov and K. I. Chukovsky, 8 vols. (Moscow–Leningrad, Khudozhestvennaya Literatura, 1960–63), VIII, 152–3. Further references to this edition are given in the text by volume and page number.
4 Aleksandr Blok, *Zapisnye knizhki 1901–1920*, edited by Vl. Orlov (Moscow, Khudozhestvennaya Literatura, 1965), 22.
5 Aleksandr Blok, *Teatr*, edited by P. P. Gromov (Leningrad, Sovetskiy Pisatel', 1981), 19.
6 Jacques-Henry Bornecque, *Lumières sur les Fêtes galantes de Paul Verlaine*, (Paris, Librairie Nizet, 1959), 176.
7 K. Mochulsky, *Aleksandr Blok* (Paris, YMCA-Press, 1948), 127.
8 *Vesy*, No. 5, 58.
9 Aleksandr Blok, *Teatr*, 21.
10 *Epopeya*, No. 2, 254.
11 Maeterlinck is named in connection with the mystics in the draft of *The Puppet Booth*, see Aleksandr Blok, *Teatr*, 18. Unlike most of his contemporaries, Blok was a severe critic of Maeterlinck's theatre, see ibid., 11.
12 Avril Pyman, *The Life of Aleksandr Blok*, 2 vols. (Oxford–London–New York, Oxford University Press, 1979–80), I, 192–3.
13 Jacques-Henry Bornecque, op. cit., 110.
14 Avril Pyman, op. cit., I, 235.
15 Aleksandr Blok, *Teatr*, 7.
16 Ibid., 10.
17 V. E. Meyerkhol'd, *Stat'i, Pis'ma, Rechi, Besedy. Chast' pervaya: 1891–1917*, edited by A. V. Fevral'sky, B. I. Rostotsky, and M. M. Sitkovetskaya (Moscow, Iskusstvo, 1968), 103.
18 Ibid., 207–29.
19 Ibid., 213.
20 Ibid., 253.
21 Ibid., 215.
22 Ibid., 218.
23 Ibid., 223.
24 Ibid., 221–2, 316.

10 From Symbolism to Modernism – Apollinaire's Harlequin-Acrobat

SUSAN HARROW

European high culture of the early twentieth century owes much to the influence of popular art forms derived from the Italian comic tradition. The history of that influence is revealed through the processes of assimilation and transformation, reconstruction and metamorphosis whereby Modernism simultaneously affirms its link with the past and declares its newness.[1] Modernism's preference for the heterogeneous favours the conflation of popular genres and types, and so it becomes impossible to disentangle the multi-coloured strands of *commedia*, circus, and street acrobatics. Modernism achieves its dazzling, unassailable synthesis when Pierrot shares the stage with the modern-day pantomime artiste and Harlequin makes his entrance into the world of the street acrobat. It is in the work of the pioneers of Modernism – Apollinaire and Picasso – that we glimpse the liberating, transforming and ultimately regenerating power of a movement which sets free the *zanni* from the *commedia*'s conventions, only to repossess them for the modern temper and re-present them in a radically new frame. Be the medium plastic or poetic, musical or balletic, the spirit of pantomime filters through the modern whilst its colour suffuses and gives life to the contours of the new art, and the artist, the perennial tightrope walker, achieves that hazardous balance between tradition and innovation.

Stylistic variations on the need to be new (and radically so) produce the multifarious 'isms' which typify the struggle for style engaged in the post-Romantic era and pursued across the centuries' divide, and this shapes reworkings of the familiar pantomime figures. There is, for example, the primitivist treatment Henri Rousseau gives to the traditional Pierrot-moon association in the richly enigmatic *Nuit de carnaval* (1886) with its miniature, luminous Pierrot and Colombine, two tiny beacons of light in a swamp of darkness. Subsequent treatments of the Pierrot figure reflect a broader shift in consciousness consequent both on artistic necessity and on social and political change.

The sense of pessimism which overtakes the modern sensibility is the comfortless refuge of the artist whose confidence in the new century is broken by the events of 1914–18. And so the serene, dream-like figure of Rousseau's portrait-landscape vanishes, to be replaced by the tortured captive of Klee's abstract composition, *Pierrot Captive* (1923). If Klee's transfiguration of Pierrot betokens the sense of alienation that permeates the literature and art of our century, anguish finds its release (and art its salvation) in irony as Pierrot-Petrushka, the eponymous puppet anti-hero of Stravinsky's ballet, returns as a ghostly apparition to mock the audience's blind faith in illusion. In an age dominated by the consciousness of life's absurdity, of its non-sense, the artist turns to the consciously absurd – to comic shows and pantomime arts – in his search for a structured space in which to play out his obsessions and desires. Turning to the cinematic arts, we find in Fellini's 1955 film *La Strada*, through the tragi-comic vision of itinerant circus life, a projection of the universal search for meaning in existence.

Such instances of the multi-facetted *commedia* and circus-inspired production of the modern era confirm our suggestion of a double conclusion for the relationship between the traditional popular arts and Modernist high culture, one which links figurative continuity to the Modernist imperative to 'make it new'.[2] Here we touch on the paradox at the centre of modern art : to be radically new is to declare a major stylistic difference in respect of the prevailing or preceding tradition as a first step towards displacing that tradition. However, the active negation of tradition is predicated on a recognition (valorization) of tradition without which there is no impetus for change, no urge to 'make it new'. It follows that modern art inevitably builds tradition into its scheme. It is with this double perspective of continuity and change, assimilation and transformation of aspects of the overlapping worlds of the *commedia* and the circus that we turn to the early twentieth-century avant-garde in France, and to the enthusiastic espousal of the popular arts by poets and painters engaged in a wholesale effort to radicalize their art, by breaking with modes of representationalism and inno-vating new forms of non-mimetic, non-idealist expression. Arguably, the most representative of the avant-garde, Apollinaire and Picasso, Modernism's 'enfants terribles', drew thematic inspiration from a range of popular art sources – pantomime, street acrobatics, comic theatre. Picasso emerges as the major visual exponent of circus and *commedia* iconography. The testimonies of contemporaries and commentators confirm the day-to-day appeal of the popular arts for

poets and painters. Gertrude Stein records the enthusiasm of the 'bande
à Picasso' for the rumbustious Cirque Medrano: 'At this time they all
met at least once a week at the Cirque Medrano and there they felt very
flattered because they could be intimate with the clowns, jugglers, the
horses and their riders.' [3] Roland Penrose lends similar importance to
the avant-garde's close association with the world of the highflying
acrobats and performing fools. He indicates in this a formative
influence for Picasso:

> For some years the most popular place of entertainment among artists
> was the Cirque Medrano . . . There, behind the scenes and outside
> among the side-shows of the fair . . . Picasso made friends with the
> harlequins, jugglers and strolling players. Without their being
> conscious of it, they became his models. With their families they
> camped beside the booths in which they performed under the warm
> glare of paraffin lamps. Their wives, their children, their trained pets,
> monkeys, goats and white ponies squatted among the props necessary
> for their acts. Detached from the everyday business of the great city,
> they lived absorbed in rehearsing and giving displays of their agility.[4]

The influence of the popular arts on Picasso's iconography is well
documented. Here I shall pursue their parallel influence on the creative
imagination of the 'painters' poet', Guillaume Apollinaire. I shall begin
with the wider context for change – the development of the style
referred to as Modernism and the impact of Cubism upon poetry.

Picasso's output in the high avant-garde period reveals a series of
breaks, shifts and reorientations that are consistent with the search for
a radically new, anti-representational style. Turning from the manner-
ism of his earlier work, Picasso pursues between 1905 and 1907 a
simpler style that anticipates the flattened surfaces and juxtaposed
planes of Cubism, and an altogether more objective, conceptual art.
This purification of style leads to the classicism and abstraction of the
major paintings of the 1915–24 period, most notably *The Harlequin*
(1915) and *The Three Musicians* (1924). Counterpointing the process of
stylistic shift and reorientation in Picasso's work throughout this
period is the constancy of circus and pantomime iconography. The
point of departure is a series of 'Circus' paintings completed between
late 1904 and mid-1905. Here tumblers, mountebanks, child acrobats
and circus families populate a world peripheral to performance. We

glimpse the artistes in off-stage moments of quiet melancholy, their air of tightlipped desolation an ironic contradiction of their colourful motley. These are solitary, static figures who wait in the wings, or huddle together, the sole inhabitants of the barren plain of *Family of Saltimbanques* (1905). The very anonymity of the *topos* in this and the related work *Young Acrobat on a Ball* (also 1905) anticipates the Cubist rejection of anecdote and context. The unmasked status of the artistes is, moreover, a metaphor for the exposing of the illusionist lie. The mellowing of the boudoir pinks, apricots and mauves of the earlier Circus paintings into sober beige and pale sand colours prefigures the monochromes of Cubism. Picasso's painting at this point reveals an unexpected, if fertile, contradiction: at one level, the rejection of narrative suggests a stylistic innovation consistent with Modernist anti-representational approaches; at another, the absence of an identifiable context confers a spiritual quality on figures whose detachment connotes purity and conveys, beyond their simple humanity, a sense of the universal in line with Symbolist preoccupations.

In this, Picasso's canvas shares certain affinities with Apollinaire's poem 'Les Saltimbanques' which, first published in the February 1909 issue of *Les Argonautes*, is generally held to date from around 1904–5, making it contemporary with Picasso's paintings. The imagery and thematic structure of 'Les Saltimbanques', not to mention its title and probable date of composition, reveal some clear parallels with Picasso's late Circus period, particularly, *Family of Saltimbanques* and *Young Acrobat on a Ball*. The poem's evocation of an anonymous 'plaine' finds a visual parallel in the denuded wasteland of both paintings. Beyond the topographical resemblance a comparison of the iconography of poem and canvases reveals marked thematic and figurative similarities. The representatives of youth and maturity, the theme of regeneration suggested by the linked hands of the spangled acrobat and the little girl in *Family of Saltimbanques*, the props of circus routine – the ball on which the girl acrobat balances, the cube on which the muscled companion sits to watch her practise, the drum which the young boy steadies on his shoulder in *Family of Saltimbanques* – find their poetic equivalent in Apollinaire's 'Saltimbanques':

> Ils ont des poids ronds et carrés
> Des tambours des cerceaux dorés
>
> They have weights both square and round
> And drums and hoops all gilded bright   (lines 9–10)

More subtle and more pervasive in both poem and paintings (and in contrast to the more prosaic monetary preoccupation 'Quêtent des sous . . .' (Begging their way)) is the atmosphere of unreality which suffuses these representations of ordinariness. In Apollinaire's poem, this gives rise to a mysterious correspondence between the circus folk and the world of nature:

> Chaque arbre fruitier se résigne
> Quand de très loin ils lui font signe
>
> Each fruit tree feels resigned to see
> Them wave and point from far away   (lines 7–8)

The acquiescence of nature before the presence of the circus folk suggests a cosmic affinity. The anthropomorphic vision conveys the idea of a quickening of the natural world instantly receptive to the mysterious power in its midst. Whilst the vague supernaturalism of the piece and the ellipsis of poetic expression combine to make this a disquieting, hermetic poem, the thematic, figurative and stylistic overlap with Picasso's late Circus works sheds crucial light on the shared preoccupations of poet and painter.

Beyond this point the stylistic gap between poet and painter widens conspicuously, Picasso pulling ahead in pursuit of the properly analytical style that would become Cubism. In 1907, when Apollinaire's search for new forms enters a neo-Symbolist phase reminiscent of Rimbaud, the accent falling less on stylistic invention than on lyric renewal, Picasso, for his part, is embarking upon a phase of radical, modernist innovation, his creative energies invested in the pursuit of a vigorous anti-representational, anti-illusionist form. Of prime interest, here, is the constant reworking of *commedia* and circus iconography in parallel with the development of the Cubist aesthetic. In the 1909 painting, *Harlequin leaning on his elbow*, the performer is transformed by Picasso's rigorously analytical treatment, the juxtaposed and interlocking flattened planes boldly redefining the traditional unity of the figure. The reappearance of Harlequin at this point confirms the iconographic alignment of the Cubist period upon the preceding Circus period. The 1908 Cézanne-inspired *Saint Anthony and Harlequin* – a Cubist interpretation of the Temptation of St Anthony – provides the thematic link by revisualizing the association of sacred and profane, spirituality and the figure of Harlequin. The later 'synthetic' phase of

Cubism, with its accent on abstraction and classicism, its alignment of flat planes of solid colour, constructs a dehumanized, denaturalized Harlequin whose selfdom is reduced to the most elemental, yet most significant of metonymic representations – the performer's motley, now given a highly geometrical treatment in *The Harlequin* (1915). In 1921 Picasso returns to the association of spirituality and the pantomime world in *The Three Musicians*. Here Pierrot and Harlequin appear alongside a Franciscan monk in a work where the bold abstractionism of synthetic Cubism is enhanced by attention to line and to the harmony and unity of the composition.

Across the changes of temper that take us from the gentle, otherworldly fantasy of the Circus period through analytical Cubism to the neo-classicism of *The Three Musicians* via the semi-realist Pierrot of 1918 and beyond to the sentimentalism of Picasso's naturalist portrayal of his son Paul in 1924 (*Paul as Pierrot*), the successive reworkings of *commedia* and circus iconography provide the constant against which we can measure the development of a Modernist aesthetic in Picasso's painting.

We find in the work of Apollinaire – across a time span that coincides with the high years of Cubist experimentation – a similar pre-occupation with pantomime figures and circus themes, and a search for a fresher, more contemporary style that involves the gradual dis-placement of Symbolist values and the introduction of non-idealist, non-representationalist perspectives. The poems 'Crépuscule' and 'Un Fantôme de Nuées' are important landmarks, for they correspond to different moments in Apollinaire's development of a Modernist poetic. Taken together, these poems enable us to chart the struggle for a specifically Modernist style, and at the same time to identify the ambiguities and hesitations inflecting the programme of aesthetic renewal. The first of them, 'Crépuscule', was published jointly with 'Saltimbanques' in 1909, and likewise is thought to have been written around 1904–5: it transforms the *commedia* Harlequin into a mystical performer in a twilight fantasy of unmistakable Symbolist inspiration. The suggestions it places in the reader's mind are stirred once more in the more outwardly Modernist but equally hermetic 'Un Fantôme de Nuées'. Composed in 1913, this poem returns to the circus theme and to the figure of the popular performer, reworking these in a complex frame which superimposes naturalist and fantastic visions and where the world of the street acrobats' performance provides access to a mythic world beyond the confines of the material. A key composition of Apollinaire's Modernist phase (1912–1914), spanning 'Zone' and the simultanist compositions and conversation poems of the pre-war period, this poem re-enacts the struggle for style and the desire for poetic renewal. Yet it remains an ambivalent expression of creative desire, for whilst it affirms certain aspects of the Modernist credo, it seems to turn back to a more markedly Symbolist lyricism: as we shall see, this later poem demonstrates clear structural and thematic affinities with 'Crépuscule'.

Whilst the limits of space dictate that this discussion of Apollinaire's performers will focus on two key poems, Apollinaire's rehabilitation of pantomime in the theatre of avant-garde experimentalism is of signal interest. In 1917 the poet-dramatist returns to the popular stage and the self-transforming power of the focal performer in *Les Mamelles de Tirésias*: although the motley has disappeared and the clown is transfigured, the boisterous pantomime spirit prevails, while the traditional themes of travesty and carnival are reworked in an avant-garde farce that combines the humour of slapstick and a form of proto-Surrealist fantasy announced by Apollinaire to be more real than reality. The same desire to transform the popular theatre leads Picasso to design the set, costumes and curtain for Cocteau's infamous *Parade* (1917): the same struggle for the modern emerges in the painter's use of the tactics of shock-Modernism to subvert the nostalgia inspired by the conspicuously sedate depictions of the stage curtain.

The appeal of circus and pantomime iconography in the work of Apollinaire and Picasso is clear. Whilst circumstantial factors such as their regular attendance at the Cirque Medrano are helpful in pinpointing influences, the continuity of inspiration and the permanency of such figures suggest a more strongly motivated choice, one closely related to the search for a new aesthetic in poetry and painting undertaken in the early years of the twentieth century as a reaction against canons prevailing at the end of the nineteenth century. The convergence of the search for style and the assimilation of pantomime elements gives rise to a series of Modernist reworkings of the popular performer figure.

The use of *commedia* figures and the avant-garde search for style demand to be situated in terms of the impact of popular culture on 'high' art, itself in the throes of modernization from around the mid-nineteenth century.[5] This sets the search for a specifically Modernist style in the wider context of a modern tradition whose origins are post-Romantic and whose development is paralleled by the remaking of the pantomime mask. It is out of the tradition of the modern that Modernism develops – both as a product of that tradition and as a reaction against it. That is, Modernism represents a continuation of the tradition of setting up alternatives to the prevailing canons in order to contest the central, cultural hegemony; at the same time, Modernism proposes itself as a radically new alternative and in so doing opposes previous attempts to radicalize.

The development of the modern tradition in art and literature coincides with a renewed interest in popular art forms. There is a clear affinity between an anti-canonic movement in literature and art and the non-elitism and marginality of the popular arts. Whilst this merits a fuller discussion beyond the limits of the present essay, it seems clear that the desire to assimilate popular forms is the natural corollary of a radicalizing action which aims to displace the bourgeois hegemony in the arts by opposing the traditionalism and conservatism of canonic forms. The struggle to set art free from conventions involves the espousal of forms previously considered too marginal, even too 'low', to constitute true art. The socio-ideological content of Romanticism – its anti-traditionalism and anti-elitism, and its call to revolutionary change – prepares the way for this, sustaining a conception of art that stresses marginality and artifice over conformity and 'truth'. It is with this shift in sensibility that the influence of the popular arts on modern high culture becomes suddenly more pervasive from around 1840. The nineteenth-century revival of interest in pantomime and the performing artiste owes much to the near-universal influence of the most famous Pierrot of the age, the mime Jean-Baptise Deburau who performed nightly at the Théâtre des Funambules between 1825 and 1839 to audiences which included Banville and Gautier.[6] The enthusiasm of Gautier, who acted as a promoter and reviewer of the Funambules, likewise that of Champfleury, who wrote pantomime scripts and who identifies the poet's inner self with the figure of Harlequin, did much to endorse pantomime as a source of artistic inspiration.

This is the Golden Age of pantomime. Having established itself as an anti-canonic, and necessarily vigorous form, pantomime asserts its independence on the margins of French theatre in defiance of the conventions of the bourgeois stage. And so it identifies with and overlaps with related forms of entertainment like acrobatics, a form increasingly represented visually and poetically in the work of Daumier and Baudelaire. The typically anti-bourgeois position this inspires is reflected in Banville's 'Odes funambulesques', where the liminary poems 'La Corde raide' and 'Le Saut du tremplin' have a distinct satirical dimension.[7] Throughout this period we note the tendency of modern writers to conflate the different entertainments of the popular stage in their pursuit of the elusive Performer. The post-Romantic phase reflects this, the twin figures of the pantomime artiste and circus performer penetrating the artistic and literary imagination as an expression of the alienation and isolation suffered by the poet or artist. Together with Banville's 'Odes funambulesques' (1857), Baudelaire's two prose poems 'Le Vieux Saltimbanque' (1861) and 'Une Mort héroïque' (1863) have given rise to considerable critical discussion of artifice, marginality and dissonance, and the absurd as a means of access to unreality.[8] Baudelaire and Banville see Pierrot as a dispossessed pariah, a social outcast, a figure of mockery, but also as a being invested with a privileged sensitivity, mundane yet strangely elevated. The parallels between poet/painter and performer are clear: Banville and Baudelaire explore the analogy between clown and creator, aerialist and artist, in terms of themes of audacity and alienation, humanity and isolation, yet they stop short of identifying the performer as the projected Other (or alter ego) of the Poet. Only with Verlaine and then more fully with Laforgue do the identities of poet and performer merge.

It is at the point where figures of clowns and acrobats are transformed by the poetic imagination that a more complete reworking of pantomime iconography is achieved. Laforgue creates Pierrot anew, substituting for Baudelaire's visualization of Pierrot his own identification with Pierrot. Thus the structuring Baudelairian duality and analogy which, as a statement of resemblance, emphasizes difference over identity, gives way in Laforgue to a more complex non-differentiation that is characteristic of the modern tendency to blur boundaries. Performer and Poet merge in Laforgue's creation, Lord Pierrot. The elevation of the pantomime fumbler into an aristocrat of a distinctly ironical disposition reveals the spirit of serious self-parody which informs the modern venture, destabilizing the traditional search for self. If Laforgue's Pierrot remains detached and controlled, Verlaine's Pierrot expresses the seering agony of the modern self: he tears away the illusion of gaiety and abandon so elegantly embroidered in the *Fêtes galantes* poems, to reveal, not the naïve, moonstruck clown (Gilles) or sprightly Pierrot of Watteau, but a figure in the grip of existential terror as he contemplates the spectre of his own death. This vacant self, adrift in a ghostly void, announces the literature of silence of the post-Modern era.

If Deburau's mime-show is the major influence on nineteenth-century aficionados of foolery and the famous mime, in the words of Robert Storey 'the godparent of the multifarious Pierrots who found their way into Romantic, Decadent and Symbolist literature', what of the European cultural mainstream of the twentieth century?[9] Certainly, the interest of the 'bande à Picasso' in the figures of clowning clods and pantomime performers, at the turn of the century, has to be understood in a frame that takes in the Medrano and extends far beyond it, for the avant-garde's reworking of the clowning theme mirrors the trans-formimg efforts of the entire modern movement and endorses the concept of a tradition of the Modern. The common purpose which unites – historically and culturally – the Pierrots and Harlequins of Picasso, Apollinaire and Max Jacob to those of Baudelaire, Laforgue, Verlaine, Toulouse-Lautrec, Alain-Fournier, Chagall, T.S. Eliot, e.e. cummings, and Klee, and in our time to the angst-filled non-entities and puppets of Beckett and Ionesco, is the assimilation, transformation and perpetuation of an endlessly reworkable cultural model. Its open-endedness produces the myriad, modern representations of pantomime and circus, clowning and *commedia*, as each artist – poet or painter, choreographer or composer – engages in his personal search for style. At this point we should consider more closely the exchange that takes place between popular stage and high culture.

At any stage in the modernizing process this exchange is defined by the appropriation, transformation and refinement of *commedia* and circus matter. The suggestion of an analogy with alchemy (an idea personified by Apollinaire's 'Arlequin trismégiste' in 'Crépuscule') is borne out by Watteau's treatment of the pantomime theme: the refinement and elevation of *commedia* figures transposed by the pastoral elegance of the *Fêtes galantes* signals the transmutation of pantomime matter. It is this determined break with the rumbustious spirit of the *commedia* and a commitment to renewal through metamorphosis that turn the brutish oafs and fleet-footed schemers of the pantomime world into the remote, elegiac creatures of Watteau's dream settings. So the players are transfigured and the pantomime cliché is made new. This raises – in respect of twentieth-century transformations – the question of what precisely is being transformed. Is Deburau's Pierrot the model? Or is it Watteau's Gilles? Determining the degree of influence is patently impossible; however, it is clear that the modern reworkings of Pierrot and Harlequin refer back – directly or indirectly – to the *commedia* tradition, itself the product of processes of assimilation and reworking of aspects of ancient carnival. When Robert Storey suggests that Deburau's interpretation is a direct source of inspiration for modern artists, we sense that what we are confronting is neither strict tradition nor pure invention but an alliance of old and new, a miraculous remaking of the pantomime cliché on the Funambules stage. What ensures the survival of the cliché is an original and audacious treatment which allows the reworking to assert its newness, displace the stereotype and come to prominence in its own right: pertinent examples of this are Sacha Guitry's play *Deburau* and Marcel Carné's film *Les Enfants du paradis* – two instances of the remodelling replacing the model as a theme for the modern stage and the screen.

Already we have gained some sense of the tradition of which the work of Apollinaire and Picasso represents an extension and a remaking. The survival of the pantomime clown and the circus acrobat depends on the revitalization of a cliché whose properties are extracted, magically transformed and 'made new' in line with the call to radicalize style. Just as Deburau, when he began to play Pierrot, was adopting the well-known *commedia* mask and, in the process, rehabilitating the original pantomime model, so the same holds true for Picasso and Apollinaire whose harlequins and tumblers are influenced directly or indirectly, maximally or minimally, by a long series of forerunners. At the same time the Modernist's originality is measured in terms of the perceived difference between the *model* and the invention. This is where the question of stylistic change comes into play. The Modernist imperative of making it new involves subsuming the *commedia* model in order to transform it, thus combining the techniques of assimilation and imitation, central to the reproduction of pantomime matter, with processes for radicalizing style. The transformation of the *commedia* model involves the reworking of one or other of its components in the context of a new artistic departure: that is, those instances where the model of reference is identified by the persistence of a significant identifying component within a new creative framework. For example, in Henri Rousseau's *Nuit de carnaval* the dusky Pierrot is identified by his familiar white conical hat and his ballooning smock. This alliance of old and new shapes the iconography of the avant-garde. We find in the work of Picasso, for example, that Harlequin remains identifiable even in the most abstract compositions: in *The Three Musicians* the rectangle of motley designates the pantomime performer, thus Harlequin's costume has the value of a synecdoche and the process engaged is one of metonymic identification set in a framework of radical formal innovation.

Clearly there is an element of mimetic representation here. Mimesis is introduced into a compositional frame that is conspicuously non-mimetic (in terms of its abstractionism), that is anti-representational in its endeavour not to reproduce but to recreate through processes of transposition and transfiguration. The Modernist balances the preservation of a tradition and the renewal of that tradition, the latter being consequent upon the negation of the inherited cliché in favour of newly-discovered imaginative possibilities and the establishment of an anti-tradition.

This raises a second issue and leads to a temporary widening of our perspective. The processes of assimilation and transformation themselves extend the tradition of literary regeneration whereby a given model is assimilated and perpetuated by a new set of forms. Literary examples abound and Cervantes' *Don Quixote*, as a Golden Age prefiguration of the modern novel, will serve to illustrate this point. Tales of chivalry provide the model which Cervantes' eponymous hero adopts as a credo and ideal. Don Quixote dreams of becoming the kind of hero inscribed in the codes of chivalry but settles for tilting at windmills. It is across the gulf between ideal and reality, desire and experience, that the ironic voice of the Modernist is heard to echo. Like Don Quixote, who adopts the accoutrements of the knightly hero, the Self emerging in Picasso's paintings or in Apollinaire's poems dons the garb of the pantomime player or circus performer and establishes an ambiguous equivalence between himself and the figure of the popular artiste – that is to say, the Self simultaneously identifies with and stands apart from the Harlequin-Acrobat, precisely because the assimilation of the performing figure through literary and visual media involves the creation of an illusion and a dramatization predicated on the assuming and casting aside of a mask. This implies a constant mediation towards, and retreat from, the Other: mediation in the projection of the Self upon the Performer whose values and qualities he espouses; retreat when the Self confronts the artifice and apprehends the purely illusory nature of his endeavour to 'become' the Other, articulated through the absent mask. The Self is filled with a sense of anomie as he beholds the gaping void between desire and its fulfilment. In our era the voice of post-Modernist irony echoes across that space, negating the search for self and announcing a literature of silence that reflects the dehumanized state of things. But this is to look beyond the reaches of Modernism to its eventual displacement, a debate outside the scope of the present study. Our concern is with Modernism and the tradition of the Modern of which it is a product. The relationship between Self and motleyed Other can be summarized as one of identification and alienation, complicity and estrangement. This is the dualism at the centre of a complex drama of the Self where the artiste – pantomime clown or circus showman – becomes a figure for the poet, the projection of the contemporary *mal de siècle* and its transcendence through art. The twin themes of transcendence and creativity provide the focus for our study of Apollinaire's poems.

Whilst our attention focuses now on Apollinaire's treatment of *commedia* and circus themes, our context remains the avant-garde's search for style and the continuation of an interest in the popular arts that develops out of the nineteenth-century Romantico-Symbolist preoccupation with the pantomime Pierrot.

It is not to Apollinaire but to his contemporary, the poet Max Jacob, that we turn for clarification of the Modernist position on comic art inspiration. In a letter to Jacques Maritain in 1936 the convergence of the processes of continuation and transformation of *commedia* figures with the Modernist search for style are the subject of an elliptical though illuminating remark.[10] Commenting on the shift from the Symbolist mode which had prevailed at the end of the nineteenth century to a rigorous Modernist consciousness in the early twentieth century, Jacob speaks of an 'art arlequin' ('la connaissance des effets à produire et leurs moyens') replacing the 'art pierrot' ('l'humble confession des états d'âme') of the previous generation. The meaning of Jacob's statement has to be sought in the new stylistic temper and the emergence of a Modernist temper that develops in opposition to the dominant canon of the past century – Romantico-Symbolism, a sensibility predicated on the pursuit of sentimentality, lyrical effusiveness, and a preoccupation with subjectivity which posits the text as the vehicle for the expression of the more profound self of the artist. With scientific progress and material innovation leading to heightened human expectations towards the end of the nineteenth century, there occurs a significant displacement within the artistic sensibility. Lingering Romantic *ennui* gives way to a new spirit in the arts and to approaches which stress creativity over expressivity, objectivity over subjectivity. Consistent with this is a new emphasis on the work of art as a self-referential object. And so the artist turns from an art of lyrical expression to an art of objective construction. For Jacob, the ousting of the pitiful Pierrot by the agile Harlequin metaphorizes the shift from the subjective art of the late nineteenth century to a formalist-inclined art of creation whereby a detached, critical imagination now prevails over the more purely lyrical sensibility of Romantico-Symbolism.

In the struggle for a new art Apollinaire emerges as an arbiter. A 'poète de transition' is Reverdy's assessment of one whose name is synonymous with the development of an energetic, avant-garde sensibility in the early years of the twentieth century as a reaction against the Symbolist ideality. The new spirit responds to the need to address reality in fresh and radical ways, that is, to replace traditional representationalism with a resolutely anti-representationalist perspective. Apollinaire's composition – spanning twenty years from 1898 to 1918 – reflects this preoccupation. In the climate of artistic upheaval and realignment of the new century, it stands as a summation of the complexities and contradictions faced by the poetic avant-garde. The collections *Alcools* (1898–1912) and *Calligrammes* (1913–18) trace the development of Apollinaire from a post-Symbolist position through to his engagement with the more innovative forms of Modernist conception in the 'Ondes' series of 1912–14. This pursues the experimental dimension of a credo reaffirmed in the last great poems and in the 1917 lecture *L'Esprit Nouveau et les poètes* where Apollinaire draws together the contrasting strands of his aesthetic. Whilst Apollinaire's commitment to Modernist renewal is serious and sustained, he refuses to break with tradition and stands poised between the Old and the New, intent on balancing their differences and effecting, where possible, the transition between the lyrical tradition and the Cubist-inspired imperatives of formal construction, non-representationalism and emotional sobriety. Invention and renewal, experimentation and reconciliation – this is the stylistic backdrop against which Apollinaire's performimg artistes make their appearance in the two poems we shall examine here – the 1904–5 poem 'Crépuscule' and the 1913 poem 'Un Fantôme de Nuées' published, respectively, in

Alcools and *Calligrammes*. These are key poems for us in that they reveal the reworking of the Harlequin-Acrobat figure in two quite different stylistic settings – one, more purely Symbolist-inspired, the other more clearly Modernist in conception. We begin by examining the more conspicuous stylistic differences which emerge from a comparative study of 'Crépuscule' and 'Un Fantôme de Nuées'. While the poems share a narrative function – that is, to recount the miracle performance of the Harlequin-Acrobat – they are constructed on quite different sets of aesthetic criteria, a factor which influences the treatment of the performer figure and the poetic construction of the performance. 'Crépuscule' is markedly Symbolist in inspiration, the supernatural atmosphere of the piece favouring the development of illusion at all levels:

> Frôlée par les ombres des morts
> Sur l'herbe où le jour s'exténue
> L'arlequine s'est mise nue
> Et dans l'étang mire son corps
>
> Grazed by the shadows that pass
> Colombine naked and cool
> While the day expires on the grass
> Studies herself in the pool   (lines 1–4)

In contrast, 'Un Fantôme de Nuées' exposes the illusion at its centre, exploiting the stylistic discrepancy between the naturalistic reconstruction of contemporary reality at one level and the exploration of a timeless, mythic dimension at another. The technical complexities this engenders are those identified with the Modernist poetic: in particular, the creation of a simultaneous vision based on techniques of juxtaposition and reconstruction points to the influence of Cubist-related stylistic criteria. Moreover, the assimilation of a cultural model derived from the *commedia* tradition is itself the subject of authorial comment (contrasting with 'Crépuscule', where the assimilation is 'silent'). This forms the basis of an initial, unambiguous differentiation of the worlds of the spectator and the *spectacle*: on the one hand, there is the world of contingent reality (identified spatio-temporally by references to 'le boulevard Saint-Germain' and 'la veille du quatorze juillet'), on the other, the mysterious realm intimated by the movements of the Harlequin.

The difference in style between the two poems has to be approached in terms of context. 'Crépuscule' was composed around 1904, one year

into Apollinaire's 'long sleep', a period of relative inactivity that
followed the completion of the first version of 'La Chanson du Mal-
Aimé' and endured until 1908 and the emergence of a 'fire aesthetic', the
moment of creative rebirth for Apollinaire.[11] This interlude is often
dismissed as a poetic void, but from it emerged several short pieces
imbued with a delicate post-Symbolist spirit. These short poems reveal
Apollinaire to be the natural inheritor and continuer of the Symbolist
tradition which he adapts and makes his own, exploring now a lighter
vein of fantasy.[12] 'Crépuscule', in combining elements of a wistful *fin de
siècle* imagination, its melancholy atmosphere and monochromatic
tones, with a subtle evocation of Harlequin's metamorphosis, transcends the pathos of Romanticism, reaffirming the transforming power
of the poetic imagination through the figure of a miraculous performer
who is the embodiment of the conquering creative spirit. A further
parallel may be drawn with certain Picasso paintings of the same period
– the same remoteness, the sense of unreality and the all-pervading
otherness of the scene, the dream-like quality of the world of ritual
performance, emerge in paintings whose monochromatic tendency –
the predominance of beiges, ochres, sand colours in the later Circus
series – was largely influenced by Symbolist painting. By the time we
reach 1913 and 'Un Fantôme de Nuées', the poetic imperatives have
altered in line with painterly influences. Cubism had continued to shape
poetic theory and practice. But now the rigour of analytical Cubism
gives way to the more fluid art of Orphism. Whilst the anti-illusionist,
anti-mimetic principles of Cubism survive in Orphism, the hard
contours of Cubism have dissolved into a harmonious, synthetic vision,
thus endorsing Apollinaire's prediction that Cubism would become
'humanized'.[13] Just as Robert Delaunay captures the spirit of the
contemporary in polychromatic, simultaneous reconstructions of Paris,
so Apollinaire's 'Un Fantôme de Nuées' registers the colour and
vibrancy of the twentieth-century world, celebrates the surprise
potential of each superficially ordinary incident and uncovers, through
the magic of the acrobatic performance, an epic dimension beyond the
material. Let us now consider each of these poems at greater length.

'Crépuscule' reveals the influence of the Romantico-Symbolist imagination upon the poet. It plunges the reader into a mystical world where
the shades of the dead roam and fairy folk mingle with sorcerers from
Bohemia. It is a world reminiscent of Verlaine's 'Colloque sentimental'.

The development of the poem reveals a greater seriousness of purpose than a concern with decors and the creation of an otherworldly atmosphere might suggest. After describing the static, classical pose of Arlequine (a reflection of the academic tendency of much Symbolist art), the poet moves into the role of narrator and commentator of the 'spectacle' about to unfold. In this the narrator acts as a mediator, relaying to the reader the miraculous performance of which he and the supernatural audience are privileged witnesses. The poem's structure suggests the formation of a series of concentric circles – circles of observation – around the figure of the performing Harlequin. The innermost ring is occupied by the fairy audience, the middle ring by the narrator and the outer ring by the reader. These circles enclose the 'spectacle', consecrating a sacred, unimpeachable space from which the profane – spectators, narrator and reader – are excluded:

Sur les tréteaux l'arlequin blême
Salue d'abord les spectateurs
Des sorciers venus de Bohême
Quelques fées et les enchanteurs

Ayant décroché une étoile
Il la manie à bras tendu
Tandis que des pieds un pendu
Sonne en mesure les cymbales

The pale harlequin on the stage
Now salutes his spectators
Some elves a Bohemian mage
Fairies prestidigitators

Then he unfastens a star
His arms work a juggler's feat
While a hanged man rolls a fanfare
On the cymbals with his feet   (lines 9–16)

The suggestion that the performance is meaningful in the absence of verbal communication, that the soundless movements impart a significant message, is conveyed by the 'spotlighting' of the Harlequin figure in lines 13–16. The shift from the all-embracing view of spectators and trestle stage (lines 9–12) to the focus on the performer plunges the world of the spectators into darkness, privileging the miracle unfolding in their midst. The different stages of the performance draw attention to its representational and symbolic import, in particular to Harlequin's ritual salutation, to the dynamics of a performance which involves his juggling a star plucked from the firmament whilst the Hanged Man beats time, and Harlequin's ultimate self-transformation. The obscure symbolism of the performance weaves a strange allegory which in turn gives rise to the baffling triptych with which the poem concludes. Leaving aside for the moment the metamorphosis of Harlequin, what are we to make of the three visions of the closing quatrain?

> L'aveugle berce un bel enfant
> La biche passe avec ses faons
> Le nain regarde d'un air triste
> Grandir l'arlequin trismégiste

> The blind one cradles a beautiful child
> The doe passes with her fawns
> The dwarf observes sadly
> The rise of Trismegistes Harlequin   (lines 17–20)

The ternary structure suggests a unity between three apparently unrelated tableaux depicting human, animal and supernatural life. The parent/child pairs ('aveugle'/'enfants'; 'biche'/'faons') connote themes of protection and vulnerability. At the same time each group seems oblivious or indifferent to the Harlequin's powers, whilst the sadness of the dwarf, who beholds the miracle transformation, tells of the impossibility of his rivalling Harlequin, and the physical contrast suggested by the dual presence of the dwarf and Harlequin, now three times great, suggests a clear opposition. The effect of this is to unite the dwarf to the 'aveugle' and the doe in terms of their triple non-identification with the all-powerful, self-metamorphosing Harlequin. The absence of reciprocity here, and the process of differentiation which the insertion of the triptych sets in motion, allows us to extend the allegory in terms of a set of counter-values which places the threefold representation of frailty, powerlessness, and resignation in opposition to the apotheosis of Harlequin-Trismégiste, the embodiment of creative virtuality.

    If the meaning behind the symbolism remains obscure, the processes of symbolization are somewhat clearer. In particular, the absence of any conclusive indication favours intimation over revelation. Indeed the poem, working from the allegorical device at its centre, seems to point us towards a truth that lies beyond the immediately communicable. The performance is a mediation towards that truth, and the poem the vehicle of that mediation. For all its simplicity and brevity, the poem is a creation of subtle complexity, constructed in such a way as to allow intimation to emerge from structure. Let us look more closely at two crucial moments in the structuring of the enigma.

The first of these concerns the status of the solitary 'Arlequine' and her relationship to the performing 'Arlequin'. The presence of these two *commedia* figures suggests an extension of their pantomime collusion. Indeed, given Apollinaire's retention of the feminine variant 'Arlequine' over the more usual 'Colombine'[14] – the syllable count being unaffected – suggestions of collusion stretch towards resemblance, even identity. In the poet's endeavour to balance opposing forces, specifically those represented by man and woman, there resurfaces the obsession with resemblance and difference that punctuates *L'Enchanteur pourrissant* and culminates with the subject's coming to consciousness of the 'éternités différentes de l'homme et de la femme' in *Onirocritique*. In 'Crépuscule' the male–female resemblance suggested by the nominal identity of the *commedia* figures 'Arlequin' / 'Arlequine' is negated by a structuring duality which emphasizes enduring differences over superficial resemblance. The sexual difference – marked syntactically by the feminine gender inflection – is reinforced thematically and structurally by Arlequine's cold indifference. Locked in frozen contemplation of her own naked body she stands apart from the other 'figurants', her isolation marked formally by the stanza boundary. The hermeticism of the opening stanza encloses the Arlequine within its own enchanted circle, whilst her narcissistic pose speaks at once of the irresistibility and the sterility of self-obsession. Her introspection (and that of the Romantico-Symbolist sensibility which her presence evokes) is overturned by the self-projection and universalizing movement of the Harlequin, the symbol of creative desire and its spectacular fulfilment. This leads us to the second question and the somewhat elided moment of Harlequin's self-metamorphosis. What is the significance of the performer's feat? Its result, at least, is unambiguous. His transformation from simple 'Arlequin' to 'Arlequin trismégiste' is predicated on his identification with the mystic Hermes Trismegistes, an instance of myth-assimilation that confers on the Harlequin the status of supreme magician and alchemist. This is a question to which the conclusion of this essay will seek to bring a possible answer.

At this point we turn to consider the second poem, for certain similarities link the 1904 and 1913 compositions, not least the thematic of acrobatics, the narrative of performance, and the figure of the miraculous performer.

The tendency of critics to neglect comparative studies of these poems (or others) across the chronological span of Apollinaire's corpus is evidence of a long-established tradition of parcelling off specific areas within the corpus whilst paying lip-service to the notion of global unity and forces for continuity that cut across the boundaries between the two major collections of poetry. The absence of comparative perspectives in the case of the two poems we are considering is confirmation that perceived differences of style outweigh similarities of theme and structure in the reckoning of many critics. Style and the treatment of theme are inseparable in any discussion of Apollinaire's Modernism, its consolidation as well as its hesitations. Indeed the major stylistic differences between poems emerge in the varying treatment of a recurring theme or figure. The aim here is to assess the impact of the search for style on the theme of popular performance and the figure of the performer. We begin by considering the pursuit of a more consistently Modernist style and the hesitations of a poet who never relinquishes his Symbolist inheritance.

Whereas 'Crépuscule' is placed under the sign of enigma, its obscure, elliptical reverie unfolding into a mysterious *dénouement*, 'Un Fantôme de Nuées' is striking in its directness of tone and its naturalness of style. A product of Apollinaire's high Modernist period (1912–14), the poem is an attempt to shake off the fetters of pure poetry and move boldly towards a new lyricism which embraces the language of everyday communication and seeks in unremarkable instances untapped sources of poetry. There is a clear echo of ideas explored in 'Zone' (1912):

> Tu lis les prospectus les catalogues les affiches qui chantent tout haut
> Voilà la poésie ce matin . . .
>
> You read handbills catalogues posters singing aloud
> That's what poetry is this morning . . .   (lines 11–12)

The informality and directness of register contrast markedly with the remote narrative voice in 'Crépuscule'. In 'Un Fantôme de Nuées' space and time markers relate to the here-and-now of empirical experience, the everyday world of Paris, its street-performers and their spectators.

The foregrounding of the trivial, banal, and incidental contributes a strong sense of reality, whilst the commemoration of the struggle for democracy ('la veille du quatorze juillet', 'la statue de Danton') is an attempt to historicize, consistent with the feeling for ordinary humanity that pervades the poem. The effect of situating the narrative within this commemorative framework is, at one level, to validate the discourse of realism and enhance the poem's verisimilitude; at another level, the commemorative aspect implies processes of symbolization that anticipate the transcendence of the here-and-now of the narrative by the miraculous child-acrobat and recall the allegorical dimension of 'Crépuscule'.

The development of the narrative reveals the symbolic subtext of the mountebank show. Each performer embodies a desire, dream or obsession: the organ-grinder dreams of the future but has to endure the burden of the past:

> Vois-tu le personnage maigre et sauvage
> La cendre de ses pères lui sortait en barbe grisonnante
> Il portait ainsi toute son hérédité au visage
> Il semblait rêver à l'avenir
> En tournant machinalement un orgue de Barbarie

> Do you see the man who's savage and lean
> His father's ashes sprouted in his graying beard
> And he bore his whole heredity in his face
> He seemed to be dreaming about the future
> Turning his barrel organ all the while   (lines 22–6)

His presence suggests the perpetuity of the life cycle and in this there is a strong echo of 'Les Trois Vertus plastiques' – 'On ne peut pas transporter partout avec soi le cadavre de son père . . . Mais nos pieds ne se détachent qu'en vain du sol qui contient les morts', ('One cannot be lugging one's father's corpse around everywhere . . . But we try in vain to release our feet from the earth under which lie the dead.')[15] The oldest acrobat bears witness to the inexorable passage of time, to age and to human decline. He wears the signs of his morbidity on his purply-pink vest:

> Le plus vieux avait un maillot couleur de ce rose violâtre qu'ont aux joues certaines jeunes filles fraîches mais près de la mort

> The oldest wore a sweater the rose-violet color you see in the fresh cheeks of young girls who are dying   (line 30)

The second mountebank is more phantomatic than real, a ghostly presence, that of a self dehumanized ('. . . un homme sans tête'). In the persona of the organ-grinder and in the trio of acrobats there is a structural and thematic reflection of the 'charlatan crépusculaire' and the forlorn trio of the concluding stanza of 'Crépuscule'. The same themes of vulnerability, powerlessness, and detachment are embodied in figures whose presence is, likewise, marginal to the miracle of performance. The curious acrobatic trio gathers ('Les bras les bras partout montaient la garde', 'Arms arms everywhere mounted guard', line 36) in anticipation of the appearance of the miracle child, the incarnation of freedom and timelessness and the focus of the onlookers' wonderment. His emergence from under the barrel-organ, like the Harlequin's salutation in 'Crépuscule', signals the show's commencement and the imminent transcendence of the world of the spectators.

It is precisely the miracle acrobat's transmutation of the substance of the everyday into mythic experience which links 'Un Fantôme de Nuées' to 'Crépuscule', where the association of the figures of Acrobat and Alchemist is given an overtly allegorical representation. Just as the twilight Harlequin effects a spectacular metamorphosis of his being, so the tiny street acrobat turns his professional routine into a music of forms, purer and more ethereal than music itself. In this way both poems respond to the desire of the creative self to transcend human limitations and explore a realm of boundless virtuality. Apollinaire affirms the necessity of such a vision in his 1908 essay 'Sur la peinture':

> . . . le peintre doit avant tout se donner le spectacle de sa propre divinité et les tableaux qu'il offre à l'admiration des hommes leur conféreront la gloire d'exercer aussi et momentanément leur propre divinité.[16]

> . . . the painter must above all create for himself the image of his divinity and the paintings he presents for the admiration of others will bestow upon them the same glory of exercising, for a moment, their own divinity.

In the 1913 poem the tension between banal and mythic – absent in 'Crépuscule', where fantasy is all-pervading – produces the stylistic complexity we identify with the Modernist poetic. This complexity centres on discrepancies arising from the interplay of realist and fantastic modes, that is, on the one hand, the naturalistic reconstruction of reality, on the other, the exploration of a timeless, mythic 'surréalité'.

Both poems provide the framework and the imaginary space for the narrative reconstruction of a performance. The means employed to this end contrast sharply, reflecting the different stylistic orientations of the poet, Symbolist preoccupations in 'Crépuscule', Modernist assumptions in 'Un Fantôme de Nuées'. In the earlier piece the supernatural atmosphere and otherworldly backdrop provide an already derealized setting for the narration of the performance, and this favours the development of an all-pervading illusion. Thus the poem's construction facilitates the non-differentiation of the two worlds and indeed suggests some affinity between the inner world of the performance and the outer world of the spectators. This affinity is confirmed at the point where the Harlequin reaches into the night sky for a star with which to juggle. The feat reveals that the power of the Harlequin is not confined to the world of the 'spectacle' but extends to the cosmos. Moreover the upwards projection and the intimation of an absolute obscured by the night sky are consistent with the strong idealist motivation of Symbolism. In the later poem a stricter delineation of the worlds of audience and performer is maintained: the difference is reinforced most prosaically perhaps in the protracted haggling over the price of the performance. The realism of the commercial element, particularly the preoccupation with lucre, stresses the materiality of the world in which the performance takes place. Here access to the illusion is secured not through any supernatural affinity of spectators and performers, but more prosaically on the basis of a commercial transaction. The effect of this is to ground the narrative in modern reality, heightening the sense of the ordinary and the unspectacular in line with a Modernist concern with things immediate, concrete and contemporary. Yet there is no espousal of realism per se and the naturalistic is offset throughout the poem by the mode of fantasy:

Je me fis une place dans ce cercle afin de tout voir
Poids formidables
Villes de Belgique soulevées à bras tendu par un ouvrier russe de Longwy
Haltères noirs et creux qui ont pour tige un fleuve figé
Doigts roulant une cigarette amère et délicieuse comme la vie

I found a place in the circle where I could see everything
Tremendous weights
Belgian cities raised at arm's length by a Russian worker from Longwy
Hollow black dumbbells whose stem is a frozen stream
Fingers rolling a cigarette as bittersweet as life   (lines 12–16)

The tendency to multiply modes of expression reflects the dialogical thrust of Modernism whereby a plurality of discourse replaces any one, continuous mode of expression. Likewise the Modernist preference for the synchronic over the diachronic, the heterogeneous over the homogeneous, the multi-directional over the unilinear, is central to the assumptions upon which the 1913 poem is constructed. The following example will illustrate this. Here, crude material considerations are a potential obstacle to the performance taking place and to the revelation of its mythic subtext:

> La musique se tut et ce furent des pourparlers avec le public
> Qui sou à sou jeta sur le tapis la somme de deux francs cinquante
> Au lieu des trois francs que le vieux avait fixés comme prix des tours
>
> Mais quand il fut clair que personne ne donnerait plus rien
> On se décida à commencer la séance
>
> The music stopped and there were negotiations with the public
> Who sou by sou threw down on the rug the sum of two and a half
>   francs
> Instead of the three francs the old man had set as the price of the show
>
> But when it was clear no one was going to give any more
> They decided to begin the performance   (lines 46–50)

The incongruous linking of prosaic and mythic orders throws up a series of opposing values: materiality/immateriality; temporality/eternity; reality/fantasy. This reinforces the poem's discontinuities, sharpening the differences between the here-and-now of the Paris street scene and the magical realm intimated by the tiny acrobat. Whereas in 'Crépuscule' the poet blurs the differences between the outer world and inner world of performance, creating an impression of total illusion in line with the synthetic function of Symbolism, in 'Un Fantôme de Nuées' he exposes the differences between these two worlds by way of a radical juxtaposition of the world of everyday reality and the mythic world acceded to through the performance. Whilst the coherence of the narrative is preserved, the two orders are strictly delineated. The contingent world is identified spatio-temporally by familiar references to Paris and Bastille Day as well as by the naturalistic description of the humdrum of human activity. This is the world of the empirical. The revelation of a mythic order is predicated on the temporary abolition of contingency as ordinary time is suspended and spatial constraints are transcended by the totalizing movements of the young acrobat:

Une jambe en arrière prête à la génuflexion
Il salua ainsi les quatre points cardinaux
Et quand il marcha sur une boule
Son corps mince devint une musique si délicate que nul parmi les
    spectateurs n'y fut insensible

. . . . .

Et cette musique des formes
Détruisit celle de l'orgue mécanique

. . . . .

Le petit saltimbanque fit la roue
Avec tant d'harmonie
Que l'orgue cessa de jouer

One leg back ready to kneel
He saluted the four points of the compass
And when he balanced on a sphere
His thin body became such delicate music that none of the onlookers
    could resist it

. . . . .

And that music of shapes
Destroyed the music of the mechanical organ

. . . . .

The tiny juggler turned cartwheels
With such harmony
That the organ stopped playing   (lines 56-9, 62-3, 65-7)

This miraculous lifting of constraints and freeing of the creative
spirit places the performance under the sign of the eternal. It is
here precisely that the ambiguity and complexity of Apollinaire's
Modernism is revealed, for in such instances of metaphysical transcendence the poet seems to turn back towards a more conspicuously
Symbolist position. The vision of harmony that unfolds draws on music
not merely as a metaphor for the agility and grace of the acrobat, but as
an intimation of spirituality and, by its purity and immateriality, the
privileged language of Symbolism. Apollinaire's Modernism can thus
be seen to be built on certain anomalies of style and temper; whether it
is a hesitant Modernism, however, is another matter. Apollinaire is
clearly representative of the synthesizing tendency of Modernism which

reacts against the previous canon not by flatly rejecting it but rather by accommodating it to Modernism, by reworking it in a new, radically contemporary frame.

The structure of the poem exposes a series of opposing values and antithetical forces. What makes for its complexity is the way these merge and overlap to produce a total vision. The means employed in this metonymic construction of poetic reality reveal some affinity with the techniques of Cubist painting. Disparate elements are introduced into the textual frame and the poet sets about juxtaposing radically different orders, aligning ordinarily unaligned realities – prosaic and poetic, empirical and fantastic, real and illusory – in frames which combine to produce a mythic vision of the modern world. We saw already how the vision of a Belgian worker hoisting cities on his shoulder transforms the conventional image of the circus weightlifter, giving this a mythic reinterpretation. The modes – naturalism and symbolism – and voices – poetic and narrative – combine to produce a poem which embraces and ultimately transcends stylistic disparities. Thus Apollinaire places the production of an autonomous poetic imaginary above the pursuit of any single stylistic option.

We need to reflect finally on the place of the performing artiste at the centre of the two poems. The figure of the acrobatic performer, Harlequin or mountebank, is a constant linking these two poems, a constant inflected by the search for style. Harlequin alights from the Symbolist stage of 'Crépuscule' and reappears in contemporary form, as an exponent of the declining art of street acrobatics, in 'Un Fantôme de Nuées'. This transformation of the artiste from mystical Harlequin into street acrobat reflects the shift from an art more conspicuously Symbolist in tone and temper to a contemporary Modernist conception informed by Delaunay's simultanism and a proto-surreal vision of the contemporary world. The initial effect is to demystify the focal performer now relocated in the modern city; at the same time his very performance confers on him the intrinsic difference which separates him from the world of the spectator and creates the conditions through which he can transcend human limitations, performance being an intimation and prefiguration of the mythic realm beyond the reality of everyday experience. And so there operates an essential remythification of the performing artiste who is the catalyst and communicator of the mythic experience. His performance is catalysing in that it summons the desire of humanity to transcend ordinary limitations. In turn the spectators' desire is projected back upon the performer who embodies their dream and its fulfilment:

> . . . chaque spectateur cherchait en soi l'enfant miraculeux

> . . . every spectator searched in himself for the miraculous child,
>
> (line 71)

In the context of a specifically modernizing situation and within a more conspicuously secular world, this metaphysical aspiration takes on special significance. It is here that Apollinaire's acrobat figure rejoins the traditional *commedia* Harlequin who subverts accepted criteria in order to create and whose energy, audacity and spirit of adventure reflect the poet's defiance of conventions, his pursuit of creative freedom and, above all, his commitment to an exuberant, all-embracing sensibility alive to the surprise potential of the modern world.

NOTES

1 The description of Modernism I subscribe to here is necessarily broad. It bears on the fundamental redefinition of stylistic criteria which occurs in the early decades of the twentieth century and marks the break with inherited canons of Romanticism and Symbolism. At the same time, Modernism represents a new orientation of the Modern and a radicalization of its anti-mimetic aims consistent with a conception of the work as an autonomous, self-referential artefact. The emphasis in this article is on the synthesizing function of the early Modernism of Apollinaire whose work internalizes the transition from Symbolism to a properly avant-garde position. Apollinaire's independent Modernism actively embraces Old and New, sustains Tradition and Adventure. The study which follows considers the Harlequin-Acrobat figure in the light of the distillation of forms and the combining of technical procedures that is the sign of Apollinaire's search for style. Studies of the Modernist phenomenon by Malcolm Bradbury, Hugo Friedrich, Theo Hermans, Octavio Paz, and Charles Russell offer particularly probing analyses.
2 Ezra Pound, *Make It New* (London, Faber and Faber, 1934).
3 Gertrude Stein, *Picasso* (Boston, Beacon Press, 1959), 7.
4 Roland Penrose, *Picasso: His Life and Work*, third edition (Berkeley, University of California Press, 1981), 110–11.
5 Hugo Friedrich, *Die Struktur der modernen Lyrik* (Hamburg, Rowohlt, 1956).

6 Louisa Jones, *Sad Clowns and Pale Pierrots* (Lexington, French Forum, 1984), 46, traces the history of the 'Funambules' and its impact on nineteenth-century literature and painting.
7 See Jones, op. cit. 177–87 for discussion of Banville, Verlaine, Catulle Mendès and the Goncourts.
8 These poems are discussed by Jean Starobinski in *Portrait de l'artiste en saltimbanque* (Paris, Skira, 1970).
9 Robert Storey, *Pierrot: A Critical History of a Mask* (Princeton University Press 1978), 94.
10 This unpublished letter is quoted by J. de Palachio in 'La Postérité du *Gaspard de la Nuit*' in *Max Jacob I – Autour du poème en prose* (Revue des Lettres Modernes, Paris, Minard, 1973), 187.
11 Apollinaire alludes to this 'big sleep' in the draft version of 'Les Fiançailles' entitled 'Les Paroles Etoiles' ('Puis après ma fuite et la mort de mes vérités poétiques / Je m'éveillai au bout de cinq ans une nuit citadine' in *Oeuvres poétiques* (Paris, Pléiade, 1965), 1068.
12 Poems of this period include 'L'Adieu', 'L'Emigrant de Landor Road' and 'Salomé'.
13 In a review of April 1911 Apollinaire declares Cubism to be 'un art dépouillé et sobre dont les apparences encore rigides ne tarderont pas à s'humaniser.' in *Oeuvres complètes*, volume IV (Balland et Lecat, 1966), 188.
14 Allardyce Nicoll, *The World of Harlequin* (Cambridge University Press, 1976), 96–7 confirms that Colombina took the name Arlechinna and that from the seventeenth century she moved closer to Arlequin, rivalling with him in agility and dressed in the same bright costume.
15 *Apollinaire: Les Peintres Cubistes*, edited by L.C. Breunig and J-C. Chevalier (Paris, Hermann, 1980 [1965]), 55.
16 Ibid.

Sources of translations

'Crépuscule' – stanza 5 is my own translation.
'Saltimbanques', 'Zone' – translated by Oliver Bernard in *Apollinaire: Selected Poems* (Penguin Modern European Poets, Penguin, 1965).
'Crépuscule' (stanzas 1–4) – translated by William Meredith in *Apollinaire: Alcools (Poems 1898–1913)*, (Garden City, NY, Doubleday and Co., 1964).
'Un Fantôme de Nuées' – translated by Anne Hyde Greet in *Calligrammes: Poems of Peace and War (1913–1916)*, (Berkeley, University of California Press, 1978).
Les Peintres cubistes – my own translations.

11 The *commedia dell'arte* in early twentieth-century music: Schoenberg, Stravinsky, Busoni and Les Six

GABRIEL JACOBS

It is no trivial matter to explain why so many creative artists of the late nineteenth and early twentieth centuries were fascinated with the characters of the *commedia dell'arte*, and the many strands of the problem are nowhere more difficult to disentangle than in the area of musical composition. Composers as diverse in their styles and aims as Debussy, Fauré, Ravel, Richard Strauss, Rachmaninoff and Symanowski all wrote pieces or movements whose titles incorporate the names of the stock characters of the *commedia*. Some, notably Schoenberg and Stravinsky, composed within the space of the decade 1910 to 1920 acknowledged masterpieces which took their inspiration directly from it.

It is not that this period is unique in having produced music based on the *commedia*: it inspired compositions almost from its very beginnings. In 1594, Orazio Vecchi wrote *L'Amifiparnasso*, a madrigal comedy the cast of which includes Harlequin, Columbine, Pantaloon and Pierrot. The same period saw similar compositions by Alessandro Striggio, Giovanni Croce, and Adriano Banchieri, while in 1639 Giulio Respigliosi (who for the last two years of his life was Pope Clement IX) wrote *Chi soffre, speri*, the first Italian comic opera (*opera buffa*), whose characters are again those of the *commedia*, and which was the start of a genre destined to be of lasting popularity. Indeed, from these first examples stem several parallel and virtually unbroken lines of musical activity related to the *commedia*, including an oral folk tradition typified by internationally known French songs such as 'Monsieur Polichinelle', 'Au clair de la lune' and 'Fais do-do, Pierrot mon p'tit frère'. But the atmosphere which characterized Europe (and especially France and Germany) in the periods immediately preceding and following the First World War produced a generation of serious composers who appear to have been quite unable to ignore the attraction of Harlequin, Pierrot and friends. This is truly the period of a musical fascination with the *commedia* which no doubt sprang from developments in the two forms of literary expression traditionally most closely linked with music – drama and poetry – and in painting.

Legitimate theatre throughout the nineteenth century had moved towards the well-made play, and thus away from the spontaneous atmosphere of the *commedia*, an atmosphere which was to be rediscovered in the early years of this century. As Evert Sprinchorn has put it:

> When the thoroughly rehearsed, minutely directed naturalistic play attained its fulfilment about the time of the First World War, a reaction set in and directors rediscovered the world of the Commedia with its gaudy colours, its frankly theatrical and often grotesque masks or types, the vigorous presence of the actor . . . and the virtual absence of any troublesome playwright. The Commedia provided a total theatre in which colour, . . . music, and acrobatics contributed to the overall effect. It was a circus with a plot, and compared to it the realistic theatre seemed a pale fragment of lost art.[1]

Poetry, too, had witnessed a steadily increasing interest in the *commedia* in the second half of the nineteenth century, and particularly in France where there was a distinct nostalgia for the melancholy playfulness of Watteau's masked figures of the previous century. It is not surprising, then, that contrasting with the move of the legitimate French theatre towards naturalism and the well-made play was an opposite one in a lower-brow culture towards extravagance and spontaneity in the form of the *pantomime*. Unlike its English namesake, which since its foundation in the early eighteenth century has never waned in popularity, the *pantomime* in France was gradually to die out in our own century, its final demise being painfully visible in a desperate appeal for public support broadcast by leading clowns, mimes and theatrical celebrities on French television in 1973.[2] The late nineteenth century, however, had been the heyday of French *pantomime* and, in the literary domain, poets above all appear to have been especially receptive to its characteristic mixture of depth and simplicity. Verlaine sketched a *pantomime* scenario in five acts (*Motif de pantomime*), though his interest in the *commedia* is more widely known from his collection *Fêtes galantes*, where in poems such as 'Clair de lune', 'Mandoline' and 'Fantoche' the stock *commedia* characters betray hints of indeterminate sadness behind their masks of gaiety. In many other Verlaine poems, too – such as 'A la promenade', 'Colombine',

'Pierrot', 'Pierrot gamin', 'Le Clown', 'Le Pitre' and 'Un pouacre' – the *commedia* provides the basic substance. And Verlaine was far from the only nineteenth-century French poet to use the *commedia* as a starting point for verse. Baudelaire, Gautier, de Banville, Mallarmé and (especially) Laforgue[3] were all touched to a greater or lesser extent by it. French novelists such as Flaubert and Edmond de Goncourt showed a certain interest in the *commedia* in their fiction,[4] but the poets felt its influence most profoundly, as was also the case in Germany (Rilke being the prime example) where pantomime and puppet theatre enjoyed considerable popularity in the nineteenth and early twentieth centuries.

However, the link between music and other art forms in this period is most obvious in its relationship with painting, since painters of the time – especially the Cubists – took popular culture to unprecedented levels of style. Both before and during the First World War and well into the 1920s, Harlequins, Pierrots and Columbines made up a substantial part of the creative output of Picasso, Gris and Severini, as well as, to a lesser extent, of Braque and Derain, and the list can be extended to include Chagall, Matisse, Metzinger, Rouault, Léger and others when allied forms of culture, such as the fairground or the circus, are included.[5] It was not just that some of these artists designed sets and costumes for new musical stage representations of the *commedia* and related genres – though this they did with enormous enthusiasm – but also that the *commedia* seemed to offer composers and painters alike a means of expressing their modernism while appearing neither to cut ties with the past nor to be living in an intellectual cocoon.

All in all, then, composers in the early part of our century turned to the *commedia* as a source of musical inspiration partly as a result of being carried along by both a poetic tide and the momentum of a long-standing musical tradition, partly as a growing reaction against naturalistic drama, and partly as a consequence of parallel developments in painting, though it should be stressed that such a bird's eye view does not reveal the multiplicity of themes and ideas linking *commedia*-related 'serious' music of this period with other forms of cultural expression such as opera, ballet, jazz, the Parisian *fête populaire* . . . indeed, all types of entertainment and artistic activity from the highly refined and rehearsed to the unashamedly low-class and extempore. Furthermore, composers, painters and writers of the period were all in one sense part of an intellectual clique, whether or not they knew each other personally, and whether or not their aim was in reality an anti-intellectual one. No artist ever works in a vacuum, but this was a time when cross-fertilization was the order of the day, and the *commedia* was one of the major pollinators.

Schoenberg: *Pierrot lunaire* (1912)

A poet of Verlaine's time – though less original and less subtle than Verlaine – the Belgian Albert Giraud, was the author of a text used by Schoenberg for what has come to be his most acclaimed composition. Giraud had brought together fifty *commedia* poems into a collection entitled *Pierrot lunaire*, published in 1884. The collection attracted the attention of the German novelist and dramatist Otto Hartleben, no doubt because it characterized – in fact, almost caricatured – the *fin de siècle* vogue for moonstruck narcissism and eroticism. In 1892 Hartleben had published a German translation of Giraud's collection, and it was a selection from this rather free rendering which became the text of Schoenberg's *Pierrot lunaire*, in which twenty-one of Giraud's poems in the Hartleben translation are set to music for contralto solo and small chamber orchestra (though the libretto is spoken rather than sung, with changes in pitch indicated in the score as so-called *Sprechstimme* notation). Schoenberg divides his composition into three parts, each showing Pierrot in a different light: he moves from despair and erotic desire, through martyrdom and visions of grotesque punishments, to expressions of buffoonery, sentimentality and nostalgia for the better times of the past.

Schoenberg was certainly acquainted with other musical settings of *commedia* poetry, such as those by Debussy and Fauré of Verlaine, and may even have known an existing setting of the Giraud collection by the German composer Otto Frieslander.[6] But it seems evident in any case that the immediate attraction of Giraud's poems for Schoenberg was their stark stylization, which in some ways makes them closer to the original *commedia* than the works of greater poets of the period. For Schoenberg's *Pierrot lunaire* is an Expressionist work which was not intended to be either pretty or realistic.

The Expressionist mood (it can hardly be called a coherent movement, let alone a school) among German creative artists between 1910 and 1925 was typified by a desire to reach inner meaning by intuition. Thus Schoenberg renounces tonality, in the view of the painter Kandinsky, as a means of freeing art from conventional aids: 'His music leads us to where musical experience is a matter not of the ear, but of the soul.'[7] The price to be paid for the resulting renewal of moral and spiritual values is *angst*. The *commedia* as perceived by Schoenberg in the poems of Giraud provided the same mood of *malaise*.

It is less clear, however, whether or not it also provided a way for Schoenberg to show his rejection of the aestheticism of the previous century. Certainly, the Expressionists wished to return art to the people, for example in music by bringing it back to the level of cabaret and music-hall. Yet modern music criticism tends to take the line that *Pierrot lunaire* should be seen primarily as an ironic comment on the decadence of a previous era rather than an attempt to recreate it. This view is upheld by Schoenberg's own comments on the work, such as one contained in a letter of 1940 in which he vehemently insists that it was always intended as a satire.[8] Taking such comments very seriously, and analysing the musical score carefully, Alan Lessem has spearheaded the view that *Pierrot lunaire* is above all else a parody, not in the sense that the composer deliberately uses musical quotation – on the contrary, the work is singularly lacking in obvious derivations – but rather that he 'mimics the play of surface qualities and stylistic mannerisms drawn from the musical traditions of the past.'[9] As for the choice of text, Schoenberg himself put the music far above any meaning which might be ascribed to it. In a letter written in 1922, commenting on a Paris performance of the work which Darius Milhaud had conducted, and with the poems spoken in a curious re-translation into French, he declared that the text was of no significance whatsoever: 'I am not responsible for what people make up their minds to read into the words. If they were musical, not a single one of them would give a damn for the words. Instead, they would go away whistling the tunes.'[10] Furthermore, in the programme for the first performances of the work, the text of the poems in German translation was preceded by a revealing note written by the composer:

> One can imagine tales where there would be no coherence, and yet associations – like dreams; poems that are simply euphonious and full of beautiful words, but with no meaning or coherence whatever – at most, a few incomprehensible strophes – like fragments of utterly various things. Such true poetry can have, at most, an allegorical meaning, as a whole, and an indirect effect, like music.[11]

One is reminded of the free-association word-pictures of Edith Sitwell, which were to be set to music in 1922 by William Walton in his *Façade*, itself an example of popular entertainment wrapped in 'serious' music,

and having strong affinities with *Pierrot lunaire*, not least in that Walton
reverses Schoenberg's arrangement of the Giraud poems as three sets of
seven songs by producing seven sets of three, and in the way the text is
spoken rather than sung – it was no accident that at its revival in 1942
Façade was preceded by a performance of *Pierrot lunaire*.[12] Clearly, as
Walton was later to do (though admittedly with a different emphasis),
Schoenberg selected his text only as a kind of evocative background to
what was essentially an experiment in musical form and style,
something which in Schoenberg's case reinforces the view that any
notion of stepping down from an ivory tower to the level of ordinary
people was at best at the back of his mind, if it was there at all.

Stravinsky: *Petrushka* (1911) and *Pulcinella* (1920)

Stravinsky saw the final rehearsal of *Pierrot lunaire* in Berlin as a
member of an invited audience, and considered it a brilliant
instrumental masterpiece, as he was later to repeat on numerous
occasions.[13] Yet he makes no comment in any of his pronouncements,
either in interviews or writings, on Schoenberg's use of a *commedia*
text, appearing to have taken for granted, as one would expect in this
period, that the *commedia* would be a natural choice of basic content in
an artistic creation. It is therefore not surprising that he too turned to it
directly at the end of the decade with the ballet *Pulcinella*, having also
used it at the very beginning, a year before hearing *Pierrot lunaire*, in his
Petrushka, a ballet belonging to the tradition of the puppet theatre. The
commedia and the puppet theatre were to all intents and purposes one
and the same thing in the minds of many creative artists in the pre-war
period. The important element of both was the fact that the characters
were dehumanized, wearing a single facial expression throughout,
either as a puppet's head or as an actor wearing a mask, but capable of
appearing in numerous guises and roles and of expressing a range of
moods. Unrestricted by individual psychological traits, the characters
of both the *commedia* and the puppet theatre could be as superhuman
as those of the classical myth and legend, but with the addition of a low-
life comic element.

The setting of *Petrushka* (the Russian equivalent of the Punch and
Judy show) is the St Petersburg Shrove-Tuesday Fair in the 1830s, with
its roundabouts and swings, masked revellers, street musicians and a
showman's little puppet theatre. The puppet Petrushka (a derivative of
Pierrot) and two other puppets are charmed into life by the Showman.

Petrushka tries to woo the Ballerina, but she rejects him and instead makes advances to his rival the Moor, something which makes Petrushka insanely jealous and causes him, in true Pierrot style, to suffer deeply. In the evening, the Moor kills Petrushka, the latter's ghost appearing to the Showman at the end of the ballet. The music is based on Russian folk songs, folk dances and chansons, as well as French music-hall ditties such as 'Elle avait un'jambe en bois'.

Pulcinella is written as variations on themes by or attributed to the eighteenth-century composer Pergolesi, with the latter's bass lines and melodies virtually unaltered but with the music occasionally thrown out of eighteenth-century focus by the use of more modern harmonies and rhythms. The story is that of *The Four Pulcinellos*, which Diaghilev may have found in a book of Pulcinella stories, or perhaps from an old manuscript already in his possession.[14] The local girls are in love with Pulcinella, but their fiancés are jealous and plot to kill him. They appear to their loved ones disguised as Pulcinella, but the latter has changed places with his double, Fourbo, who pretends to succumb to the blows of Pulcinella's enemies. The real Pulcinella disguises himself as a magician and brings Fourbo back to life. Pulcinella eventually arranges all the marriages, and himself marries Pimpinella.

Picasso was commissioned to design the sets for the first production of *Pulcinella*, but there was trouble. Diaghilev, the director of the Ballets Russes which performed it, wanted *commedia* designs, while Picasso provided designs more in the style of the Offenbach period. Picasso then produced, as a compromise, an eighteenth-century set in the form of a theatre with baroque decorations, but all this was later scrapped and replaced with a moonlit Neapolitan scene. So Diaghilev eventually had his own way and the *commedia* element was pushed to the fore.

Both *Pulcinella* and *Petrushka* fit the notion of a *commedia*-like subject matter used to express nostalgia tinged with parody (for instance, the use of eighteenth-century music in *Pulcinella* – reminiscent of the way in which Verlaine and other poets turned to Watteau – and its presentation, at least as the work was seen by contemporary critics, as a pastiche),[15] and as a reaction against high-brow aestheticism (for instance, through the direct use of popular song and music-hall numbers in *Petrushka*).

That Stravinsky should have turned to the music-hall was to be expected. The French music-hall in the early part of the century was still the stage for *pantomimes*, and the Folies-Bergères and the Théâtre

Michel in Paris, as well as numerous provincial theatres such as the Palais des Beaux Arts in Monte Carlo, occasionally put on some which were in the true tradition of the *commedia*. And yet, transposed into the music of Stravinsky, an awkward artificiality creeps in. In reality, Stravinsky's music-hall songs were no more a close representation of the actual music-hall than his rag-time pieces were of rag-time, or Schoenberg's *Pierrot lunaire* was of the real *commedia*. That is not to detract, of course, from the undoubted musical genius of either composer, but merely to point out that the heart of both the *commedia* and the music-hall – their spontaneity[16] – was transformed by Schoenberg and Stravinsky into something requiring painstaking preparation (*Pierrot lunaire* was performed for the first time only after months of rehearsals and re-touching) and which, in the end, gave rise to works as inaccessible to the general public as any intellectual monument. Robert Storey puts the disparity in a nutshell: 'In the famous photograph of Stravinsky with his Petroushka, the urbane composer, impeccably dressed, capable of nothing that would compromise a well-bred gentleman, seems bored – though patient, forbearing, polite at having been posed with a fool.'[17]

What is more, Stravinsky just as much as Schoenberg dismisses the subject matter of his *commedia*-based works as being of little significance, talking for example of *Petrushka* as 'this composition which – let us not forget – is in an exclusively musical form and in which the dramatic action need not be taken into account'.[18] The fact is that for both Schoenberg and Stravinsky, all the nostalgia for bygone moments of gaiety and innocence, all the closeness to popular culture, were of little importance when compared to their high-brow musical ambitions. The nearest Stravinsky ever came to writing music actually to be performed in the true tradition of popular culture was when, during the Second World War, he was commissioned by the Barnum and Bailey Circus in New York to write a ballet to be performed by elephants dressed in tutus, the result being the *Circus Polka*. While the piece is touched by Stravinsky's genius, it was not well received by the actual practitioners of the circus art for whom it was written. According to an observer who watched the rehearsals and several performances, whereas the elephants had always been happy dancing to well-known waltz tunes and dreamy songs, Stravinsky's complicated rhythmic structure confused them: 'It robbed them of their feeling of security and confidence in the world about them – so alien to their native condition of life. It would have taken very little at any time during the many performances of the ballet music to cause a stampede'.[19] Being out of touch with the artistic demands of elephants is not of course a reason for concluding that Stravinsky, for all his look of a well-bred gentleman, was also out of touch with the people, but the story provides an interesting illustration of the gap between 'serious' music based on popular culture, and popular culture itself. In the words of Mikhail Bakhtin, 'the essence of grotesque realism is degradation, that is, the lowering of all that is high, spiritual, ideal, abstract'.[20] Such a degradation appears to have been an impossibility for the musical intelligentsia to which Stravinsky so firmly belonged.

Busoni: *Arlecchino* (1917)

The first performance of Busoni's opera *Arlecchino* took place with that of his *Turandot* in Zurich in 1917. The two together were to be taken, according to the composer, as examples of 'la nuova commedia dell'arte',[21] linked as they are by the use of masked figures and stock characters. Busoni composed *Turandot* on the basis of Carlo Gozzi's original play but, as he put it, 'closer in tone to a pantomime',[22] and he takes a quite different approach to the story from that of Puccini in the latter's more celebrated version of it, giving his characters much more black humour and biting satire.[23]

But the link between *Arlecchino* and *Turandot* is actually less marked than that between *Arlecchino* and Busoni's final (unfinished) masterpiece *Doktor Faust* (1925). Indeed, although the two works are separated in time by some eight years, they complement each other perfectly in theme, since the ideas for both were originally identical in Busoni's mind. In the early puppet versions of *Faust*, Casperle (a German Harlequin/Pierrot figure) is Faust's comic counterpart, and it is plain that for Busoni the two figures were inseparable (he notes in his diary in 1910: 'Faust – Casperle!').[24] In fact, he originally intended his *Doktor Faust* to be punctuated with scenes of comedy by Casperle, though in the end the latter's intended role was fulfilled by Harlequin in *Arlecchino*. What is more – and reinforcing the notion of a blurred division between the *commedia* and puppet theatre in the minds of creative artists in this period – *Arlecchino* is described in the printed score as a musical *capriccio*, but in the manuscript as a 'Marionetten Tragödie'[25] even though no puppets or representations of them are actually used; and when the curtain rises on *Doktor Faust*, it reveals another on which is painted a puppet theatre.

Arlecchino is set in Bergamo, Harlequin's home town. Harlequin runs off with the wife of the elderly tailor Matteo, and reappears as a recruiting sergeant, as a husband who duels with and kills the noble-born Leandro whom Harlequin discovers making love to his own wife Columbine, and as the victor who pronounces a moral epilogue. The absurd is never far away: for example, the Abbate sings a song in praise of a donkey (the *asinus providentialis*). There is also satire, more so than in *Pierrot lunaire*, *Pulcinella* or *Petrushka*, and especially on the Italian opera which is parodied in various styles from Scarlatti to Verdi, with direct quotations from Mozart's *Don Giovanni* and Donizetti's *Bergamasco*. And there is satirical comment on contemporary events – *Arlecchino* was composed and performed at the height of the greatest catastrophe the civilized world had ever seen, and Busoni takes the opportunity to make his opera something of a pacifist (as well as an anti-bourgeois) manifesto.

Thus *Arlecchino* contains many of the stock figures of the *commedia*, and is used, very much in its tradition, as a vehicle for satire. But like the *commedia*-related works of Schoenberg and Stravinsky it is less an accurate reflection of the *commedia* proper than a means of intellectual expression. Indeed, the real starting point for the work is to be found as much in Cervantes (whose works were known in detail to Busoni) as in the *commedia*: 'Arlecchino's speeches,' Busoni declares, 'are just as seriously meant as those, on a monumental scale, of *Don Quixote*.'[26] His aim therefore appears to have been to elevate the character of Harlequin to that of a commentator on the tragedy of the human condition. Yet the message remains hermetic, the work never becoming popular even with the intelligentsia at whom it was aimed. Edward Dent suggests that the reason for its lack of success lies in the terse libretto, which was written by Busoni himself and made even more terse by his reducing it further at a late stage in the composition of the work: 'The whole opera,' Dent comments, 'moves far too quickly for the average German audience'.[27] Like Schoenberg and Stravinsky, Busoni evidently wished to make the musical form, not the subject matter, the core of his work, despite his assertion that Harlequin's speeches were to be taken seriously and despite the element of didacticism.

The genesis of *Arlecchino* had been Busoni's presence at an attempt to revive the old-style seventeenth-century *commedia* in a performance of the mask comedy *L'Inutile Precauzione* (1692) in a theatre in Bologna in 1912.[28] Busoni comments: 'The Arlecchino cut a most impressive figure; he was personified by an actor who bestowed upon him a tinge of monumentality. Nowhere the low comedy of the Germans.'[29] But in avoiding such low culture in *Arlecchino*, Busoni produces a kind of refinement which clashes with what the *commedia* traditionally represented, and his 'nuova commedia dell'arte' becomes, in the final account, an intellectualized construct. One of the attractions of the *commedia* for creative artists of this period was that it put no limits on imagination, but its original essence of being low-class has been lost in *Arlecchino*, as it has also been in the corresponding compositions of Schoenberg and Stravinsky (perhaps even more so), the result being an equal loss of general appeal. In an explanatory note in the score of his *Rondò Arlecchinesco*, composed shortly before the full *Arlecchino* as an example of Italian carnival music, Busoni talks of Arlecchino's message being universal: 'Now he boldly asserts his principles through the trumpet; now he whistles at the world with the voice of the piccolo; threatens with the double basses, languishes with the cello, scampers away with violinistic agility.'[30] Such a use of individual orchestral instruments to represent moods or actions is not only hallowed in musical tradition generally, but can be clearly traced back within the history of the *commedia* and allied forms of popular culture. A strikingly similar example can be found in a playbill for a French *pantomime* of 1802, *Le Tribunal invisible*, which proclaims that it is accompanied by the careful use of orchestral resources: 'the plaintive flute is appropriate to the sufferings of the persecuted heroine; the double bass accompanies the tyrant; the comic action is preceded by a lively tune.'[31] But despite the fact that such an approach is rooted in the popular tradition, it is nevertheless clear that universality for Busoni meant a comment on humanity rather than universal accessibility.

It should be noted that throughout his life, Busoni was almost obsessed with the literature of the fantastic, from the tales of Ernst Hoffmann to those of Edgar Allan Poe.[32] It was therefore in one sense more natural for him than for Schoenberg or Stravinsky to be attracted by the *commedia*, which in none of its traditional forms submits to a rational order of things. And it was typical of him that his interest in a subject should extend to an in-depth study of it. In 1912 he was on tour in England (he was a concert pianist of international repute), thus missing the first performances of *Pierrot lunaire*. On his return to Germany he invited Schoenberg to perform it for him privately in front of a small audience in his own house. Schoenberg agreed, and conducted the performance. Busoni was overwhelmed by the power and originality of the piece,[33] but he appears to have been at least as much interested in the subject matter as the music, discussing the origins of Pierrot as would a theatre historian:

> It would have to be proved genealogically that Pierrot is a native of Bergamo. He is probably a borrowed Italian masque figure (Arlecchino comes from Bergamo) who was transformed by French comedy (Molière?). Pierrot's costume is reminiscent of the Italian Bajazzo or Pagliacco (man of straw), who is however neither a masque nor theatre-character but a carnival figure.[34]

The letter not only shows the influence of *Pierrot lunaire* on Busoni (within a few weeks he had produced the first draft of the libretto of *Arlecchino*, and had decided that his Harlequin would speak rather than sing, as does the soloist in Schoenberg's piece),[35] but also his intense interest in popular culture, an interest which extended in 1913 to his spending some considerable time sketching out a ballet, never to be completed, set in a common Parisian dance hall, *The Dance of Life and Death*, based on 'gypsy dancing, pantomime, a grand waltz and can-can, street dancing, a suicide dance on the parapet of a bridge, a religious dance and dance of death', and intended to be of popular appeal.[36] But the resulting treatment of such melodramatic scenes in *Arlecchino* shows the same disparity between a genuinely popular art form and the distanced transmutation of it that can be discerned in Schoenberg and Stravinsky.

It is often argued that serious composers are intellectuals who will not be satisfied with a descent into triviality, and who therefore write not for the masses but for a refined audience. It has to be said, however, that while such a view may be valid when applied to grand opera, it is not a notion that either Schoenberg, Stravinsky or Busoni would unequivocally have accepted – hence Schoenberg's wish for his tunes to be whistled by the audience leaving the auditorium rather than their seeking any deep meaning in the text; hence Stravinsky's surprise at his being dubbed a revolutionary by the critics following the first performance of *The Rite of Spring* ('I was made a revolutionary in spite of myself,' he was later to say),[37] despite the fact that nobody had ever heard music like it; hence Busoni's wish to avoid writing music in the heroic German intellectual tradition as characterized by Wagner ('I am no more a Wagnerian than a Christian,' he declared while putting the finishing touches to *Arlecchino*).[38] It is true that all three composers used the *commedia* to a greater or lesser extent for parodic purposes, something which had always been part of its tradition. Yet, with the perhaps mixed benefit of hindsight, it can be seen that this apparent fit with the tradition of the *commedia* is less than perfect in the hands of composers who chose, for whatever reasons, to ignore its real essence.

Les Six

The group of six composers based in Paris in the early years of the 1920s who became known as Les Six – Georges Auric, Louis Durey, Arthur Honegger, Darius Milhaud, Francis Poulenc and Germaine Taillefer – were naturally influenced by musical figures of the stature of Schoenberg and Stravinsky, and all six were well acquainted with their *commedia*-related compositions (though no direct influence of Busoni can be discerned). Honegger was proud to admit that he wrote *Le Dit de jeux du monde* after the manner of Schoenberg and Stravinsky; Germaine Taillefer was capable of playing the entire score of *Petrushka* from memory; and Milhaud and Poulenc visited Schoenberg in Vienna in 1922, Milhaud and Schoenberg conducting *Pierrot lunaire* in turn as an experiment.[39] In certain cases, the influence is patent, as for example in Milhaud's *Salade* which, like *Pulcinella*, is described in the score as a 'ballet chanté', uses eighteenth-century music, and is based on a *commedia* episode with Punchinello as its main character.

However, the real mentor of Les Six was Eric Satie, who had been extolled in the little work by Jean Cocteau entitled *Le Coq et l'Arlequin*, published in 1918, which became a manifesto for the six composers. The book consists of a series of texts and (sometimes contradictory) epigrams and aphorisms, extolling Satie and denouncing to varying degrees Wagner, Debussy, and even Stravinsky. As Robert Siohan has noted, *Le Coq et l'Arlequin* 'is distinguished by its youthful verve, a dry and ready wit, a readiness to juggle with meanings, and to take advantage of misunderstandings, all of them qualities that were closely allied to the spirit of the Italian *Commedia dell'Arte*'.[40]

Le Coq et l'Arlequin opens, in its dedication to Georges Auric, with the curious statement: 'I admire the Harlequins of Cézanne and Picasso but I do not like Harlequin', and the dedication ends with the cry: 'Up with the Cock! Down with Harlequin!'[41] For Cocteau, the cock is a creature of the day who openly declares what he has to say, while Harlequin is 'the cock of the night',[42] a character whose mask and costume reflect his despicable personality – multi-coloured and thus multi-faceted, and presenting a face other than his own. But in denouncing Harlequin, Cocteau is not of course denouncing the spirit of *commedia*. On the contrary, *Le Coq et l'Arlequin* is very much a eulogy of low-class culture ('The café-concert is often pure; the theatre is always corrupt' is one of its aphorisms).[43] So it is not surprising that the *commedia*, and popular culture generally, figure prominently in the work of Les Six, as well as in that of Satie. Auric's *Gaspard et Zoé* includes a café-concert waltz. Durey composed a *commedia*-type series of piano pieces entitled *Scènes de cirque* (though they were never published).[44] Honegger wrote his pantomime-ballet *Fantasio* for the mime Georges Wague. Poulenc composed several pieces with *commedia*-related titles, such as *Bal masqué* and *Le Jongleur*, and some *Chansons gaillardes* based on seventeenth-century crude drinking and love songs; his *Cinq impromptus* for piano are written in a music-hall style, and *L'Embarquement pour Cythère* (a *valse-musette* for two pianos, evoking the Nogent-sur-Marne pleasure gardens of his youth) was composed as a direct result of his admiration for Watteau. Milhaud's *Salade*, in the words of Paul Collaer, is 'rich in tunes invented by the composer, juxtaposed as naturally as one could wish with popular songs';[45] and each movement of his *Carnaval d'Aix*, a suite of twelve pieces for piano and orchestra extracted from *Salade*, stands for a *commedia* character. Satie, who belonged to the previous generation of composers but who was the main musical driving force behind Les Six, wrote a pantomime-ballet entitled *Jack in the Box* (it was not discovered until after his death), and his *Sports et divertissements* (twenty short piano pieces) consist of representations of games and carnival entertainments à la *commedia*. All six composers and Satie collaborated on the music for Cocteau's *Le Boeuf sur le toit* which some contemporary critics saw as an adaptation of the *commedia*, with Harlequin and Columbine replaced by stock characters from American films,[46] and five of the six (Durey had bowed out) also worked together on Cocteau's mime play *Les Mariés de la Tour Eiffel*.

The most important *commedia*-type piece composed by Satie, and performed for the first time in the same year as Busoni's *Arlecchino*, was *Parade*, a ballet conceived by Cocteau and produced by Diaghilev. Its subject matter is that of a *théâtre forain* – an itinerant group of players who set up their stage on a street in Paris and try to attract the attention of passers-by with a 'parade', the traditional sideshow of street theatres. *Parade* contains elements of the circus (a pantomime horse and acrobats appear, and a drop-curtain designed by Picasso for the première showed a circus horse and clowns), vaudeville, and song and dance idioms of the exact kind envisaged by Busoni for his *Dance of Life and Death*. The scenes are divided into music-hall numbers. Auric is said to have remarked that *Parade* presented 'all the sorrow of the travelling circus . . . the nostalgia of the barrel organ which will never play Bach fugues'.[47] Picasso's sketches for the set and costumes (his first stage designs) gave rise to some extra characters – the Managers – who organize the publicity for the show and who, in the words of James Harding, 'by their superhuman nature, would reduce the dancers to the stature of puppets'.[48] The Parisian high-society audience reacted angrily to the first performance of this idiotic ballet with its absurd music (which includes scoring for typewriter), and there were scenes reminiscent of those at the first night of Stravinsky's *The Rite of Spring* four years earlier.

However, while Les Six continued throughout the 1920s and beyond to incorporate into their works elements of the music-hall and other forms of popular culture (including the newly introduced jazz which, in its low-class appeal in 1920s Paris and its reliance on improvisation, has certain affinities with the *commedia*), the importance of such elements had diminished by the middle of the decade, and the *commedia* had been all but abandoned as a source of musical subject matter. In part, the reason lies in the fact that by the time *Le Coq et l'Arlequin* was published, its basic thesis was no longer as revolutionary as Cocteau imagined it to be. The absurd cacophony of *Parade* may have shocked bourgeois Parisian audiences at a time when the real backdrop of the war seemed to demand either didactic comment or romantic escapism (and for those audiences, preferably the latter), but the battle against what Cocteau and Les Six saw as the blurry landscapes of Debussy and the monumental towers of Wagner had already been fought, and to some extent won, by Schoenberg and Stravinsky, paving the way for a new type of music and having such a profound effect on its history. In this sense, *Le Coq et l'Arlequin*, while helping to raise Satie to the rank he deserved and continues to hold, was merely following an established line, though it is also worth noting in this context that Cocteau's attacks, especially on Debussy, went much further than anyone had gone before, indeed to the point of distortion. Throughout *Le Coq et l'Arlequin* Cocteau wages an unrelenting war on Debussy. Take, for example: 'Enough of clouds, waves, aquariums, water sprites and perfumes of the night; we need a down-to-earth music, *an everyday music*', or: 'You cannot get lost in the Debussy fog as you can in the Wagner mist, but you can catch a cold in it.[49] Such a view of an entirely 'misty' Debussy is quite unjustified, as amply evidenced by his *Suite bergamasque* (with its *commedia* overtones), his *Gollywog's Cakewalk* and similar 'everyday' pieces constructed with a 'down-to-earth' staccato focus. To dismiss Debussy as all clouds and seas is to ignore both his wit and his eclecticism. As Léon Vallas rightly comments:

> Occasionally Debussy made the classification of his works a difficult task by writing compositions of an utterly unexpected type. In the *Children's Corner*, published in 1908, he displayed a sense of humour which some of his earlier compositions had already revealed, though the seriousness of 'Pelléas' had made people forget this characteristic.[50]

Equally importantly, while Les Six willingly collaborated with Cocteau, Satie and each other, their short flirtation as a group with the *commedia* and allied forms of popular culture was but a veneer of unity, as is evidenced by how rapidly they diverged once the bourgeois had been thoroughly *épatés*. And some among their number were clearly aware of that schism between popular culture as appreciated by the people, and popular culture as treated by intellectuals. As early as 1920, Honegger was to say (with refreshing honesty): 'I am no worshipper of the fair-grounds, of the music-hall, but, on the contrary, of chamber music and symphonic music, and when they are at their most serious and austere.'[51] At the other extreme, Auric soon became a hugely successful composer of film music, writing nearly a hundred scores with no high-brow pretensions (his best-known piece was the theme song for John Houston's *Moulin Rouge*). Les Six had looked to popular songs for inspiration; Auric actually wrote them, and it would be too facile to contend that he did so merely for financial reasons.

Conclusion

From about 1910 until the mid-1920s, the *commedia* represented for many composers a means of expressing a general nostalgia for the past but also a distaste for the values of the preceding era, and – especially – a means of substituting the ordinary and the universal for the heroic and the exceptional. As Pierre Duchartre was to put it at the very end of the period (1925) and thus with the benefit of an immediate retrospective view (though he may not have realized that it was in fact the end of an era): 'Not Othello, not Hamlet, not Phèdre or Chimera, not characters who churn up their minds with uncommon emotions. The Commedia dell'Arte is a world complete in itself where anyone can find nourishment.'[52] And yet these same composers, by the very fact of being avant-garde, were also removed from that world.

The history of popular art is such that it continues for long periods underground, now and then surfacing as landmarks of the greatest artistic achievement (one has merely to think of Rabelais in this context). When handled by composers of the early part of our century, it was capable of being the basis of greatness, as with Schoenberg and Stravinsky, and to a lesser extent with Busoni and certain moments in the music of Satie, Honegger, Poulenc and Milhaud. However, it was also capable of producing a somewhat uneasy union of low-class and high-class cultures. The interest shown by these composers in popular art was a reaction against Romantic pathos, yet the *commedia* with its melodrama and melancholy comedy was the very essence of senti-mentality. By turning it into a high-class art, they allowed such sentimentality to retain a central position – indeed, if anything, to exaggerate it – but at the same time they remained aloof from it. Their aim was to show human suffering and joy acted out not in some aristocratic or other-wordly setting but in the streets, in the circus, in fairgrounds; yet in the end they could do no other that create something which was abstracted from that setting. They produced an art which rebelled – consciously or unconsciously – against a bourgeois concert-going public, and which therefore gained notoriety, but which did not of course take on the mantle of greatness merely because of that. *Pierrot lunaire* and *Petrushka* are supreme masterpieces which have deeply influenced the course of twentieth-century music not because they attempted a fusion of popular art and its intellectualization, but almost despite that attempt. Cocteau complained bitterly that at the first performance of *Parade*, 'the audience took the transposition of the music-hall to be bad music-hall'.[53] Perhaps the audience was right.

NOTES

1   Giacomo Oreglia, *The Commedia dell'Arte*, translated by Evert Sprinchorn (London, Methuen, 1968), xii–xiii.
2   See Louisa Jones, *Sad Clowns and Pale Pierrots: Literature and the Popular Comic Arts in 19th-Century France* (Lexington, Kentucky, French Forum Publishers, 1984), 238.
3   Edward Lockspeiser in his *Music and Painting* (London, Cassell, 1973), 98–109, argues that the *commedia*-related works of composers in the early years of the

twentieth century took their inspiration above all from the writings of Laforgue.

4   The Goncourt brothers are usually credited with stimulating French interest in Watteau and the eighteenth century generally, with works such as *L'Histoire de la société française pendant la Révolution* (1854), *L'Art du XVIIIème siècle* (1855–9) and *La Femme au XVIIIème siècle* (1862).

5   For interesting explorations of the relationship between music and painting in this period, especially as applied to Cubism, see Donald Mitchell, *The Language of Modern Music* (London, Faber and Faber, 1963), 76ff; and Kenneth Silver, *Esprit de Corps: The Art of the Parisian Avant-Garde and the First World War, 1914–1925* (London, Thames and Hudson, 1989), *passim*.

6   See Alan Lessem, *Music and Text in the Works of Arnold Schoenberg: The Critical Years, 1908–1922* (UMI Research Press, 1979), 122.

7   Wasily Kandinsky, *On the Spiritual in Art*, edited by Hilla Rebay (New York, Guggenheim Foundation, 1946), 36.

8   See Josef Rufer, *The Works of Arnold Schoenberg: a Catalogue of his Compositions, Writings and Paintings*, translated by Dika Newlin (London, Faber and Faber, 1962), 82; letter dated 31 August 1940.

9   Lessem, *op. cit.*, 126.

10   Erwin Stein (ed.), *Arnold Schoenberg Letters*, translated by Eithne Wilkins and Ernst Kaiser (London, Faber and Faber, 1964), 82; letter of 30 December 1922.

11   Quoted in Willi Reich, *Schoenberg: A Critical Biography*, translated by Leo Black (London, Longman, 1971), 77–8.

12   See Frank Howes, *The Music of William Walton* (Oxford University Press, 1974), 20.

13   See, for example, Robert Craft and Igor Stravinsky, *Conversations with Igor Stravinsky* (London, Faber and Faber, 1959), 69; Stravinsky and Craft, *Expositions and Development* (London, Faber and Faber, 1962), 68; Stravinsky and Craft, *Dialogues and a Diary* (London, Faber and Faber, 1968), 104; Stravinsky, *Themes and Conclusions* (London, Faber and Faber, 1972), 189–90.

14   See Eric Walter White, *Stravinsky: The Composer and his Works* (London, Faber and Faber, 1966), 245.

15   See Robert Siohan, *Stravinsky*, translated by Eric Walter White (London, Calder and Boyars, 1965), 91–3. Modern critics tend to take the view that *Pulcinella* is not primarily a pastiche, but there is certainly a satirical element in it.

16   The question of improvisation in the *commedia* has been much debated, but few doubt that there was always an important element of spontaneity.

17   Robert Storey, *Pierrots on the Stage of Desire: Nineteenth-century French Literary Artists and the Comic Pantomime* (Princeton University Press, 1985), 313–4.

18   Igor Stravinsky, 'Quelques confidences sur la musique', lecture given 21 November 1935, *Conferencia*, Journal de l'Université des Annales, 15 December 1935; my translation.

19   George Beal, 'Entr'acte: Stravinsky and the elephants', in *Concert Bulletin* for the Boston Symphony Orchestra for 13, 14 and 15 January 1944; quoted in White, *op. cit*, 374–5.

20 Mikhail Bakhtin, *Rabelais and his World*, translated by Helene Iswolsky (Cambridge, Mass., MIT Press, 1968), 19–20.

21 See Antony Beaumont, *Busoni the Composer* (London, Faber and Faber, 1985), 223.

22 Letter of 1 November 1916, quoted in Beaumont, op. cit., 241.

23 For a comparison between the *Turandot* of Busoni and that of Puccini, see Mosco Carner, *Puccini: A Critical Biography* (London, Duckworth, 1958), *passim*.

24 Entry for 16 October 1910, quoted in Edward Dent, *Busoni: A Biography* (London, Eulenburg Books, 1974), 293–4.

25 See Beaumont, op. cit., 221.

26 Letter of 15 April 1917, quoted in Beaumont, op. cit., 222, where Cervantes's influence on Busoni is discussed.

27 Dent, op. cit., 236.

28 See Dent, op. cit., 195.

29 Quoted in Beaumont, op. cit., 208.

30 Ibid., 215.

31 Reproduced in Irène Mawer, *The Art of Mime* (London, Methuen, 1942), 76; my translation.

32 See Dent, op. cit., 170.

33 In a letter of 18 October 1912, quoted in Beaumont, op. cit., 208–9.

34 Ibid., 209.

35 According to Beaumont, op. cit., 209.

36 See H.H. Stuckenschmidt, *Ferrucio Busoni: Chronicle of a European*, translated by Sandra Morrism (London, Calder & Boyars, 1970), 145–6.

37 Igor Stravinsky, *Poetics of Music in the Form of Six Lessons* (Harvard University Press, 1947), 10.

38 Letter of 15 April 1917, quoted in Beaumont, op. cit., 32.

39 See James Harding, *The Ox on the Roof: Scenes from Musical Life in Paris in the Twenties* (New York, St. Martin's Press, 1972); respectively 63–4, 44 and 109–10.

40 Siohan, op. cit., 91.

41 Jean Cocteau, *Le Coq et l'Arlequin: notes autour de la musique* (1918), reproduced in *Le Rappel à l'ordre* (Paris, Stock, 1926, to which page numbers refer), 13–4; all translations from this text are mine.

42 Ibid.

43 Ibid., 29.

44 See Harding, op. cit., 62–3.

45 Paul Collaer, *Darius Milhaud* (Antwerp, Société Belge de Musicologie, 1947), 113; my translation.

46 See Harding, op. cit., 78.

47 Ibid., 37.

48 Ibid., 35.

49 Cocteau, op. cit., 28 and 41.

50 Léon Vallas, *Claude Debussy: His Life and Works*, translated by Maire and Grace O'Brien (New York, Dover Publications, 1973; reprinted from the Oxford University Press edition of 1933), 183.

51 Quoted by Paul Landormy, 'Arthur Honegger', *La Victoire*, 20 September 1920; translation by Fred Rothwell in an English version of the article, *The Musical Times*, 1 September 1929, which is re-quoted by Geoffrey Spratt, *The Music of Arthur Honegger* (Cork University Press, 1987), 221.
52 Pierre Duchartre, *La Comédie italienne* (Paris, n.p., 1925), 332.
53 Cocteau, op. cit., 34.

12 Dario Fo and the *commedia dell'arte*[1]

CHRISTOPHER CAIRNS

The extraordinary vogue for the *commedia dell'arte* as a performance language in the contemporary theatre has given rise to two distinct conventions. First, the 'archaeological' reconstruction of the working methods, costumes, masks and relationships between the well-known stereotype characters, refined and polished to a high degree of professional performance by such companies as TAG Teatro of Venice and the Carrara family, who tour Europe with their re-elaborations of classic scenarios such as *La Pazzia di Isabella*.[2] Secondly, we have the adaptation or 'selection' of styles from past traditions of *commedia* for modern uses: a bringing face to face with contemporary social and political causes of a deep-rooted European theatrical tradition, particularly since the 1960s. It is to this second *modern* convention that Dario Fo's *Harlequin* belongs, a convention that has seen many and diverse experiments, such as the adaptation of *commedia* to a travelling show, in which the poet and teacher Giuliano Scabia has appeared in Italy as a kind of Harlequin-devil; or the depiction of Harlequin as a very modern Algerian immigrant into France in Ariane Mnouchkine's *L'Age d'or*, first presented at the Théâtre du Soleil in Paris in 1975.[3] And there have been other adaptations, such as those of the more radically innovative San Francisco Mime Troupe, El Campesino, and Schumann's Bread and Puppet Theatre in the United States.[4] The *commedia dell'arte* is a style and performance language in these adaptations, taking contemporary social and political issues by the throat, as it were (American involvement in Vietnam is an example), but selectively adapting the traditional attributes of mime and improvisation to the contemporary world, or inventing new character-stereotypes of decisively modern relevance, such as the San Francisco Mime Troupe's creation of the Lawyer, Politician, College Student and Feminist.

    Dario Fo's relationship with the *commedia dell'arte* came to a head in 1985 but grew from a long-standing similarity between the *commedia's* dependence on audience reaction and Fo's own background as a performer. His emphasis on mime (originally from Lecoque) and ability to improvise in direct address to the audience are all characteristics which derived from his background in variety, but which he and his company developed from the sixties onwards. When their new ideological stance prompted an even closer relationship with the audience in discussions after or during the show of the issues it raised, this was also, in a sense, a further sophistication of *commedia* techniques. In London in 1988, Fo admitted that he had come late to the formal study of the *commedia dell'arte*, but had found with some surprise that he had been involved in similar theatrical practice (with different roots, in variety, the circus, the silent film) already for many years.[5]

Against this background of instinctive sympathy for the *commedia dell'arte* (and research is showing how many *commedia* characteristics had appeared in his previous productions),[6] Dario Fo came to his *Harlequin* production in 1985 as a result of the promptings of academics. He admits that:

> When Ferruccio Marotti and Franco Quadri asked me to undertake a 'Laboratory [workshop] on Harlequin', and a show to be performed at the Venice Biennale, I accepted at once: I have always been interested in the *commedia dell'arte*, it's my territory.

He goes on to define the ideological parameters of his standpoint, showing his particular Harlequin to be an evolution from the *giullare* of *Mistero Buffo*, since

> The *commedia dell'arte* companies were, after all, giullari organised into groups. During the Renaissance, in harmony with the spirit of the times (this was the era in which the arts, trades and business began to be organised) even the theatre began to organise itself. At a certain moment, those who had been dilletanti travelling players went to a notary and constituted theatre companies with contracts.[7]

In the same interview, Fo admitted that he had gone back to the roots of the *commedia dell'arte* in the creation of the Harlequin show. He had started with the basic *canovaccio* or synthesis, and improvised on the basis of this, seeking the starting point for the evolution of each situation or gag in ancient models, often building on a terse citation of an object or prop (for instance the *lazzo* of the ladder, which he was to build into a long episode in the final show). Ferruccio Marotti has said that the original scenarios were provided for Dario Fo by Delia Gambelli (whose researches on the classical figure of Harlequin are well known)[8] and himself. But he also stresses the consonance of Fo's (radical left-wing) ideological stance from the seventies, and what he considers to be the ancient roots of *commedia*. Marotti spoke to Sergio Parini in these terms in 1985, stressing that Harlequin was never a stereotype susceptible of facile classification like Zanni (a servant from Bergamo) or Pantaloon (a merchant from Venice), and was not limited to a recognizable type, language or regional place of origin. Secondly, Harlequin was a universal gadfly, a creature *di disturbo*, and far from the polished stereotype immortalized by Goldoni in the eighteenth century.

> The reinterpretation of Harlequin as a figure *di disturbo* was based on some documents discovered by Delia Gambelli and myself. Witness the first document which exists on the character. This is an anti-Harlequin libel written at the end of the sixteenth century by a French comedian who, eaten up by jealousy at the success of Martinelli [Harlequin] makes Harlequin descend into Hell in search of the proprietor of a well-known brothel. Martinelli replied to this affront by reaffirming his own artistic superiority: 'It is true – he said to his colleague [and enemy] – I did go down into Hell, but even there, I made everyone laugh, even the devils.'[9]

Marotti went on to show that this aggressive, almost anarchic line was followed above all by the two earliest famous Harlequins, and two of the most celebrated, Tristano Martinelli and Dominique Biancolelli, who broadened the function and applicability of the stereotype from Zanni (who must always be the servant, always inferior, physically and visually 'lower' than the Magnifico) to play potentially many parts, impersonating not only the servant, but also an inquisitor, even a woman. And since it is these two Harlequin actors who were principally the subject of Delia Gambelli's researches, it is not hard to see where Fo's authentication lies for his own distinctively subversive Harlequin. This image also fits his own 'subversive' personality as a theatre performer – from the politically downtrodden *giullare* of *Mistero Buffo*, or indeed from the early Chaplinesque *Poer nano* to (perhaps its other extreme) a Pope who can similarly turn the tables on the conservative establishment in the cause of social justice (of 1990).[10] And just as this is firmly in tune with the downtrodden cult of the 'little man' of the twentieth century, the anti-hero of many guises and forms, it is also reminiscent of the many other *engagé* and newly radical adaptations of *commedia*, such as those of the San Francisco Mime Troupe that we have noted. Thus it can be seen how relatively little distance separates the committed left-wing Dario Fo (who will send up and satirize almost any received orthodoxy, including that of the Italian Communist Party) and a slightly anarchic universal type reminiscent of the earliest Harlequins in their stage personalities whose most obvious modern incarnation is Chaplin.

The 'Laboratory on Harlequin' took place at Sta Cristina (near Gubbio) in Italy, where, over a six-week period, academics would read examples of early scenarios (such as those by Flaminio Scala, or the notebooks of Biancolelli), and Fo would make sketches of many of the *lazzi*. He was then left entirely free to improvise on the basis of this evidence, noting down his impressions in this graphic form. The whole process was monitored by technicians, TV cameramen and others, so that the resulting tapes could be played back in the evenings and the improvisations assessed. This body of filmed material is a precious resource which will one day allow the process of evolution to be observed very closely, just as the notes taken by two Rome university students (along with hundreds of photographs) will shortly be published in book form.[11] Marotti's summing-up shows exactly where this initiative was driving in the early summer of 1985, and reflects the result: a show that (even if it seems to lack some structural unity to an audience expecting a 'play') is nonetheless consistent with its ambition:

> The objective was to overturn the official concept according to which the *commedia dell'arte* is tied to the idea of 'comedy', that is a performance in three or four acts. Our researches in the University of Rome in recent years show that the majority of the pieces for the great Harlequins of the sixteenth and seventeenth centuries (Martinelli and later Biancolelli) were a collection of farces, comic situations of 10–20 minutes' duration, the 'Comedy' was only the container of these various farces, of the *lazzi*. This is the Harlequin I am referring to in this show.[12]

Before considering the show itself, we should mention that there were two further products from the fruitful collaboration of Dario Fo with the groves of academe: the first is Fo's *Manuale minimo dell'attore* (*The Tricks of the Trade*), published in 1987, but clearly written during the period (more or less) of the gestation and performance of the

Harlequin show. There is substantial evidence in its pages – indeed the whole first book is devoted to *commedia* – of the theories elaborated during the summer of 1985; the Italian edition carries a drawing of Harlequin by Fo on its front cover, and the English edition (imminent as this goes to press) has a number of photographs from the show itself.[13] Secondly, Fo was asked to direct and design productions of Molière's *Le Médecin malgré lui* and a rarely performed Molière farce, *Le Médecin volant*, at the Comédie-Française in Paris in the summer of 1990. The latter is barely a scenario-synthesis, and Fo was able to fill this out with elaborations on *lazzi* drawn from antique Italian *commedia* scenarios. Importantly, just as the process of evolution of *Harlequin* was visualized through sketches (published in *Alcatraz News*), so too was the preparation process for the Molière production, the results of which are to be published in Paris.[14] The benefits of this process of 'physical visualization', for the observation of the creative process of theatre, from the hand of an actor who is also an artist, can hardly be overstressed.

But there is one other way of considering the period Harlequin 'selected' by Dario Fo for his own *commedia* performance: a consideration of the tradition's modern derivatives. If the lessons of the *commedia dell'arte* have come down to us (archaeology apart) directly and most explicitly through farce, pantomime, the circus, music hall and the various performance uses of the clown image and survival of mime (not excluding Punch & Judy), why should not Fo, argues Ugo Volli,[15] reinvent the tradition in terms of these modern derivatives? Even if, as he also suggests, the results show some fallback on gags and theatrical devices already used before, and seen in other contexts, this is precisely what Fo freely admits in his accounts of his late arrival at historical *commedia*. His discovery, as we have seen, was that *commedia*-derived skills were already in his repertoire, having been acquired through his experience of mime and variety. In fact he remains faithful to his own performance roots which themselves facilitated his adoption of the mask of Harlequin – a mask uncluttered with the narrowness of stereotype characteristics, or regional (and linguistic) stamp, and a Harlequin who is, in the end, Fo himself, as he must be.

> Naturally [speaking of early Commedia actors] they were people who had at least 2,000 gags and jokes under their belt. I would never have been able to carry out this task [Harlequin] at twenty years of age. I can only do it now thanks to all the research I have done on this theatre.[16]

And Fo spoke in 1988 of being able to improvise on a theme with few or no notes precisely because of a lifetime's activity as a performer in the theatre.[17]

Turning now to the *Harlequin* show, first performed at the Venice Biennale on 10 October 1985, and on tour in Italy until March 1986, there is much evidence of development from the early draft of the script (which Dario Fo's son, Jacopo, confessed 'my father has not finished writing'[18] when the first number of *Alcatraz News* went to press in November), to the version which was being performed in February and March 1986. Of course, this is entirely characteristic of Fo: the adaptation of material, addition of scenes and detail, in response to audience reaction is as much part of the working methods of Dario Fo and Franca Rame as it must have been for the earliest *commedia* troupes. 'The audience is the sole arbiter' is a sentiment often expressed down the long history of the tradition.[19] In fact the edition of the script now considered definitive by the author (my copy marked: *aggiornata, aprile 86*) represents the *end* of the performance schedule, not the beginning, and is a transcript made from a recording of the perform-ance given at the Teatro Ciak, Milan on 2 March 1986. Comparing these two versions makes it clear that the 'laboratory' yielded much that never reached final performance, just as many of the sketches already referred to have no tangible relationship with the show performed, for the same reason. Finally (as if to prove the truth of an infinitely variable and volatile text) we have the inclusion in an early script of two observers of the 'laboratory' of a sketch ('The Flying Cat') *as if* performed but which had gone from the performance by February 1986,[20] as well as the example of *Arlecchino fallotropo*, which was included in the Milan performance on 15 February, but excluded on 25 February, possibly to leave time for an increased volume of situations related to references to current affairs. Thus we have a shifting volume of material, true to the spirit of the *commedia dell'arte* ('feeding off' its audience in every respect), always related to the performers' percep-tions of audience reception. For the purposes of the present discussion, therefore, four versions of the script have been used: the early draft published in *Alcatraz News* in November 1985, a sound tape of the show performed on 15 February 1986, a videotape of that performed on 25 February and the performance script (transcript) of 2 March 1986. In what must be an economical description, there is clearly no space here for a discussion of all the many minor variants, destined elsewhere, in any case.[21]

The prologue in front of the curtain is a feature of all modern performances by Dario Fo (often a hilarious performance in itself), testing the vibrations of the audience, settling people into their seats as has become traditional, and itself echoes *commedia dell'arte* practice in the character's self-introduction to the audience alone on stage. In the case of *Harlequin* it takes the form of a 'lecture' on the *commedia dell'arte* with a collection of masks displayed on a screen and costumes for Harlequin in different periods – from Martinelli in the sixteenth century to Goldoni's in the eighteenth – as well as costumes for Colombina and Franceschina. Fo explains that his own leafy costume indicates an 'early' Harlequin, the subversive one, *di disturbo*, and not later versions made famous by Goldoni. The prologue, then, is the prologue to the show, not an integral part of the *commedia dell'arte* storyline, which comes afterwards. It defines Fo's own interpretation of the arch-subversive, the defender of obscenity and scurrility (he claims that Harlequin used to defecate on stage, then pelt the audience with the fruits of his labours, shouting: 'Good luck! It brings good luck!'). He explains how the *canovaccio* (scenario) was used, how the indications of *lazzi* are built on in performance, using the 'Phallicthropic Harlequin' sketch as an example, in which a monster Phallus grows and grows as a result of drinking an overdose of his master's love (virility) potion. The sketch employs a full range of Fo's talents with mime (attempts to conceal the 'monster' from curious female onlookers include camouflage as a cat and as a baby), and he afterwards performed the sketch in London in 1988. Fo then proceeds to illustrate moments from the history of the *commedia dell'arte*, sometimes substituting the names of contemporaries (such as Italian cabinet ministers) for historical personages for topical effect, in a process which seems entirely gratuitous and linked to the 'lecture' situation by the slenderest of threads. The following priceless morsel (which had the audience in stitches) is based on the 'cartoon' image of the subject in the minds of the audience, and is linked to its situation only by a gag about the electric chair, which is gratuitously anachronistic anyway:

> It's amazing isn't it? We must have a highly developed sense of humour, mustn't we? To accept . . . . as a Minister of Defence: just think of it! Incredible! All fat and buttery! A soft and fluttering defence, an elastic defence! Imagine giving . . . . a kick! Buaah! Your foot would sink right in and come out all sticky and covered with pudding and crème caramel, glue, honey; after a week you'd still be covered in sticky . . . . ![22]

The prologue proper now begins as a prelude to the *commedia dell'arte* performance, with music, tumbling, acrobatics and song, in a colourful interlude which has Fo playing (or making noises with) an antique all-enveloping trombone. The whole of the prologue scene is based not (as traditionally) on an explanation in summary of the period story to be recounted by the play (although the earliest script did have a sketch-version of this that was later abandoned), but on the situation-comedy of the stage itself: the curtain has got stuck. Marcolfa (played by Franca Rame) is discovered mopping the stage floor, and protests that the audience seem like voyeurs; a ladder must be sought to mend the curtain, and the source, acquisition and description of this, as well as its eventual raising, are an opportunity for a string of surreal jokes attending this oldest of stage props (the ladder, pole or plank, from Charlie Chaplin to Benny Hill), which are yet entirely consistent with the surreal and magical world inhabited by this early Harlequin. First it is so long that the actor holding either end will disappear into the wings (only to reappear on the wrong side); then it is erected, and becomes a lookout mast on a fishing vessel; erected with the help of guy ropes, it metaphorically and physically draws in the audience, as two ropes are held by members of the audience: 'No! don't give it to him; he's an intellectual; they always let go when things get interesting!'[23] Finally, Fo pretends almost to let it fall onto the front stalls, claiming four dead the previous evening, a gag (potential danger for the audience) used by him both before and since,[24] importantly when an extended piece of ladder-play threatens to precipitate the actress into the audience in his direction of the Molière farces at the Comédie-Française. As we have seen before, in *Harlequin*, this situation is the hook for a string of organ transplant jokes, topical for 1985, again involving certain venerable senior politicians.

In all this, the very structure of the stage and its props are the situation: the 'prologue' itself never gets off the ground. In the show performed in the winter of 1986, an extended monologue was inserted for Franca Rame, in which she relates the story of the Magnifico's wife Isabella, sexually frustrated, who must learn from the prostitute her husband is known to frequent how to win back her husband. The lesson given to the wife by the prostitute, Eleanora, provides the actress with a unique opportunity to deliver to all women in the audience a lesson (replete with mime, obscene detail and voice-effects, such as sighs and sobs) in the techniques of seduction – and this is openly addressed to the audience when she advises them to take notes, quells an objection from the second row, and changes her mind about the number of times they made love that night when she realizes it is unrealistic. The monologue is a translation into period costume, with the licence conferred by the *commedia dell'arte*, of the love-chase from a female standpoint, reminiscent, in some respects, of Franca Rame's monologues and one-act plays, but here almost an ironic treatment of feminist polemic. Significantly, apart from the one moment when she rebukes the protester in the audience, the scene is played wholly in character and in *grammelot*: Marcolfa as the washerwoman is perhaps closer to the working-class origins of *A Woman Alone* than the more sophisticated protagonists of *The Open Couple* and *An Ordinary Day*.[25]

So the story of Isabella's reconquest of her husband, the Magnifico, is all that remains of the original prologue storyline from the first draft script. Originally, the 'plot' told of young Flavio (disguised as a woman to avoid conscription into the Flanders wars), who goes into service in Pantaloon's house and falls in love with Isabella, dropping all 'her' pots and pans with the emotion of meeting her.[26] All this disappeared in performance (although a Pantaloon with stinking breath does survive in a sketch), and the period 'story' surfaces only very occasionally during the ladder episode, such as when a *zanni* is reminded by Fo-Harlequin that he cannot protest he is overworked because trade unions had not been invented in 1585.

By now it is clear that the *Harlequin* show was a series of situation gags (originating from antique models) but based loosely on the characteristics of Harlequin, and only linked with the Renaissance *commedia* theme by the situation of performance itself (the stage, costume, Fo's mask, stage props). It comments on the *commedia dell'arte*, in a sense, rather than reliving or reinventing it. Harlequin himself is its only connecting thread in the end. His 'paradoxes' – the extension of the real into an imaginary surreal or grotesque, such as when he 'rubs out' the audience offending Marcolfa by watching her work with a mime of cleaning a blackboard – are typical of the characteristics described by scholars like Molinari, or of the Harlequin described by Fo himself, who will mime being a chair to embrace his love when she sits down.[27] Another example, from later in the show, is where Fo-Harlequin puts half a cold chicken to his ear, claiming to be able to hear the sea. The action of the mime associates the actual object the audience sees with another, similar one it knows well.

The characteristics for which Harlequin was famous also include hunger, and the original script included an episode in which Harlequin

1.   'The Gravediggers' sketch from Dario Fo's *Harlequin*: Fo throws a skull and a skeleton protests (see pp. 257–8).

discovers a heap of rubbish, thanking God for such a precious find. Sifting through the remains of countless meals, he identifies the different social classes whose meals he now shares, doubtless with liberal doses of mimed attributes, and comes upon an unused candle, which he eats as a great delicacy. The scene was cut from the final performance but echoes the famous *zanni* hunger scene (in which Harlequin or a *zanni* mimes eating parts of himself, so great is his hunger) that Fo performed at the National Theatre in London in January, 1991. Hunger, too, was the initial theme of the *Cantata dei Pastori* ('Song of the shepherds'), present in the first draft, but abandoned in performance. Two *zanni* spy a blackbird, then a cat, then a dog, waiting for each animal to eat up the former in order to catch them all at once. Predictably, the animals escape and the *zanni* have to be content with the crumbs the blackbird was pecking. This is followed by the arrival of the Virgin Mary *en route* for Jerusalem and needing porters. Understanding *Pellestrina* (on the coast not far from Venice) for *Palestina*, the *zanni* attempt to take her there by a boat which is almost wrecked in a storm and only saved by invocations to the Virgin (who of course is present). Thus the mistaken-identity gag is sustained to the end, supported by songs sung in chorus. Apparently from an original by Perrucci, and analysed with variants by the authors of *Io Fo Arlecchino*, who style it an 'operetta', the whole episode was no longer in the show in performance.

The same fate befell 'The Flying Cat', a sketch which appears in the early draft as the triumph of Harlequin's astuteness and cunning over received wisdom. Harlequin quizzes Eularia, who appears to be a walking dictionary: he bets with her that she cannot answer all his questions; she raises the stakes by prevaricating with answers *around* the question, while he mimes various chronometers to indicate the passage of time. This guessing game, with Eularia now asking the questions, goes on through a rising crescendo of mimed attributes of the fabulous animal – called, in the end, the flying cat – until the monster appears from the wings of the finale blowing bubbles as part of the world of fantasy and imagination that Harlequin inhabits, and the triumph of childlike fantasy over conventional wisdom is complete. Harlequin is vanquished on this occasion by Eularia's superior tactics. The sketch was clearly a powerful vehicle for the mime talents of Dario Fo, and appears, as we have seen, as if in performance in the summary of *Io Fo Arlecchino*, though not in the final performance.

The sketch entitled 'The Gravediggers' did survive into final performance and endured, with variants, down to the end of the performance schedule. It takes place in a graveyard where Harlequin and Razzullo are digging the grave for a man who drowned himself in a bowl of water. But the fable Harlequin now recounts is of a suicide in a vat of wine (the opportunity for mime and voice-effects), and the episode is a comic *tour de force* of Harlequin's traditional assaults on conventions, a surreal circus of obscenities (Harlequin explains the derivation of 'scatology' in a mock-serious discourse, and urinates on a skull), pantomime effects (two skulls speak and a skeleton emerges), physical business (skulls are slapped and thrown about like footballs), and a mock-serious funeral conducted by a homosexual priest which ends in a fight, further deaths, and dinner with the 'despairing' widow. The whole is commented on by Fo-Harlequin in a systematic dismantling of conventional taboos: death, the Church, the family, with surreal touches like the following:

> WIDOW   Aahh! I've been widowed a second time.
> [the widow's lover has just been killed in a fight]
> HARLEQUIN   God, for a hundred performances now, the dead man's brother has ended up dead – with his head resting on the priest's buttocks![28]

This episode – alone in Fo's *Harlequin* – is self-contained and moves from the situation of the suicide by drowning to the fable of the wine suicide, to knockabout with clown-skulls (who ironically play the part of respect for the dead), and ends in a mini-farce of the funeral, complete with *De Profundis* and music, in which Fo-Harlequin mercilessly lampoons the solemnity and gravity of such occasions. Just as the many uses of the ladder prop in the prologue (secured with guy ropes) echo many of Fo's favourite stage effects using theatrical devices before and since *Harlequin*,[29] so too the animation of the skulls, in a sort of ludicrous parody of the scene from *Hamlet*, re-uses the puppet and marionette effects from other times and contexts.[30] Here, more than elsewhere, Harlequin is, in Fo's words: 'destroyer of conventions. His interventions are often completely gratuitous, and his morality always derives from paradox . . .'[31]

The second half of Fo's *Harlequin* contained the episode of the Key and the Lock, a classic sexual metaphor, and the sketch with the animals, which builds on Harlequin's traditional fear. The Key episode begins with a device typical of the bizarre logic of paradox in the world Harlequin introduces: a joke with a table and the attempt to lift it with a lever. Once again, the *situation* causes the table to be brought onstage; the result is mockery of the pretensions of science to accomplish miracles. The table will bear the Lock (a giant stage-prop some three feet square,) tended, oiled and decorated by Franceschina (played by Franca Rame), while Harlequin's Key is on a similar scale, carried like a rifle over the shoulder. Endless elaborations of the predictable scenario follow: Harlequin supplies oil for cleaning the Lock, it is tempted by a *zanni* with a golden key, until, refusing penetration by Harlequin's key, the Lock is finally persuaded by the traditional blackmail when Harlequin produces a picnic lunch, and Franceschina realizes she is hungry. In the early version of the script, conception followed penetration, and five little keys clatter onto the stage, but in performance Harlequin returns to his key to find a substitute rubber floppy inflatable key in its place – it has died – and the sketch ends as a tragedy of love.

In the concluding episode, Harlequin's traditional fear of animals provides the excuse for a variety of pantomime beasts, and a play on the fiction/reality dualism of men and animals. Harlequin illustrates this by fear of a dog, conversation with a donkey (in the fantasy world of magic that pantomime confers), finding that it had formerly belonged to a drunken priest who had suffered a heart-attack after making love to a girl! Anticlericalism apart, the climax comes after a practical joke played on Harlequin by two *zanni* who impersonate a pantomime lion to frighten him. Determined on a show of courage to win the love of Franceschina, Harlequin undertakes feats of bravado with the lion, believing it contains his two friends, while in reality, a *real* lion has escaped from a ship in port. A number of jokes derive from this situation of 'mistaken identity', including such circus favourites as the head (or hand) in the lion's mouth, 'feeding' sausages to the animal's 'rear actor' and a lesson in roaring.

Looking back on Fo's *Harlequin*, one is struck again by Marotti's claim that the essence of the *commedia dell'arte* was the *lazzi*, never the story, which was only their shell, Practitioners of 'strict tempo' *commedia* like Carlo Boso teach young actors never to lose sight of the storyline – or you will lose your audience. The format chosen by Dario Fo, utilizing, as we have seen, all the resources of his performance experience and background, does move the Harlequin show perceptibly nearer the relative structural anarchy of music-hall. And yet the audience in the circus tent will react with wide-eyed delight at clowns and a high-wire act without worrying about hypothetical organic

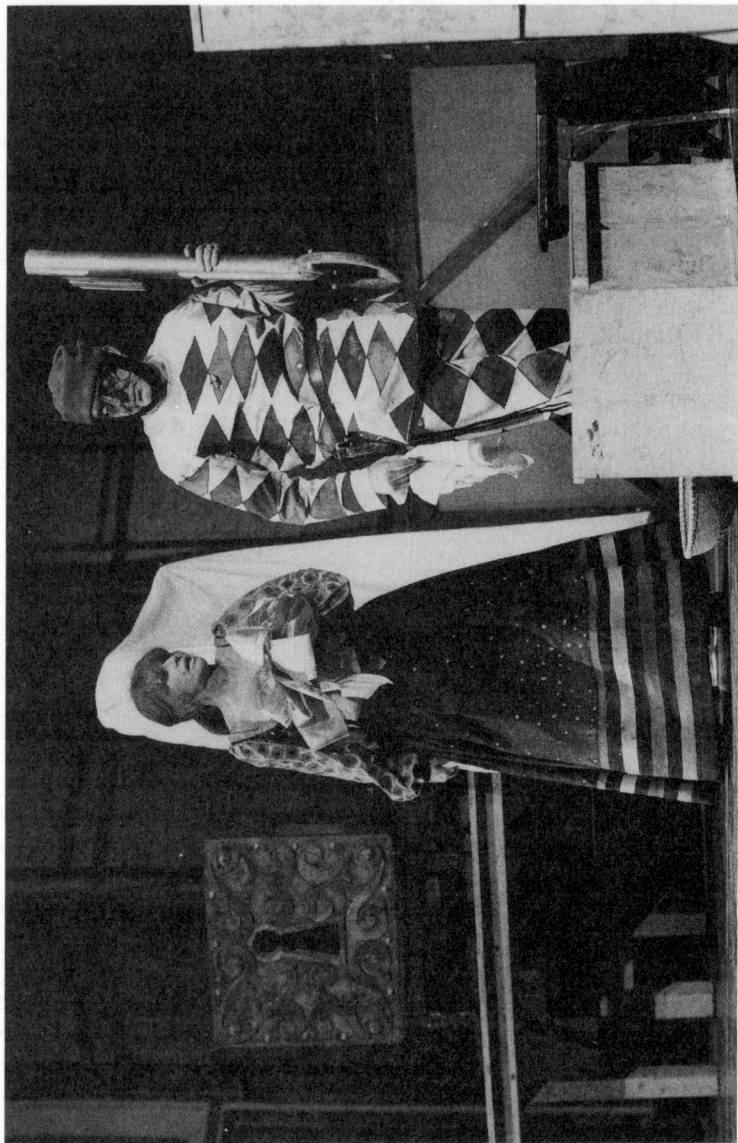

2. The Lock and Key episode from Dario Fo's *Harlequin*: Harlequin (Fo) presents his key but is scorned by Franceschina (Franca Rame). (See pp. 258–9.)

connections. Alone among the sketches – tied in a loose bundle by Harlequin's traditional attributes, in a word, his biography – is Franca Rame's monologue, which is both period-orientated (as built on 'Renaissance' concepts of corsetry), and in tune with the storyline (the relationship between Isabella and Eleanora). For the rest, costume, spirit, the paradox and the imagination, the authentic sources of *lazzi*, are all part of the *commedia dell'arte*, but mingle irresistibly with other undeniable strengths of Fo's comic stage personality, which no amount of justification and research in the world will turn into a Harlequin of history. The very twentieth-century targets, from the anachronisms of satire of cabinet ministers to Fo's propensity for 'gags off the wall', are, in the end, the result of Fo's stage personality, as robustly satisfying as it ever was, which tends to spill out in performance and breaks free from the 'academic' framework of the *commedia dell'arte*, in an instinctive rapport (itself authentic) with audiences in the here and now, which will not be boxed and pigeon-holed. And in the end, this is itself what the *commedia dell'arte* means today: the *freedom* to adapt to 'modern' purposes a pan-European theatrical tradition which encompasses experiments as diverse as the *Age d'or* of Ariane Mnouchkine, the complexities and multi-discipline approach of Eugenio Barba, and the determinedly 'modern' innovations of the San Francisco Mime Troupe. With the innate subversive charge of the radical, Fo *is* today's Harlequin (at least since the death of Chaplin), and the encounter (confrontation?) in 1985–6 with academic pretensions was a liberating of his stage personality, not a caging of it.

Typically, in his *Manuale minimo* . . . , he begins precisely with a satirical treatment of the scholarly controversy surrounding the *commedia dell'arte*, in a sense, distancing himself from it as from all the pedantries of academically disputed orthodoxies:

> Yet, where I succeeded in reaching the sublimely impossible was the point in which Meldolesi of Dams at the University of Bologna,[32] although he was giving a course on avant-garde theatre at the time at Holstbro[33] in Denmark, was made to leap here to Rome by my magic, and obliged to take part in a debate which, in reality, will take place at Stresa next year. In this case I simply speed up time by 10,000 light-units and make the event happen when it suits me . . . here in Rome, for example . . . I get loads of people together and without even seeking their approval, I throw them into the audience.
>
> Taviani,[34] up you get! . . . Come on, no 'buts', I know you're actually in Palermo at this minute . . . and you can't see how I managed to get

you here . . . I can't explain, it's a trade secret. Come on, repeat word for word your lecture from Pistoia . . . What do you mean, which one? The one on Harlequin, of course, where you said you thought he was a character extraneous to the *commedia dell'arte*, so much so that you said he wasn't even Italian but French in origin. . . There, good . . . now you stay put while I get Eugenio Barba[35] to reply to you, who at the moment is in New York . . . Don't worry about the time difference . . . Here he is, Eugenio, reply to him . . . You don't want to? Well, I'll make you say what you wrote in your essay three years ago . . . in the chapter: *Harlequin – an oriental mask*.

Stop, everyone, there's Marotti[36] asking to speak . . . he's speaking from Bali where he's on holiday at present . . .[37]

In the end, Fo makes them all go to lunch – in their respective places and time-zones, and exclaims: 'Ah, at last! A bit of peace and quiet and *normality*!'

NOTES

1 I am grateful above all to Dario Fo and Franca Rame for their co-operation and the loan of photographs from the Fo-Rame private archive (published by kind permission of Mimmorossi of Perugia, in all cases except Fig. 2, which is by Bruno Medici, of London). Thanks are also due to them for the sound and videotape, as well as performance script of *Harlequin*. All translations of Italian sources cited are by the author.

2 TAG Teatro's production, originally from a Scala scenario, was also performed at the Royal Festival Hall, London, in January 1989 and January 1990, to critical acclaim.

3 See the very informative report on 'La Commedia dell'Arte negli anni ottanta', by various authors in *Lettera dall'Italia* 9 (1988), 23–42.

4 See James Fisher, 'The Show Booth: Commedia dell'Arte on the twentieth-century American stage' in *New England Theatre Journal*, 1, (1990), 61–77, and the same author's *The Theatre of Yesterday and Tomorrow: Commedia dell'Arte on the Modern Stage*. I am grateful to Professor Fisher for allowing me to see a draft of his book prior to its publication.

5 From a videotaped interview with the author in London on 13 November 1988.

6 For the influence of *commedia* on *Trumpets & Raspberries* see Ed Emery, 'Dario Fo's *Trumpets and Raspberries* and the tradition of *commedia*' in Cairns (ed.), *The Commedia dell'Arte from the Renaissance to Dario Fo* (Lewiston–Queenston–Lampeter, The Edward Mellen Press, 1989), 330–5. A long list of similarities is given in the forthcoming work cited below in n. 13.

7 *Alcatraz News*, 1 (November, 1985), 15–16 (interview with Sergio Parini).

8 Delia Gambelli, 'Quasi un recamo di concertate pezzette: le composizioni sul comico dell'Arlecchino Biancolelli' in *Biblioteca Teatrale*, 1 1971, 47–95, and *idem*, 'Arlecchino dalla preistoria a Biancolelli', ibid, 5 1972, 17–68.

9 Interviewed by Perini in *Alcatraz News*, op. cit., 14, quoting the Scala scenario. It is entirely characteristic of Fo's elaboration from imagination of the antique source that he should add his own invented sequel to this story in the pages of his *Manuale minimo . . .* (op. cit., 8, see below, n. 13):

> Harlequin replies with a pitiless libel in which he cuts up the jealous poet, publishing it in his turn. In this Harlequin goes down into Hell for a second time but this time has his critic accompany him. The two, like Dante and Virgil (it's logical that the part of Dante is played by Harlequin), pass through the various circles of Hell meeting famous personages from French public life. Everyone treats the son of Zanni with great kindness but administers kicks in the face of the evil-speaking poet, who ends up head down in a vat of urine . . . and in saucepans of cats' excrement boiling hot . . . and also in cold excrement which is more disgusting still.
>
> They begin to play dice with the devil: Harlequin-Dante wins, evil-speaking Virgil loses and is tormented by the devils. Harlequin saves him from being skinned alive by the ferocious devils . . . grateful for this, the poor chap asks his pardon and admits he has behaved badly . . . magnanimously, Harlequin blesses him . . . (and so on in this vein)
>
> The finale is not the authentic one, I've added it myself, extrapolating from a Scala scenario, the author of Harlequin. But I think it fits well . . . don't you think?

10 Fo plays the Pope in *Il Papa e la Strega*, converted by direct experience of a clandestine drug clinic to the point where he renounces the Italian law criminalizing drugs (and abandons a number of other Vatican 'conservative' tenets). The play toured Italy in 1989–90, and is published by Methuen in English translation.

11 Cielo Pessione and Patrizia Fulcinetti, *Io Fo Arlecchino* (I am grateful to the authors for sight of a sample of their work).

12 *Alcatraz News*, op. cit., 15.

13 *Manuale minimo dell'attore* (Torino, Einaudi, 1987) to be published by Methuen as *The Tricks of the Trade* (trans. Joe Farrell).

14 Information from conversations with Dario Fo in Rome (March, 1990) where he was working on the sketches of scenes from the Molière plays in his dressing-room before performances of *Il Papa e la Strega*. I am grateful to Michael Imison for the loan of a videotape of the Molière farces.

15 *Lettera dall'Italia*, op. cit., 33.

16 Dario Fo, interview cit., in *Alcatraz News*, 15–16.

17 Videotape cit., in n. 5 above.

18 Jacopo Fo, 'A proposito di Arlecchino' in *Alcatraz News*, op. cit., 13.

19 I have in mind the experiments with Commedia of Sand and Vactangov in the

nineteenth century in general, and in particular, R. G. Davis (of the San Francisco Mime Troupe in 1968), quoted by Fisher, op. cit., 74–5.

20 Pessione and Fulcinetti, op. cit. (contents summary), compared with the script in *Alcatraz News*, op. cit., 39–49.

21 Ibid. (forthcoming).

22 The pre-performance prologue, of course, is not in any script, but is derived from sound and videotapes of performances in February 1986. In early shows it is clear that Fo-Harlequin wore the traditional black mask of the character (see Fig. 1), as the publication of the Italian *Arlecchino Fallotropo* (*Manuale minimo* ... op. cit., 70–71) makes clear: 'He dons the mask of Harlequin'. Yet he seems to have abandoned it by February 1986, since the videotape shows him with a dark-painted face. The London 1988 performance was not in costume (Fig. 2).

23 The involvement of the audience with this stage 'contraption' involving guy ropes echoes many past performance situations for Dario Fo, but more recently, in *Il Papa e la Strega*, the incident where the Pope swings from the chandelier on ropes making swimming movements, and Franca Rame confesses that he fell when their tour reached Bologna. In mock surprise at their laughter, Fo pretends the spectators are hoping he will fall again: 'then we'll all fall about!'

24 The incident quoted in the last note is an example, where Fo, swinging on his ropes, mimes fear, as the arc of the swing reaches out over the front rows of the stalls.

25 *A Woman Alone* is in Dario Fo and Franca Rame, *Female Parts: One Woman plays* (London, Pluto, 1981–but forthcoming in *A Woman Alone and other plays*, Methuen, 1991), *The Open Couple* and *An Ordinary Day* are one volume (Methuen, 1990).

26 In *Alcatraz News*, op. cit., 27–8.

27 See, for example, Cesare Molinari, *La Commedia dell'Arte* (Milano, Mondadori, 1985), particularly pp. 107–11. Fo in *Alcatraz News*, interview op. cit., 16.

28 In the earlier version, the emphasis of the funeral-farce was quite different, since the widow reverses the traditional respect for the dead on such occasions by accusing him of multiple infidelities ('two nuns, three novices, four brides, even three little girls') in a macabre and ironic reversal of the situation, kicking the corpse (from which spurts of water appear). Finally all fall into the tomb amidst protests at overcrowding! (*Alcatraz News*, op. cit., 90–91).

29 Such devices are richly evident in Fo's latest play, *Zitti! Stiamo Preciptando!* which has two puppet look-alikes, as many times in the past.

30 Ibid.

31 *Alcatraz News*, op. cit. 16.

32 Claudio Meldolesi, of the University of Bologna, and author of (among much else) *Su un comico in rivolta: Dario Fo, il bufalo, il bambino* (Roma, 1978).

33 The home of Eugenio Barba's Odin Teatret.

34 University critic, expert on Barba, and author of *Il Segreto della Commedia dell'Arte* (Firenze, 1982), as well as *La Commedia dell'Arte e la società barocca* ... (Roma, 1989) etc.

35 Writer, director of Odin Teatret, pupil of Grotowski and founder of ISTA

(International School of Theatre Anthropology).

36 Ferruccio Marotti, of the University of Rome, who was centrally involved in the Harlequin show, as we have seen.

37 *Manuale minimo* . . . , 8. It is clear that Fo's satire of these university luminaries on the international conference circuit is aimed at their ability to fit in so much world travel.

Index